HOW THE ECONOMY WORKS
and Other Essays

By the same author

Insurance Funds and their Investment (*with G. L. Schwartz*)

The Post-War Financial Problem and Other Essays

Business Finance

Studies in an Inflationary Economy

Long-Term and Short-Term Interest Rates in the United Kingdom

Benham's Economics (*editor of 8th edition*)

How the Economy Works
and Other Essays

F. W. PAISH

Macmillan

First published 1970 *by*
MACMILLAN AND CO LTD
Little Essex Street London WC 2
and also at Bombay Calcutta and Madras
Macmillan South Africa (publishers) Pty Ltd Johannesburg
The Macmillan Company of Australia Pty Ltd Melbourne
The Macmillan Company of Canada Ltd Toronto
Gill and Macmillan Ltd Dublin

SBN (boards) 333 11067 6

Printed in Great Britain by
HAZELL WATSON & VINEY LTD
Aylesbury, Bucks

Contents

Acknowledgements

The author wishes to thank the following publishers, publications and institutions for permission to re-publish the various articles and papers:

Manchester University Press

Long-Term and Short-Term Interest Rates in the United Kingdom (1966)

The Banker

Deposit Rates after Mr Jones (vol. 117, no. 500, Oct 1967)
The Two Britains (Feb 1964)

Lloyds Bank Review

The Management of the British Economy (no. 76, Apr 1965)
How the Economy Works (no. 88, Apr 1968)

University of York

Government Policy and Business Investment (the second Sir Ellis Hunter Memorial Lecture, 8 June 1965)

Scottish Journal of Political Economy

Inflation and the Balance of Payments in the United Kingdom, 1952–67 (the third Scottish Economic Society Lecture, 17 April 1968; vol. xv, Nov 1968)

The Institute of Economic Affairs

Rise and Fall of Incomes Policy (Hobart Paper 47, June 1969)

Preface

THE eight papers and articles which comprise this book were written and published between the years 1964 and 1969. No attempt has been made to revise them, although in postscripts to three of them, written in the middle of 1969, some statistical tables have been revised as well as continued. Retrospective revision of official statistics has therefore made some of the information out of date, although in no case, it is believed, to the extent of invalidating the general lines of the argument.

While each chapter deals with a different aspect of the economic situation, there is necessarily a good deal of overlapping in the background material which provides the setting for each particular discussion. In some cases later chapters serve to bring up to date information given earlier; in others a similar function is performed by the postscripts.

My thanks are due to many friends for help with particular chapters, and more generally to the Economic Adviser of Lloyds Bank, Mr J. R. Winton, and to the staff of his department, for much statistical assistance; and to Mr S. Brand, of Stewarts and Lloyds Ltd, for invaluable help in checking and correcting many of the tables.

The five years covered by this book have constituted one of the most interesting and exciting periods in the recent economic history of the United Kingdom. Starting at a time when the economy was already suffering acutely from excess demand and from a large adverse balance of payments, it provides examples of many forms of economic restraint, fiscal, monetary, hortatory and legal. Of these, only the third seems to have been wholly ineffective. Of the remainder, fiscal policy, largely in the form of higher indirect taxes borne ultimately by the consumer, seems to have had the largest and most rapid effects. Direct control of hire-purchase terms has also had marked effects, although only over a relatively narrow sector of consumer demand. The effects on the liquidity of the system of a restrictive monetary policy, reinforced by the large interest-free loans to the Government required by the selective employment tax and the import deposits scheme, have been seen most obviously in the fall in house-building and perhaps also in the check to stock accumulation. They have also probably contributed to the fall in the expenditure (in real terms) of public authorities and have perhaps helped to slow down the much-needed rise in private-sector fixed investment. Attempts at the direct control of employment incomes, after an initial success in 1966–7, have subsequently failed and have now been almost completely abandoned.

The combination of the devaluation of sterling in November 1967 with severe measures to restrict internal demand have resulted in the emergence, in the second half of 1969, of the first really adequate balance-of-payments surplus since 1958. This, together with the consequent improvement in international confidence in sterling, has already enabled the Government to make very large repayments of the enormous volume of short-term foreign debts incurred between 1964 and 1968. The situation, while greatly improved, is, however, not yet securely stabilised.

There are two main weaknesses. After devaluation, the Government was faced with the necessity of diverting resources from personal consumption and public expenditure, not only to exports, but also to industrial and commercial fixed investment, then at a level insufficient to provide for the future growth of the economy, and to stock accumulation, then negative. In the first year after devaluation a larger share of the national product than expected (see Table 6.10, p. 160) was diverted from personal consumption and public expenditure, but much of it went into stock accumulation and less than had been hoped into exports. In the second year, on the other hand, the resources needed for the great improvement shown in the balance of trade came entirely out of stock accumulation, which in the third quarter of 1969 was again negative. If stock accumulation recovers to a normal level in 1970, this alone will absorb more than a third of the estimated rise in productive potential.

A second potential source of weakness is the probability of a greatly accelerated rise in personal consumption. In 1968–9 there was a rise of over 7 per cent in income from employment. This was much larger than the rise of about 4½ per cent a year which has in the past accompanied an unemployment rate of 2·4 per cent. There seem to have been two main causes for this increase. One explanation, confirmed by the much higher number of unfilled vacancies than has in the past accompanied this level of unemployment, is that the introduction of redundancy payments in 1965 and of earnings-related benefits in 1966 has enabled many of the unemployed to wait for the work they prefer instead of having to accept what is available, and so has tended to slow down the flow of transitional unemployment through the pipelines. Consequently, the average number of unfilled vacancies in 1969 was at a level which in the past has been associated with an unemployment level of only about 1·8 per cent and a rise in employment incomes of over 6 per cent a year.

The remainder of the increase in the rise of employment incomes seems to have been due to the success of the Government's policy of diverting resources out of personal consumption. As a result, the rapid rise in money incomes has been accompanied by very little rise in real incomes, and employees have therefore very naturally tended to use whatever monopoly power they have in an effort to achieve a rate of rise in real incomes which would have been inconsistent with the basic objectives of government policy. This explanation is confirmed by the increased and increasing number of strikes and other forms of protest, both official and unofficial.

The rapid rise in income from employment in 1968–9 was reconciled with a rise of less than 1 per cent in real personal consumption mainly by a rise of 5 per cent in prices of consumer goods and services, of which about 2 per cent was due to higher indirect taxes. During 1970 the effects of the higher taxes imposed in 1969 will die away, and even without an acceleration (which seems only too likely) of the rise in personal money incomes, by the second half of 1970 consumption is likely to be rising at a rate of between 2½ per cent and 3 per cent a year. This would absorb at least half the estimated rise of productive potential.

If we add the effect of the expected rise in consumption to that in stock accumulation, it is clear that, even without any further improvement in the balance of trade, very little margin will be left for the planned increases in public expenditure or for the desirable further rise in industrial and commercial investment.

Unless, therefore, it is prepared to gamble on the development of an international business recession, which would probably turn the terms of trade in Britain's favour and enable an increased volume of imports to be paid for by a reduced volume of exports, the Government has no margin for any net relaxation of the fiscal and monetary restraints on home demand. At such a time, it will need great political courage to resist the inevitable pressures for reductions in taxation and the relaxation of monetary and other controls. But if it fails to resist, it will run a very grave risk of losing all that has been so painfully gained during the past few years, of inaugurating a new period of excess demand, and of laying the foundations of a new crisis in 1971 or 1972.

London F. W. P.
March 1970

I

Long-Term and Short-Term Interest Rates in the United Kingdom[1]

I

THE RELATIONSHIP BETWEEN LONG-TERM AND SHORT-TERM RATES

THESE three lectures on long-term and short-term interest rates will be arranged as follows. The first lecture will examine, in the light of first principles, the relationship which we should expect on various assumptions between the rates of interest on any two loans of different lengths. The relationship will be examined first on the assumption that no change in interest rates is expected and subsequently on the assumption of the expectation of a change in one or the other rate. The second lecture will discuss the nature of expectations about the future level of interest rates, and will attempt to deduce from historical data what expectations were during two particular past periods. The third lecture will deal with the forces determining the absolute level of the long-term rate and therefore (given the relationship between rates) of the whole constellation of interest rates.

I start my first lecture by making a number of simplifying assumptions, most of which will be removed progressively during the discussion.

1. All transactions take place within a single, free and competitive market.
2. There are only two types of transactions: the making and repayment of loans for a shorter period, such as three months, and the making and repayment of loans for a longer period, such as ten years.

[1] First published by Manchester University Press, 1966.

3. Loans are not marketable, and cannot be repaid before due date.
4. There are no costs, not even the subjective costs of the operators' trouble.
5. All members of the market have perfect credit-worthiness. That is to say, every member is sure of being able to borrow as much as he wants at any time at current rates of interest.
6. No one thinks that either interest rate is more likely to change in one direction than in the other. This means that the average future short-term rate is expected to be equal to the existing short-term rate, and that comparisons between the long-term rate and the expected average future short-term rate relate equally to the long-term rate and the existing short-term rate.
7. All members of the market have perfect foresight. To facilitate the subsequent removal of this assumption, it is broken down into three parts: (*a*) All members have the same expectations about interest rates. (*b*) All are quite sure that their expectations will prove correct. (*c*) Their expectations do in fact turn out to have been correct.

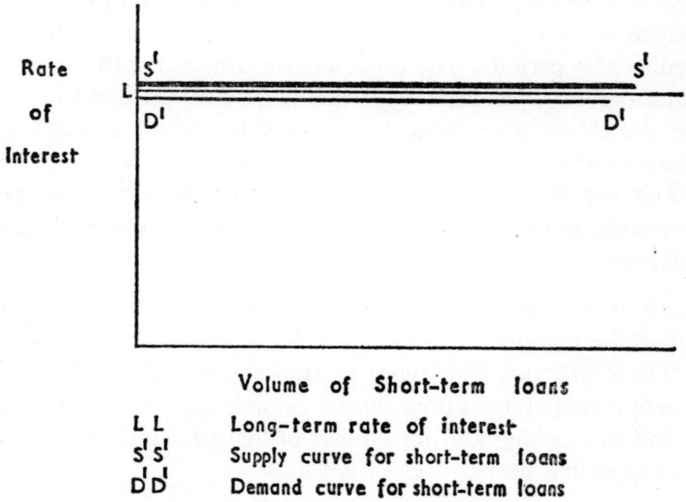

Fig. 1.1 All assumptions retained

With all assumptions retained, the long-term rate, the expected average future short-term rate and the present short-term rate must always be the same. If the average future short-term rate were expected to be the smallest amount above the long-term rate, everyone would want to lend, and no one would want to borrow, on short term, while if it were the smallest amount below the long-term rate, everyone would want to borrow on short term and no one to lend. We therefore have the position shown in Fig. 1.1.

In Fig. 1.1, *L–L* represents the long-term rate of interest, *S′–S′* the supply curve for short-term loans and *D′–D′* the demand curve for short-term loans. The vertical axis measures the rate of interest and the horizontal axis the quantity of short-term loans supplied and demanded.

Removal of assumptions: (7*c*) *Realisation of expectations*

The first assumption to be removed is 7(*c*), that expectations are in fact realised, leaving 7(*a*), that all expectations are the same, and 7(*b*), that all expectations are held with certainty, still in force. The removal of 7(*c*) gets rid of the worst of the logical difficulties inherent in the assumption of perfect foresight, while leaving the *ex ante* position unchanged. Fig. 1.1. therefore continues to apply to the relationship between the long-term rate and the short-term rate. The removal of 7(*c*) does, however, remove any simple connection between the rates of interest which people were expecting and the rates which were actually recorded.

Removal of assumptions: (7*b*) *Certainty of expectations*

The next assumption to go is 7(*b*), the certainty of expectations. While people still all expect the same thing, they are no longer sure that their expectations will be realised. Instead, therefore, of being sure that the short-term rate will remain unchanged for the whole long-term period, they accept the possibility, perhaps even the probability, that the rate will change, though they have no idea in which direction.

In our new situation, let us start by considering the choice facing a lender who thinks it very unlikely that he will need his money back before the end of the long-term period. By lending on long term he can make sure of receiving a known rate of interest for the whole period. If, instead, he elects to make a series of short-term loans, he has what seems to be an equal chance of receiving a larger or a smaller interest yield. If, therefore, he prefers certainty to uncertainty, he will not be prepared to lend on short term unless he expects to get a higher yield, over the long-term period, than if he had lent on long term. How much higher the expected average short-term rate has to be depends partly on how sure he is that he will not need the money before the end of the long-term period and partly on his attitude to uncertainty; but he will be prepared to lend on short term at the long-term rate only if he thinks that there is a distinct possibility that he will need the money within the long-term period and that therefore he may be obliged to pay a short-term rate for part of the period above that which he is receiving on his long-term loan; or, alternatively, if he is quite indifferent to uncertainty.

Similarly, a borrower who expects to need the money for the whole of the long-term period will prefer to make sure of how much he has to pay by borrowing on long term, unless the expected average short-term rate is below the long-term rate. He will be prepared to borrow on short term at the long-term rate only if there is a distinct possibility that he will need the money for only part of the long-term period, so that he may have to re-lend at below the rate he is paying on a long-term loan; or if he also is quite indifferent to uncertainty.

If, therefore, the market consists only of borrowers who are likely to need money for a whole long-term period, and of lenders who are unlikely to need repayment within the long-term period, and if all members dislike uncertainty, lenders will not lend on short term unless the expected average short-term rate is above the long-term rate, while borrowers will not borrow on short term unless they expect the average short-term rate to be below the long-term rate. There will thus be no short-term loans made, unless some members of the market prefer uncertainty to certainty. We thus have the position shown in Fig. 1.2(*a*).

As soon as we introduce into the market lenders who think that they may, or still more will, want their money back before the end of the long-term period, and borrowers who think that they will cease to need it, the situation changes. A long-term lender who

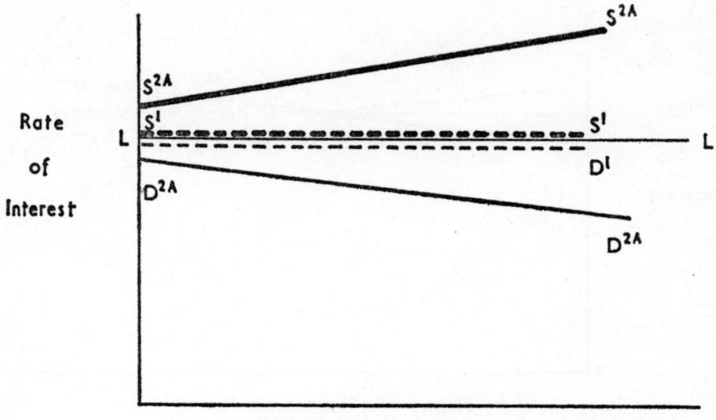

Fig. 1.2(a) Uncertainty 1

needed his money back before the end of the long-term period would have to borrow in the short-term market, possibly at a higher rate of interest than he was receiving, while a long-term borrower who ceased to need the money would have to re-lend it in the short-term market, possibly at below that rate which he was paying. The advantages of certainty which each would obtain up to the date of re-borrowing or re-lending would therefore be offset by the disadvantages of uncertainty after that date. At some point of expectations the disadvantages would equal the advantages, and the member would be willing to lend or borrow on short term at exactly the long-term rate. Beyond that point the lenders would be prepared to lend on short term even if the expected average short-term rate was below the long-term rate, while borrowers would be prepared to borrow on short term even if it was above it, provided that both sides disliked uncertainty. We now get the position shown in Fig. 1.2(*b*).

Since in Fig. 1.2(*b*) the curves are drawn symmetrically, the equilibrium position of the short-term rate is shown as equal to the long-term rate. There is no reason why this should be so. With different assumptions about the relative expectations and attitudes to uncertainty of borrowers and lenders, the equilibrium position of the expected average short-term rate could be either above or below the long-term rate.

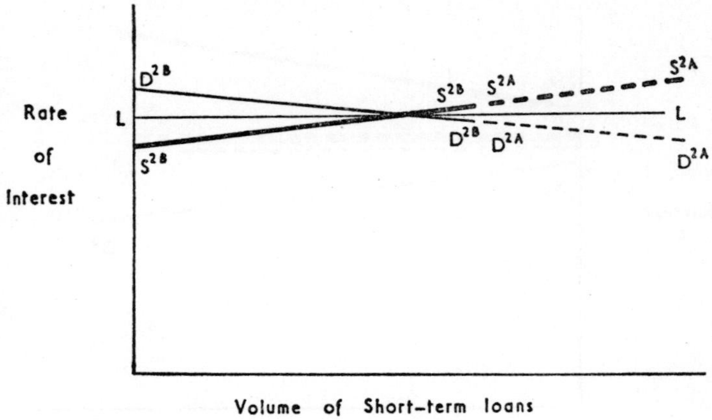

Fig. 1.2(b) Uncertainty 2

Removal of assumptions: (5) *Perfect credit-worthiness*

The next assumption to be removed is that of perfect credit-worthiness. It now becomes possible for a member's financial standing to deteriorate, so that it may no longer be possible for him to borrow as much as he wants at market rates, or perhaps at all. A creditor is also faced with the risk that his debtor may become unable to repay his loan on maturity, a risk which tends to increase with the duration of the loan. A short-term debtor may therefore find it expensive or impossible to renew or replace his maturing loan, while a long-term creditor may find it expensive or impossible to borrow any money he may need before his loan matures. The amount of the additional risk of illiquidity incurred by the long-term lender and the short-term borrower will vary greatly from person to person. The borrower who feels sure that he will need the money for only a short time and the lender who feels sure that he will not need his money back before the end of the long-term period are taking little or no risk by borrowing short and lending long. These operators are found in Fig. 1.2(*b*) respectively at the extreme left-hand end of the demand curve and at the extreme right-hand end of the supply curve, that is to say, on the D^{2B} and S^{2A} curves. At the other extremes are the borrowers who know or strongly expect that they will need the money for the whole of the long-term period and the lenders who know or expect that they will need the money back in much less than the long-term period. These borrowers would not be prepared to borrow short unless they were offered a rate of interest well below the long-term rate, while these lenders would be prepared to lend money on short term even at rates well below the long-term rate. Thus in Fig. 1.3 the extreme left-hand end of the demand curve and the extreme right-hand end of the supply curve remain unchanged, but the right-hand end of the demand curve and the left-hand end of the supply curve are well below the long-term rate.

If the short-term rates at which some borrowers and lenders are prepared to operate are a long way below the long-term rate, the lower ends of the demand and supply surves may approach a zero rate of interest. On the continued assumption of no operating costs, and on the further assumption that there are no costs of holding cash, the lower ends of both curves may reach, but not cross, the zero line. If the only choice for lenders were between long-term and short-term loans, it is very possible that some lenders would value liquidity so highly that they would prefer to accept a negative rate of interest on short-term loans rather than a positive rate on long-term loans. But if we assume that cash can be held without cost, they will prefer to hold cash rather than accept a negative rate, and the yield on short-term loans cannot therefore fall below zero. It also seems likely that, with no operating costs, the demand

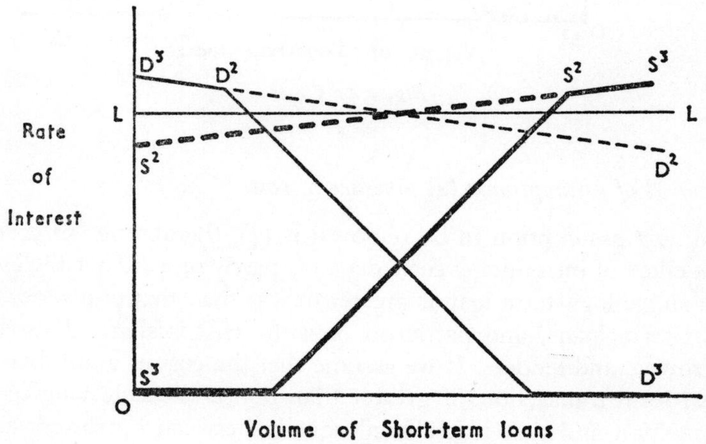

Fig. 1.3 Illiquidity

from short-term borrowers will become infinitely elastic at a zero rate of interest. We therefore reach the position shown in Fig. 1.3.

Fig. 1.3 shows the demand and supply curves for short-term loans intersecting at a level well below the long-term rate. That the equilibrium level for the expected average short-term rate will be below the long-term rate is, however, not quite certain. If the market consists only of short-term borrowers, such as merchants financing seasonal requirements, and long-term lenders, such as life-assurance offices, we might be left with only the extreme upper ends of our supply and demand curves, and with an equilibrium short-term rate above the long-term rate.

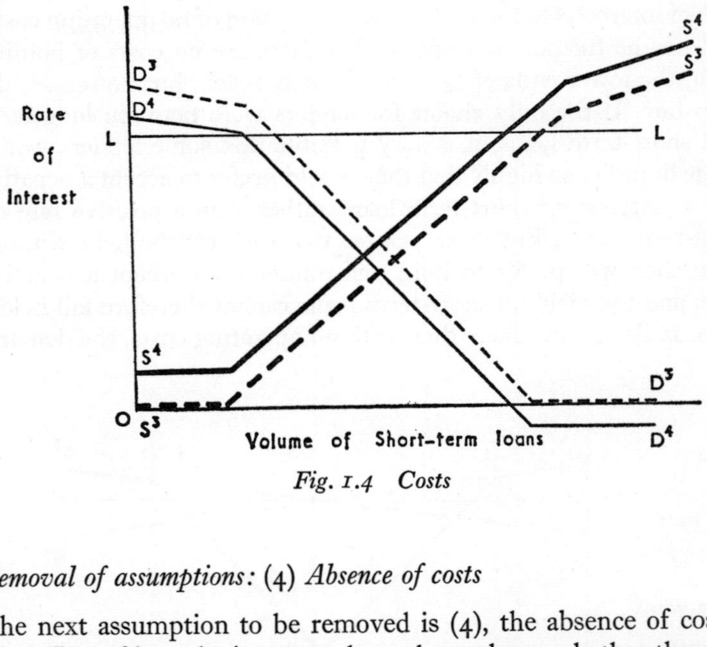

Fig. 1.4 Costs

Removal of assumptions: (4) *Absence of costs*

The next assumption to be removed is (4), the absence of costs. The effect of introducing costs depends partly on whether the cost of a single long-term loan is greater or less than that of a series of short-term loans, and partly on how the cost is shared between borrowers and lenders. If we assume that the cost of a number of short-term transactions is greater than that of a single long-term transaction and that it is shared equally between borrowers and lenders, the effect of its introduction will be to raise the supply curve and lower the demand curve by equal amounts, thus reducing the volume of short-term transactions without affecting the margin between the long-term and the short-term rate of interest. It will, however, affect the minimum rates at which any borrowers and lenders will be prepared to operate. If cash can be held without cost and some share of costs is borne by lenders, the lowest rate which any lender will accept must exceed zero by at least the cost of the transaction. Since this cost will be largely independent of the length of the loan and will increase less than proportionately with its size, very short-term loans will tend either to be very large or to carry a very high rate of interest. Similarly, at the lower end of the demand curve, demand will not become infinitely elastic until the short-term rate offered to borrowers is sufficiently below zero to cover their costs. These effects gives us Fig. 1.4.

Removal of assumptions: (3) *Absence of marketability*

The effect of introducing marketability for short-term loans only is to increase their attractiveness greatly for holders of cash but little for existing long-term lenders, who, by definition, are not greatly interested in liquidity. The move out of cash into short-term loans will shift their supply curve to the right, reducing the short-term rate of interest, widening the margin between the long-term and the short-term rates and increasing the volume of short-term transactions. The fall in the short-term rate will cause some borrowers to borrow short instead of long and will bring down the long-term rate also, though not sufficiently to prevent some widening of the gap between long-term and short-term rates.

The introduction of marketability for long-term rates only will cause a shift of short-term lenders, and perhaps also of cash-holders, into the long-term market. The long-term rate of interest will therefore fall and the margin between the long-term and short-term rates will narrow. This fall in the margin will cause some borrowers to move from the short-term to the long-term market, but the margin between the rates will remain narrower than before. It is uncertain, however, whether the narrowing of the margin will be greater or less than the fall in the long-term rate, and therefore whether the short-term rate will rise or fall.

If we introduce marketability for both long-term and short-term loans, the one certain result will be that the long-term rate will fall. Since marketability only of short loans leads to a fall in the short-term rate, while the effect of marketability only of long-term loans on the short-term rate is uncertain, is seems probable, though not certain, that marketability for both will cause the short-term rate also to fall. It is also likely, but not certain, that the margin between the long-term and short-term rates will narrow. Whether the volume of short-term loans will increase or decrease seems to be quite uncertain. A possible result of making both short-term and long-term loans marketable is shown in Fig. 1.5.

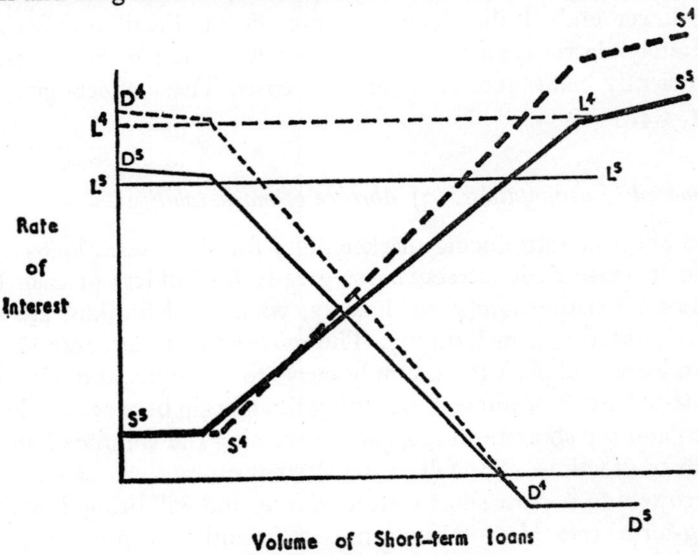

Fig. 1.5 Marketability

Removal of assumptions: (2) *Only two loan periods*

One result of introducing marketability for existing loans is that, so far as lenders are concerned, we must abandon the convenient simplification of limiting the possible number of loan periods to two. If loans are marketable, a lender can buy a partially expired loan to mature on whatever date he wishes. A lender who knows exactly when he wants his money back can avoid all risk (except that of default) by buying a loan with just the unexpired duration that he needs. If long-term and expected short-term rates are equal, that is what he will do. It will, however, be possible to induce a lender to lend for a longer period than that for which he knows he has the money available by offering him a sufficiently higher rate for a long-term than for a short-term loan. If his expectation of no change in interest rates is fulfilled, the lender will receive a rate, for the period for which he holds, that is higher, not only than the short-term rate but also than the long-term rate. If, for instance, the ten-year rate is 5 per cent and the five-year rate $4\frac{1}{2}$ per cent, the market price for a 5 per cent loan with only five more years to run will be about $102\frac{1}{4}$. The yield on a 5 per cent

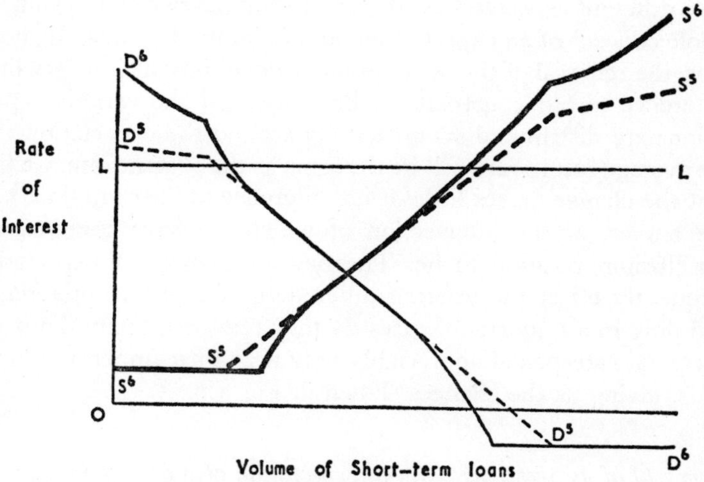

Fig. 1.6 Lack of unanimity

ten-year loan re-sold after five years will therefore be about 5·4 per cent. If, however, his expectations are not fulfilled, and at the end of five years the ten-year rate has risen to 6 per cent, the resale price will be only about $95\frac{1}{2}$ and the yield to resale only 4 per cent. The shorter the period for which the lender has the money available, the less will be the attractiveness of lending on long term, especially when the cost of dealing is taken into account; but there must always be some margin between long-term and short-term rates which will induce a lender who has the money available for less than the long-term period to lend on long term instead of short. The introduction of marketability, and consequently of a multiplicity of lending periods, does not prevent us from using a supply curve similar to that in Fig. 1.5 for determining the relationship between the rates of interest on loans for any two periods.

Removal of assumptions: (7*a*) *Unanimity of expectations*

Hitherto we have assumed that everyone expects the future average short-term rate to be the same as the present short-term rate, although with varying degrees of confidence. If we now remove this assumption and allow the members of the market to have different expectations, we seem to run the risk of allowing the whole concept of an expected rate to evaporate. Fortunately, however, the removal of the assumption of unanimity makes very little difference to our construction. Provided that the various expectations are distributed symmetrically around the expectation that the average future rate will be the same as the present rate, we find that the change makes little or no difference to the central parts of the curves, at the intersection of which we have assumed the equilibrium position to lie. The new differences of expectation frequently offset the existing differences of liquidity preference, and only in a minority of cases do they reinforce them. Thus the curves are steepened appreciably only near their upper and lower ends, giving us the changes shown in Fig. 1.6.

Removal of assumptions: (6) *No expectation of a change in rates*

Of our original assumptions only two are now left – that all transactions take place in a single, free and competitive market, and that the mid-point of market opinion is that interest rates are as likely to rise as to fall. The conclusions that we have reached on these assumptions are neither numerous nor precise. They are that the interest rate for the shorter of any two periods is likely, though not certain, to be lower than that for the longer period; and that, so long as holding cash is assumed to involve no costs, the short-term rate will be sufficiently above zero at least to cover the lender's transaction costs, including the cost of his own trouble. We now proceed to examine the effects of removing the assumption that the mid-point of market expectations is that interest rates are as likely to rise as to fall.

Before we can start this examination we have to deal with a question which we have hitherto postponed – that of defining just what we mean by 'an expected average rate of interest'. There are two possible definitions. If we merely wish to ascertain what the average of a varying short-term rate has been over a given past period, all we have to do is to cumulate the rates for the period and then find that constant rate which would have cumulated to the same total over the same period. Thus either a 2 per cent rate for one year followed by an 8 per cent rate for one year, or an 8 per cent rate followed by a 2 per cent rate, will cause £100 to increase to £110·16 by the end of the second year. Since 5 per cent for two successive years will cumulate to £110·25, it follows that either 2 per cent followed by 8 per cent, or 8 per cent followed by 2 per cent, gives an average yield of just under 5 per cent. But when we come to measure an average future rate, this method of calculation is appropriate only for those lenders and borrowers who are quite sure that they will wish to continue to lend or borrow on short term for the second year. As soon as it becomes possible that a lender will want his money back or a borrower to repay at the end of the first year, he is no longer indifferent whether the 2 per cent or the 8 per cent yield comes first. For him it would seem that the method of discounted cash flow is more appropriate. Under this method, each successive payment of interest (here assumed to be made annually in arrear) and the ultimate repayment of capital are discounted back to the beginning of the period at such a constant rate of interest as will produce the original amount lent. Where rates remain, or are expected to remain, unchanged throughout the period, both methods will, of course, give the same result. But with a changing rate the results of the two methods may differ substantially. Under the first method, either 2 per cent for five years followed by 8 per cent for five years, or 8 per cent for five years followed by 2 per cent for five years, gives an average yield of just under 5 per cent. By the second method, 2 per cent for five years followed by 8 per cent for five years gives an average yield of about 4·6 per cent, while 8 per cent for five years followed by 2 per cent for five years gives one of about 5·4 per cent. As it seems unlikely that there are many investors who would be indifferent whether the 8 per cent or the 2 per cent rate came first, the second definition is the one we shall adopt in the following discussion.

Let us start our examination of the effects of introducing an expectation of a change in interest rates by considering the simple case where it is expected that the short-term rate will fall by a given amount over a given period and thereafter remain stable at the lower level reached. Let us assume that it is expected that the one-year rate, at present 6 per cent, will have fallen to 4 per cent in a year's time and will thereafter remain at 4 per cent. Let us also assume that, when no change of rate is expected, the yield on an irredeemable loan (such as $2\frac{1}{2}$ per cent Consols) is 1 per cent higher than on a one-year loan. An investor continually investing and reinvesting in one-year loans can therefore expect to get 6 per cent for one year and thereafter 4 per cent a year for ever. Using our second definition of a future average rate, we find that the average yield from now to perpetuity is 4·08 per cent.[1] As the end of year 1 approaches, this yield falls gradually to 4 per cent. Since the level of the irredeemable rate is assumed to be 1 per cent above the expected average future one-year rate, the irredeemable rate will fall correspondingly, from 5·08 per cent to 5·0 per cent. The movements in the one-year rate, the expected average future one-year rate and the irredeemable rate are shown in Fig. 1.7.

We obtain a similar result if, instead of the short-term rate, the long-term rate is expected to fall. A lender who expects the yield on an irredeemable loan to fall from its present level of 5·1 per cent to 5·0 per cent in a year's time is expecting the price of a 5 per cent loan to rise from 98 to 100. In addition, he will receive a flat yield of 5·1 per cent. Excluding considerations of tax or expenses, this gives a total yield for the first year of 7·1 per cent. Since we are assuming that he will accept a yield on a one-year bond 1 per cent lower than on an irredeemable, this gives an equilibrium rate of 6·1 per cent for a one-year bond. Similarly a borrower, expecting

[1] £6 at the end of year 1 discounted for one year at 4·08 per cent has a present value of $£6 \times \frac{100}{104{\cdot}08} = £5{\cdot}8$.

£4 a year in perpetuity, first payment to be received at end of year 2, has a present value of $£100 \times \frac{4}{4{\cdot}08} \times \frac{100}{104{\cdot}08} = £94{\cdot}2$. Total £100.

to be able to issue a 5 per cent irredeemable loan at 100 in a year's time, as compared with 98 now, will be willing to pay up to 6·1 per cent for a one-year loan to enable him to postpone making his long-term issue. Since no further changes in rates are expected after the end of the first year, the irredeemable rate will then settle down at 5 per cent and both the current and expected future average one-year rates at 4 per cent.

While the expectation of a fall either in the short-term or in the long-term rate will always cause the current short-term rate to

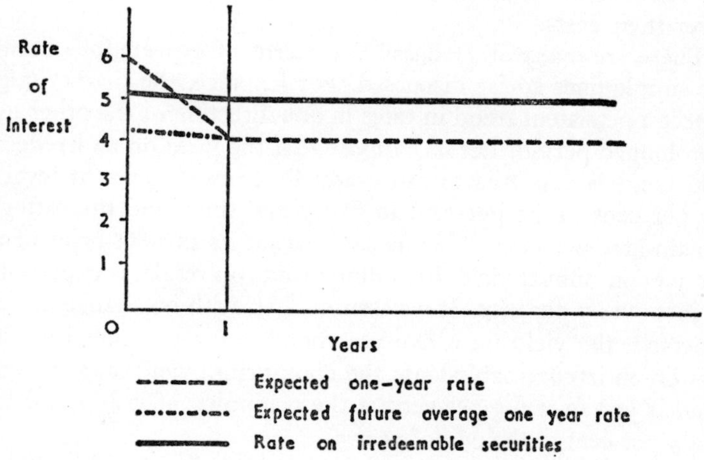

Fig. 1.7 *Long-term rate and expected change in short-term rate*

stand at less than its usual margin below the long-term rate, whether or not it will actually stand above it will depend on the size of the expected change in relation to the size of the normal margin, when no change in rates is expected.

Conversely, the expectation of a one-year rise in the short-term rate implies the expectation of a much smaller rise in the average future short-term rate and in the long-term rate, while the expectation of a rise in the long-term rate implies the expectation of a similar rise in the future average short-term rate and a much larger rise in the current short-term rate. When a rise in either rate is expected, therefore, the current short-term rate will stand exceptionally far below the long-term rate. The movements, however, may not always be symmetrical with those caused by the expectation of a fall in rates, for so long as there is no cost of holding cash, the current short-term rate cannot fall below the absolute level at which it covers the lender's operating costs. The expectation of a rise in the long-term rate so large that the equilibrium level of the current short-term rate would be insufficient to cover the lender's costs (or below zero if we assume that the lender has no costs) would therefore result in some potential lenders holding cash in preference to lending on either short or long term, and the remaining short-term lenders being able to obtain a rate sufficient to cover their costs.

There are many other possible patterns of expectations besides the simple ones so far discussed. For instance, the market might expect a persistent trend in rates in one direction or the other over a prolonged period. Let us suppose that the yield on an irredeemable bond is expected to fall gradually from its present level of 5·5 per cent to 5·0 per cent in five years' time, and thereafter to remain at 5 per cent. This means that, at its present price of 91, the average annual yield, including profits on resale, is expected to be just over 7 per cent. If we assume that, with no change of rates expected, the yield on a five-year bond is 0·5 per cent less than that on an irredeemable loan, the equilibrium yield on a five-year bond is just over 6·5 per cent at the beginning of year 1 and falls to 4·5 per cent at the end of year 5.

The equilibrium one-year rate at the beginning of each successive year will depend on the amount by which the irredeemable rate is expected to fall during the ensuing year. If the irredeemable rate is expected to fall by 0·1 per cent in each year, and if we again assume a margin of 1·0 per cent when no change in rates is expected, the equilibrium one-year rate is about 6·4 per cent at the beginning of year 1, falling gradually to about 6·1 per cent at the beginning of year 5 and then sharply to 4 per cent at the end of year 5. The movements in the irredeemable rate, the five-year rate, the expected average future one-year rate and the current one-year rate are shown in Fig. 1.8.

Thus the expectation of a prolonged gradual fall in the long-term rate implies an exceptionally high relative level for the short-term rate so long as the expectation of a further decline persists. Similarly, the expectation of a prolonged gradual rise in the long-

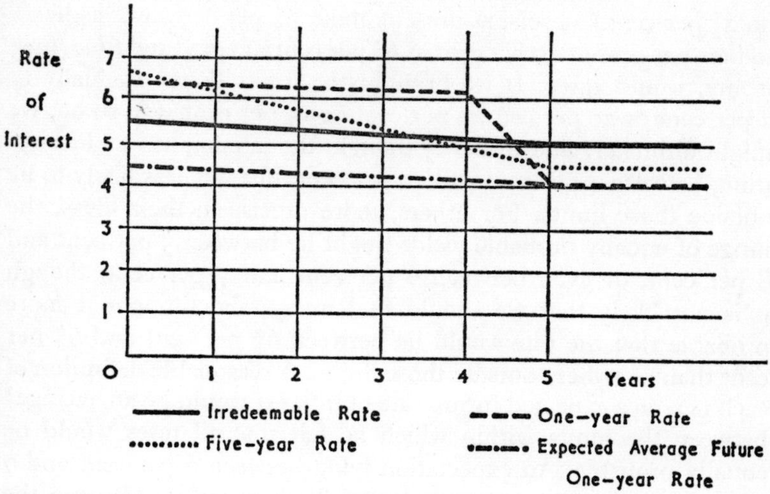

Fig. 1.8 Changes in short-term rates with expected prolonged change in long-term rate

term rate implies an unusually wide gap between the long-term and short-term rates as long as the expectation lasts.

In this discussion of the effects of an expectation of a change of rates, the calculations have been made on the assumption that the expectation is held with complete certainty. If an expectation is held with less than certainty, its effect on the relative levels of interest rates will be less than if it had been held with certainty. The effect of an expectation of a large change held with less than certainty would therefore be similar to that of a smaller change held with greater certainty. What is meant by varying degrees of certainty of expectation will be discussed in Lecture II.

II

EXPECTATIONS

Anyone who has given any thought at all to the subject must have some expectations about the future level of interest rates. Some people, perhaps, would deny this, and maintain that they had no idea at all about the level of interest rates in, say, ten years' time. But if we were to ask them whether they thought that the yield on $2\frac{1}{2}$ per cent Consols, at present about $6\frac{1}{2}$ per cent, was as likely to be 1 per cent or 40 per cent as $6\frac{1}{2}$ per cent in ten years' time, few, if any, would agree. If we brought the limits down gradually to 2 per cent or 20 per cent, 3 per cent or 15 per cent, and so on, we might ultimately find that they thought the rate might well be anything between 4 per cent and 10 per cent, but was less likely to lie outside those limits. For others, more precise in their ideas, the range of equally probable yields might lie between 5 per cent and 8 per cent, or even between 6 per cent and 7 per cent, though it is not likely that we should find many who thought it more probable that the rate would lie between $6\frac{3}{8}$ per cent and $6\frac{5}{8}$ per cent than anywhere outside those limits. A reasonable definition of each person's expected future rate of interest would be an average[1] between the limits within which he felt that all rates would be equally probable. An expectation lying between 6 per cent and 7 per cent, or between 5 per cent and 8 per cent, would mean the expectation of a $6\frac{1}{2}$ per cent rate. Both expectations would be of no change in the rate, though they would be held with different degrees of confidence. Similarly, expectations between 6 per cent and 9 per cent, and between 7 per cent and 8 per cent can both be said to be of a rise in the rate to $7\frac{1}{2}$ per cent, while if they are between 4 per cent and 7 per cent and between 5 per cent and 6 per cent, both show an expected fall to $5\frac{1}{2}$ per cent.

As was suggested at the end of the last lecture, the effect on the relationship between long-term and short-term interest rates of a given expectation of a change in either the long-term or the short-term rate will depend not only on the size of the expected change but also on the confidence with which the expectation is held. If we revert for the moment to the assumption of similar expectations throughout the market, this will mean that the effect of a given expectation will approximate more closely to what it would be if it were held with complete confidence the narrower is the range of equal probabilities for each member of the market. If members of the market, while having the same expectations, have differing amounts of confidence in them, then the effect of a given expectation of a change in rates will have more effect the larger the propor-

[1] Strictly speaking, this should be a geometric average, but the use of an arithmetic average makes little difference unless the spread is very wide.

tion of the market which holds it with a high degree of confidence. Finally, if members of the market can also hold different expectations, the strength of the effect will depend, not only on the degrees of confidence with which individual members hold their views, but also on how widely the expectations of different members are dispersed. If both a high proportion of members hold their views with confidence and a high proportion of these have very similar expectations, we should expect the results to approximate closely to those calculated in the last lecture for expectations held with complete certainty. If, on the other hand, members either hold their views with considerable uncertainty or differ widely between each other in their expectations, we should expect the effects of any change expected by the average of market opinion to be no greater than that of a much smaller change expected with confidence and unanimity.

If we accept that all members of the market have some kind of expectation about the future rate of interest, however wide the margin of uncertainty, the next question we have to ask is upon what these expectations are based. It is doubtful if many of them are derived from any full and careful analysis of the economic factors involved. Nor is it likely that members of the market will receive any clear guidance from specialists in the subject. No doubt there are occasions when some particular factor, such as a threat of war or of an impending balance-of-payments crisis, is so clearly dominant that short-period prediction can be made with confidence, if not always with success. But in general there is no sufficient consensus of opinion among experts about the factors involved, their relative importance, or even the methods of analysis to be employed, to allow any general view to emerge of sufficient authority to provide a confident guide for operators in the capital market. It is doubtful, for instance, whether the approach to the subject which I shall put forward in the third of these lectures would be acceptable to more than a minority of economists.

It would seem likely that the most important factor in determining any particular individual's expectations about future rates of interest is his knowledge, whether by personal experience or by other means, of the past levels of interest rates. If interest rates have for a long time moved within a narrow range about a constant level, he will tend to regard such a level as 'normal', and to expect a return to it as soon as the market rate diverges from it. If, on the other hand, market fluctuations have in the past been wide, although about a constant level, his range of uncertainty will be wider and his expectation that the rate will have returned to its 'normal' level by any particular future date will be less strong. While if his experience has been of rates standing for years at a time at each of a number of widely different levels, he will be likely to expect each shift of the rate to endure at its new level for some time.

The time for which a change in the current rate will have to persist before members of the market cease to expect it to return to its former 'normal' level is probably a function of the length of time for which the 'normal' level had been maintained, while the degree of certainty with which the expectation is held will tend to be a function of the past fluctuations about the 'normal' rate. If, as the result of a prolonged period of stability, the concept of the 'normal' rate is strongly imprinted, it may be many years before the market ceases to be more ready to expect rates to move in the direction of a return to the old level than to move further away from it. Thus if the old 'normal' long-term rate was $3\frac{1}{2}$ per cent, a fall in the current rate from $4\frac{1}{2}$ per cent to 4 per cent is more likely to give rise to expectations of a further fall than a rise from $4\frac{1}{2}$ per cent to 5 per cent is to give rise to expectations of a further rise. If, on the other hand, a prolonged rise in interest rates, punctuated by only temporary checks or falls, has given rise to expectations of a further rise, it may take a long period of stable or falling rates to convince the market that in future rates are as likely to fall as to rise further.

This suggestion, that the most frequent reason for people's expectations about future interest rates is their conception of what constitutes a 'normal' rate, or possibly a 'normal' trend, is so far no more than an hypothesis. I want now to try to test it by reference to historically recorded market rates. We have seen that, when a fall in either the long-term or the short-term rate is expected, the current short-term rate is higher, relatively to the long-term rate, than when no fall is expected. Similarly, when either rate is expected to rise, the short-term rate is further below the long-term rate than when no change is expected. If, therefore, we could know what the margin between the two rates would be with no change in rates expected, we could, by comparing the spread between current market rates with this normal spread, estimate in which direction the market was expecting one or other rate to move, and even, if we could estimate the degree of certainty with which the expectation was held, form some idea of the magnitude of the expected movement.

For such an investigation to be useful, we must find conditions in which the two of our original assumptions which have not yet been removed are fulfilled: that the transactions take place within the same market and that the market is a free and competitive one. To compare rates in two different markets is to introduce a time-lag of unknown and possibly varying duration; and although such a comparison might be a valid exercise in comparative statics, it might prove most misleading in a dynamic world. We cannot therefore usefully compare rates of interest on bills, which are dealt in on the discount market, with those on bonds, which are dealt in on the stock exchange. Again, the need for a free market rules out many periods since 1914 when government restrictions were in force to a greater or smaller extent; while the need for a fully competitive market seems to rule out the whole period since the first world war, when the Government became so important an operator on the market for fixed-interest securities that it has been able to exercise considerable monopoly influence, if not on the general level of interest rates, at least on the relationship between rates on loans for different durations.

The two examples which I have chosen for testing our hypothesis are therefore taken from the period before 1914. The first, in which the relationship between the long-term and short-term rate depends upon expectations about the short-term rate, is taken from the experience of the London discount market between 1890 and 1899; the second, in which the relationship depends on expectations about the long-term rate, is taken from the London stock exchange between 1902 and 1914.

The first test of our hypothesis is the simplest possible – a comparison between the rate on a six months' fine bank bill and the average rate on the two successive three months' bills covering the same period. Thus the rate on a six months' bill issued in the middle of January and maturing in mid-July is compared with the average rate on a three months' bill issued in mid-January and another issued in mid-April. If operators in the market expect the rate on the April three months' bill to be the same as on the January three months' bill, the three months' rate should be just enough below the six months' rate to compensate the buyer (*a*) for the lower liquidity of a six months' bill and (*b*) for the fact that half the interest obtained by holding two successive three months' bills will be received in mid-April, whereas nothing is received on a six months' bill until July, less any extra cost (or trouble) involved in buying two bills instead of one. If we could deduct from the six months' rate just enough to cover these items, we should find the remainder equal to the expected average yield on two successive three months' bills and also, when no change in rates was expected, to the current three months' rate. If, however, we find that the current three months' rate is different from the adjusted six months' rate, it implies that the current three months' rate is different from the expected average rate for the next two three months' periods, and therefore that the rate for the second three months' period is expected to be different from that for the first. If the current three months' rate is below the adjusted six months' rate, it shows that the market is expecting the three months' rate to rise; if it is above it, the market expects the three months' rate to fall.

Our first problem is to find the appropriate deduction to make from the six months' rate to adjust for lower liquidity and later receipt of interest. There is no completely valid way of making this adjustment, for it depends on the relationship between expectations, and we can deduce the expectations only if we know the adjustment. If, however, we can assume that, over a long period and with the level of rates at the end of the period about the same as at the beginning, errors of expectation tend to cancel out, we can perhaps take the average difference between the three months' rate and the six months' rate over the whole decade as an indication of the size of the adjustment needed. We find that over the whole ten years the average six months' rate is almost exactly 10 per cent higher than the average three months' rate. We shall accept this as indicating what the margin between the two rates would be if the market thought that the three months' rate was as likely to rise as to fall. We therefore deduct 9 per cent from the six months' rate before comparing it with the three months' rate for the same day.

The days chosen for the comparison are as nearly as possible in the middle of each calendar month. Whenever the adjusted six months' rate is above the three months' rate for the same day, it is taken as an indication that the three months' rate for the second half of the six months' period is expected to be twice as much above that for the first half of the period; where the three months' rate is lower than the adjusted six months' rate, it indicates that the rate for the second three months is expected to be twice as much below the first; and where the two rates are the same (differences of less than 0·1 per cent are disregarded), they indicate that no change in the three months' rate is expected. An example will make the method of calculation clear:

	per cent
Six months' rate, Jan–July	4·0
less 9 per cent	−0·36
Adjusted six months' rate	3·64
Three months' rate, Jan–Apr	3·25
Amount below six months' rate	0·39
Expected three months' rate, Apr–June	
3·25 + 0·39 × 2 = 3·25 + 0·78 =	4·03
Three months' rate, Jan–Apr	3·25
Expected average three months' rate for six months' period	3·64

Thus a six months' rate of 4·0 per cent accompanied by a three months' rate of 3·25 per cent is taken as indicating an expectation that the three months' rate will rise from 3·25 per cent in January to 4·03 per cent in April.

We are now ready to turn to our first experiment. I have calculated the expected changes in the three months' rate between the first and second halves of the six months' period starting in the middle of each month from January 1890 to December 1899, or 120 observations in all. The results are summarised in Table 1.1, which shows the number of rises, falls and no changes expected in each year and compares them with the number which actually occurred.

Table 1.1 shows that, over the whole decade, the adjusted six months' rate was above the three months' rate, indicating the expectation of a rise in the three months' rate, in 46 months out of the 120, and below it, indicating the expectation of a fall, in 45 months.

The number of rises actually realised was 44 and the number of falls 52. Over the whole period, therefore, total numbers of expectations and of realisations were not very widely different. If, however, we divide the decade into sub-periods, the results are very different.

There are four obvious sub-periods. There are two years at the beginning of the decade in which the three months' rate fluctuates widely, between 1·0 per cent and 6·0 per cent in 1890 and between 1·50 per cent and 3·88 per cent in 1891, but in which the average levels are within what had hitherto been a 'normal' range. Taking these two years together, the number of rises and falls expected (though not always their occasion) agrees closely with the number realised. Then there ensue four years of exceptionally cheap money, with the three months' rate falling as low as 0·5 per cent (in 1894), and rising above 2·0 per cent in only eight months out of the forty-eight. During these years the market, in spite of continual disappointments, seems to persist in expecting the rate to

TABLE 1.1

THREE MONTHS' BILL RATE, 1890–9: EXPECTATIONS AND RESULTS (SUMMARY)

Year	*Average 3 months' rate per cent*	*Rises*		*Falls*		*No change*	
		Expected	*Realised*	*Expected*	*Realised*	*Expected*	*Realised*
1890	3·6	2	5	9	5	1	2
1891	2·5	7	5	3	7	2	—
1890–1	3·0	9	10	12	12	3	2
1892	1·5	7	4	1	5	4	3
1893	2·1	5	2	2	6	5	4
1894	1·0	9	3	—	5	3	4
1895	0·8	6	3	2	4	4	5
1892–5	1·3	27	12	5	20	16	16
1896	1·5	1	5	4	4	7	3
1897	1·8	5	5	7	5	—	2
1898	2·6	4	6	8	6	—	—
1896–8	2·0	10	16	19	15	7	5
1899	3·3	—	6	9	5	3	1
1890–9	2·1	46	44	45	52	29	24

recover. During the whole four years there are no less than 27 expectations of rises, as against only 12 realised, and only 5 expectations of falls, as compared with 20 realised. The most erroneous year was 1894, when 9 rises were expected and only 3 realised, while no falls were expected and 5 realised.

The third period, from 1896 to 1898, shows a marked contrast with the second. The market failed to expect the upward turn of rates, so that it expected only 10 rises, as against 16 realised, and expected 19 falls as against 15 realised. Finally when, in 1899, the rate turned sharply upward to nearly the average level of 1890, the market was quite unable to foresee the rise, with no rises expected, as against 6 realised, and greatly overestimated the falls, with 9 expected and 5 realised.

These results suggest some tentative conclusions. In years, such as 1890–1, when the average level of rates remains within the range of what has come to be regarded as normal, the experience of the market enables its expectations, on the average, to agree pretty well with the actual results. In 1890–1 the average rate was 3 per cent. Of the ten months in which the rate stood above 3 per cent, seven were followed three months later by a fall, while of the thirteen months in which the rate stood below 3 per cent, eight were followed by a rise. Thus an operator who assumed that 3 per cent was a 'normal' rate, so that falls below it would be followed by rises and rises above it would be followed by falls, would have been right twice as often as he would have been wrong. When, however, these years were followed by four years of abnormally cheap money, with the three months' rate averaging little more than $1\frac{1}{4}$ per cent, the delayed adjustment of its ideas of what constituted a normal rate led the market badly astray. Of the 27 rises expected, only 9 actually occurred (the other 3 rises coming when no change was expected), while of the 20 falls which actually occurred, only 5 were expected.

By the end of 1895 the market's idea of what constituted a 'normal' rate seems to have undergone considerable adjustment. Although the average three months' rate in 1896 was only $1\frac{1}{2}$ per cent, or the same as in 1892, only 1 rise was expected, as compared with 7 in 1892, with 4 falls and 7 no changes it looks as if by now $1\frac{1}{2}$ per cent was accepted as 'normal'. This impression is confirmed by the experience of 1897 when, with an average rate of 1·8 per

TABLE 1.2

THREE MONTHS' BILL RATE, 1890–9: EXPECTATIONS[1] AND RESULTS[2]

	Expectations									Actual results								
	+			o			−			+			o			−		
Year	No.	Spread	Av.	No.	Spread	Av.	No.	Spread	Av.	No.	Spread	Av.	No.	Spread	Av.	No.	Spread	Av.
1890	2	1·00–1·88	1·44	1	2·75	2·75	9	2·88–6·00	4·38	5	1·00–4·00	2·70	2	2·88–4·00	3·44	5	4·13–6·00	4·93
1891	7	1·50–2·88	2·07	2	2·25–2·50	2·38	3	3·00–3·88	3·38	5	1·50–2·25	1·93	—	—	—	7	1·88–3·88	2·82
1890–1	9	1·00–2·88	1·93	3	2·25–2·75	2·50	12	2·88–6·00	4·13	10	1·00–4·00	2·31	2	2·88–4·00	3·44	12	1·88–6·00	3·70
1892	7	0·88–1·12	1·02	4	1·63–2·38	1·94	1	2·50	2·50	4	0·88–1·12	1·03	3	0·88–1·75	1·21	5	1·12–2·50	1·93
1893	5	1·25–2·38	1·62	5	1·63–2·50	1·90	2	3·75–4·25	4·00	2	1·25–1·62	1·43	4	1·38–2·38	1·66	6	1·62–4·25	3·03
1894	9	0·50–1·44	0·81	3	1·06–1·75	1·40	—	—	—	3	0·50–0·81	0·69	4	0·56–1·44	0·81	5	0·75–1·75	1·24
1895	6	0·56–0·81	0·68	4	0·62–1·19	0·82	2	1·12–1·38	1·25	3	0·62–0·75	0·66	5	0·56–0·81	0·66	4	0·81–1·38	1·12
1892–5	27	0·50–2·38	0·99	16	0·62–2·50	1·55	5	1·12–4·25	2·60	12	0·50–1·12	0·95	16	0·56–2·35	1·05	20	0·75–4·25	1·86
1896	1	0·69	0·69	7	0·56–1·88	0·95	4	1·00–3·75	2·75	5	0·62–2·62	1·35	3	0·56–1·06	0·77	4	1·00–3·75	2·34
1897	5	0·88–2·00	1·24	—	—	—	7	1·50–2·94	2·26	5	0·88–2·00	1·24	2	2·50–2·94	2·72	5	1·50–2·88	1·88
1898	4	1·19–1·81	1·47	—	—	—	8	2·38–3·88	3·20	6	1·19–2·38	1·77	—	—	—	6	2·94–3·88	3·48
1896–8	10	0·69–2·00	1·28	7	0·56–1·88	0·95	19	1·00–3·88	2·76	16	0·62–2·62	1·46	5	0·56–2·94	1·55	15	1·00–3·88	2·64
1899	—	—	—	3	2·00–3·50	2·54	9	2·19–6·25	3·55	6	2·00–3·62	2·83	1	2·12	2·12	5	2·50–6·25	4·05

[1] Three months' rate at time of
+ Expected rise in three months' rate
− Expected fall in three months' rate
o No change expected in three months' rate

[2] Three months' rate at time of
+ Actual rise in three months' rate
− Actual fall in three months' rate
o No change in three months' rate

cent, the market's expectation of 5 rises and 7 falls was closely fulfilled, and still more by that of 1899, when the market seems to have been quite unable to adjust its ideas back to an average level which would have seemed quite 'normal' at the beginning of the decade.

The impression that operators in the discount market were influenced by their acquired concepts of what constituted a normal rate and that they were slow to adjust them is confirmed by the more detailed analysis set out in Table 1.2. This shows, for each year of the decade, the levels of the three months' rate which coincided with expectations respectively of rises, falls and no change. It will be observed that in every year except one (1897) the highest rate which is expected to be followed by a rise is lower than the lowest rate which is expected to be followed by a fall. This confirms the impression that rates are expected to rise when they are regarded as 'low' with reference to some absolute standard, and to fall when they are regarded as 'high'. In periods when the rate fluctuates around a fairly constant level, this method gives quite satisfactory results; but when there is a marked trend, or a discontinuous change, in the average level of rates, there seems to be a considerable lag in adjusting the concept of what now constitutes the average rate about which the actual rate can be expected to fluctuate. The most striking example of too high a 'normal' occurs in 1894, when rates of up to 1·44 per cent are expected to be followed by rises, whereas no rate of more than 0·81 per cent was in fact followed by a rise. The opposite effect is seen in 1896, when the period of cheap money was beginning to come to an end. In that year only one rise was expected, to follow a rate of 0·69 per cent, whereas in fact five rises occurred, following rates of up to 2·62 per cent. By 1897, however, the market's idea of a normal rate seems to have caught up with the changing conditions, so that in that year expectations are closely fulfilled, but in 1898 it again begins to fall behind the rising trend, while in 1899 the market seems to have persisted in disbelieving in the permanence of the sharp further rise in rates, so that it expected no fewer than 9 falls and no rises. We thus have some evidence both of the persistence of the concept of a normal rate and of its gradual shifting under the pressure of experience.

Whereas my first example was concerned with expectations

about the shorter of two interest rates, and was taken from the London discount market, my second is concerned with expectations about the longer rate, and is taken from the London stock exchange. It covers the relationship between the yields on 2½ per cent Consols and those on medium-term Exchequer Bonds during the years 1902–13. It is in several ways less satisfactory than my first example. Ideally, we need to compare Consols with bonds of a constant life. For this we should need new issues of, say, three-year bonds every month. In fact such issues were made only at considerable intervals, so that we have to use the same bond over a period of many months, during which its remaining life is continually shortening. Thus, if we start with a three-year bond, after a year we are comparing the yield on Consols with that of a two-year bond, and after two years with that of a one-year bond. Fortunately, however, this difficulty is not as serious as it looks, since during this period the yields to maturity of bonds with lives of between one and five years do not differ from each other very much. A second, and minor, difficulty is peculiar to this period. The only suitable bond for the last part of the period matured in 1915, when interest rates were much affected by the war. It is therefore assumed, for the purpose of this exercise, that these bonds matured in July 1914, when their market price was in fact very close to their redemption price.

A much more serious difficulty is that of deciding what margin to assume between the yields on Exchequer Bonds and on Consols in conditions where there was no expectation of a change in either interest rate. It does not help us much to take an average over a long period, for conditions have changed so greatly that no inference drawn from it would be valid. For the sixty years from 1902 to 1961 the average flat yield on 2½ per cent Consols was about 9 per cent higher than that on medium-term bonds; but during the first half of this period the average yield on the bonds was about 4 per cent higher than that on Consols, while during the second half of the period, which included nearly twenty years of 'cheap money', it was 27 per cent lower. If we fall back on *a priori* reasoning we are not much better off. In the first lecture we saw that, when no change in rates was expected, liquidity considerations would lead to a tendency for the short-term rate to be below the long-term rate. But we also saw that, where considerations of liquidity were unimportant to both borrowers and lenders in that particular market, the short-term rate could conceivably be equal to, or even above, the long-term rate. We cannot be sure that these exceptional conditions did not exist in the market for British Government securities in the years before 1914. It seems likely that at that time a large proportion of the holders of government securities consisted of investors, such as trustees, who were unlikely to need to realise capital, and who might have attached importance to avoiding the trouble of frequently having to re-invest the proceeds of maturing securities. At the same time it seems that the Government found it convenient to continue to renew the modest amount of Exchequer Bonds in existence even though it could have funded them into long-dated or irredeemable stock at some saving of interest. We cannot, therefore, be quite sure that, even with no expectations of a fall in interest rates, the yield to maturity on Exchequer Bonds would have stood below that on Consols.

There is, however, one thing of which we can be quite sure, and that is that investors' expectations must have been very different from what actually happened. In Table 1.3 are set out, for January, April, July and October of each year from 1902 to 1913, the gross yields to maturity of five successive series of Exchequer Bonds. Against these are set the flat yields on 2½ per cent Consols, and also the yields after allowing for any capital gains or losses, on the assumption that the Consols were sold on the dates on which the Exchequer Bonds matured. These I call 'yields to re-sale'; they are the exact equivalent, *ex post*, of the yields to maturity on dated securities.

It will be seen that the flat yield on Consols was consistently below the yield to maturity on Exchequer Bonds from 1902 until April 1908, and thereafter consistently above it. From 1902 until 1908 the average flat yield on Consols was 2·8 per cent, as against an average yield to maturity on bonds of 3·2 per cent, whereas from 1908 to 1914 it was 3·1 per cent, as compared with the average Exchequer Bond yield to maturity of 2·9 per cent. For the whole period the average flat yield on Consols was 3·0 per cent, or 0·1 per cent less than the yield on Exchequer Bonds.

If we look at the 'yield to re-sale' of Consols, instead of the flat yield, the results of holding Consols instead of Exchequer Bonds

TABLE 1.3

YIELDS ON SHORT BONDS AND CONSOLS, 1902–14

Date	3% *Exch. Bonds 1905* *Yield to maturity*	2½% *Consols* *Flat yield*	*Yield to re-sale (Dec 1905)*
1902 Jan	3·4	2·7	1·3
Apr	3·1	2·7	1·2
July	2·9	2·6	0·6
Oct	3·2	2·7	1·3
1903 Jan	3·1	2·7	1·3
Apr	3·4	2·8	1·9
July	3·1	2·7	1·3
Oct	3·8	2·8	2·9
1904 Jan	4·0	2·9	3·4
Apr	3·4	2·8	3·3
July	3·2	2·8	2·3
Oct	3·3	2·8	3·1
	3% *Exch. Bonds 1907*		*Yield to re-sale (Oct 1907)*
1905 Jan	3·1	2·8	0·0
Apr	2·9	2·8	−2·1
July	3·0	2·8	−2·2
Oct	3·0	2·8	−1·5
1906 Jan	2·9	2·8	−3·4
Apr	2·9	2·8	−4·4
July	3·1	2·9	−3·9
Oct	3·4	2·9	−2·4
	3% *Exch. Bonds 1909*		*Yield to re-sale (Oct 1909)*
1907 Jan	3·3	2·9	1·3
Apr	3·4	2·9	1·5
July	3·2	3·0	2·3
Oct	3·2	3·0	3·0
1908 Jan	3·2	3·0	2·5
Apr	3·0	2·9	−0·6
July	2·7	2·9	−1·8
Oct	2·8	2·9	0·5

Date	2¾% *Exch. Bonds 1906–15* *Yield to maturity*	*Consols* *Flat yield*	*Yield to re-sale (July 1914)*
1909 Jan	2·8	3·0	1·4
Apr	2·7	2·9	0·9
July	2·8	3·0	1·2
Oct	2·8	3·0	1·3
1910 Jan	2·8	3·0	1·2
Apr	2·9	3·1	1·6
July	2·9	3·0	1·2
Oct	3·0	3·1	1·7
	3% *Exch. Bonds 1915*		
1911 Jan	3·1	3·2	2·0
Apr	2·9	3·1	0·9
July	3·0	3·2	1·5
Oct	3·0	3·2	2·4
1912 Jan	3·0	3·2	2·5
Apr	2·9	3·2	2·0
July	3·1	3·4	4·4
Oct	3·3	3·4	5·3
1913 Jan	3·0	3·3	4·2
Apr	3·0	3·3	4·3
July	3·1	3·4	7·0
Oct	3·1	3·4	7·5
1914 Jan	3·0	3·5	
Apr	2·5	3·3	
July	2·9	3·3	

are very much more unfavourable. There was no date between January 1902 and April 1912 when the yield to re-sale on Consols was as high as the yield to maturity on Exchequer Bonds. During most of the time it was between 1 per cent and 2 per cent lower, while during most of 1905–6, as well as for a short time in 1908, it was substantially negative. Not until the middle of 1912 did it become more profitable (for those who sold in July 1914) to invest in Consols rather than Exchequer Bonds.

In Table 1.4 an attempt is made to deduce from these changes in the relative yields on Exchequer Bonds and Consols what the expectations of investors were about the future price of Consols. In view of the difficulty in determining what the relationship between the yields would be if interest rates were thought to be as likely to rise as to fall, the calculations are made on two alternative assumptions, the first (assumption A) that the yields would be the same, and the second (assumption B) that the yield on Consols would be 10 per cent higher than that on Exchequer Bonds. The differences between the yield to maturity on Exchequer Bonds and (A) the flat yield on Consols or (B) the flat yield on Consols plus 10 per cent represent (on the assumption that at this period tax considerations can be ignored) the average annual rises or falls in the price of Consols which would be needed to make the yield (A), or the adjusted yield (B), on Consols equal to the yield to maturity on Exchequer Bonds. From these in turn are calculated what the prices of Consols would need to be on the date of maturity of each series of Exchequer Bonds.

It will be seen that the whole period from 1902 to 1913 falls into two very distinct parts. In the first, up to the middle of 1908, the expected future price of Consols, on both assumptions, is above the current price. After the middle of 1908 the price expected on assumption A lies consistently below the current price, while the price expected on assumption B starts by being only very slightly above the current price and finishes by being the same as the current price. It therefore looks as if until 1908 investors consistently expected the price of Consols to recover towards its earlier level, while after 1908 they expected it to fall further or at best to remain unchanged. Since the peak price of Consols was reached in 1897, it would seem that the idea of a return to, or towards, the previous 'normal' level was so deeply implanted that it took more

TABLE 1.4

ACTUAL AND EXPECTED PRICES OF 2½ PER CENT CONSOLS, 1902–13

Date		*Current price of 2½% Consols*	*Expected average annual change in price of Consols (%)*		*Expected price of Consols at end of period*	
			A	*B*	*A*	*B*
			Period to December 1905			
1902	Jan	94·0	+0·74	+1·08	96·7	97·9
	Apr	94·1	+0·44	+0·75	95·5	96·6
	July	94·5	+0·26	+0·55	95·3	96·3
	Oct	93·0	+0·51	+0·83	94·5	95·4
1903	Jan	92·8	+0·41	+0·72	93·8	94·7
	Apr	91·0	+0·65	+0·99	92·6	93·4
	July	92·3	+0·39	+0·70	93·2	93·9
	Oct	88·5	+0·98	+1·36	90·4	91·1
1904	Jan	87·9	+1·16	+1·56	89·9	90·5
	Apr	88·1	+0·56	+0·90	88·9	89·4
	July	89·4	+0·40	+0·72	89·9	90·3
	Oct	88·1	+0·46	+0·79	88·5	88·9
			Period to October 1907			
1905	Jan	88·2	+0·27	+0·58	88·8	89·6
	Apr	90·9	+0·15	+0·44	91·0	91·8
	July	90·5	+0·24	+0·54	90·9	91·5
	Oct	88·4	+0·17	+0·47	88·6	89·3
1906	Jan	89·8	+0·12	+0·41	90·0	90·4
	Apr	90·8	+0·15	+0·44	91·0	91·4
	July	87·8	+0·26	+0·57	88·0	88·4
	Oct	85·4	+0·47	+0·81	85·7	86·1
			Period to October 1909			
1907	Jan	86·9	+0·42	+0·75	87·8	88·6
	Apr	85·8	+0·49	+0·83	86·8	87·5
	July	84·0	+0·22	+0·54	84·4	85·0
	Oct	82·6	+0·18	+0·50	82·9	83·4
1908	Jan	83·4	+0·21	+0·53	83·6	84·1
	Apr	87·0	+0·13	+0·43	87·1	87·5
	July	87·5	−0·16	+0·11	87·4	87·6
	Oct	84·6	−0·16	+0·12	84·5	84·7

TABLE 1.4—*continued*

Date		*Current price of 2½% Consols*	*Expected average annual change in price of Consols (%)* A	B	*Expected price of Consols at end of period* A	B
			Period to July 1914			
1909	Jan	83·5	−0·19	+0·09	82·6	83·9
	Apr	85·0	−0·27	+0·03	83·9	85·1
	July	84·1	−0·17	+0·11	83·3	84·5
	Oct	82·6	−0·23	+0·05	81·7	82·7
1910	Jan	82·8	−0·22	+0·06	81·9	83·0
	Apr	81·1	−0·18	+0·11	80·4	81·4
	July	82·1	−0·15	+0·14	81·6	82·5
	Oct	80·1	−0·12	+0·18	79·7	80·6
1911	Jan	79·3	−0·05	+0·26	79·1	80·0
	Apr	81·5	−0·17	+0·12	81·0	81·7
	July	78·9	−0·17	+0·13	78·5	79·2
	Oct	77·6	−0·22	+0·08	77·1	77·7
1912	Jan	77·3	−0·23	+0·07	76·8	77·4
	Apr	78·0	−0·30	−0·01	77·5	78·0
	July	74·1	−0·27	+0·04	73·6	74·2
	Oct	73·0	−0·13	+0·20	72·8	73·2
1913	Jan	74·9	−0·33	−0·03	74·5	74·9
	Apr	74·9	−0·33	−0·03	74·5	74·9
	July	73·0	−0·33	−0·02	72·8	73·0
	Oct	72·8	−0·34	−0·03	72·6	72·8
1914	Jan	72·5				
	Apr	75·8				
	July	75·8				

than ten years of falling prices to remove it; even then it was replaced by the expectation of a stable, or at most a slightly falling, price. Not until the recovery in gilt-edged prices which accompanied the incipient depression of the first half of 1914 did the expected price fall appreciably below the price actually recorded.

It may be noted that the discontinuous change in the pattern of expectations in the middle of 1908 occurred, not as the result of a further fall in prices, but at a moment when the price of Consols had made a substantial, though temporary, recovery. It looks as if investors had by then adjusted their concept of a 'normal' price so far that they regarded the price reached in the middle of 1908 as equal to it, if not above it. They therefore seem to have concluded that no further rise could be looked for, or even that a fall might be expected. In the third of these lectures we shall see that in the middle of 1908 the long-term rate of interest also shows a discontinuity of another type.

III

THE LEVEL OF INTEREST RATES

My first two lectures have been concerned primarily with the relationship between long-term and short-term interest rates, and I have said little about the absolute level of rates. In this lecture I shall discuss the factors determining the absolute level of the long-term rate, and thus (given the relationships between rates) the equilibrium levels of the whole constellation of interest rates.

My approach to this question is basically Keynesian, though with some variations. I hold the view that the long-term rate of interest depends primarily on the relationship between the quantity of money and the national money income. I do not share the view of the Radcliffe Committee that money, in this country and at the present time, is such a nebulous concept that attempts to measure its quantity have no meaning. It is true that all assets, or at any rate all transferable assets, share with money the function of a store of value – indeed, in recent years many of them have been better stores of value than money. But the essential function of money, which distinguishes it from all other types of assets, is that of a medium of exchange – that it is widely and generally accepted in payment of debts. There are no doubt places where this function has at times been performed by many different types of assets, and where the distinction between money and non-money is blurred – as, for instance, a country where trade bills are passed freely from hand to hand in payment of debts – but this country at the present time is not one of them. In this country today, the function of money is confined strictly to three types of assets: coin, Bank of England notes and bank deposits. I do not think that we need trouble ourselves with the distinction between current accounts and deposit accounts, so long as they are kept with the same banks. In such conditions deposit accounts are merely current accounts held idle, like bank-notes in a safe with a time-lock on the door; though balances can of course be held idle on current account as well as on deposit account.

All the money in existence at any given moment can be divided, conceptually if not statistically, into two parts, one of which is held for the purpose of financing transactions while the other is held merely as a highly liquid store of value and is temporarily idle. The first part we can call active balances and the second idle balances.

Active balances are again divided into two parts – and it is here, I think, that I diverge from the Keynesian approach – one of which is held for the financing of transactions which give rise to incomes, while the other is held for the purpose of financing capital transactions, that is to say, for the making and repayment of loans and for the purchase of existing assets. On the strictest definition, income balances would consist only of those used for payments for services, either of persons or of assets, while the purchase of any physical object would be classed as a capital transaction, since it would involve merely the replacement of one asset by another. It would, however, be inconvenient to treat an ice-cream as a capital investment with a high rate of depreciation; and for practical purposes I treat income transactions as including, not only payments for services, but also all transactions concerned with the current flow of new goods and services: payments from members of the public to shops, from shops to manufacturers, from manufacturers to suppliers of materials, and from all of them back to the public in payment of wages, salaries, rent, interest, dividends, and so forth. The money thus goes round and round in what I call in Fig. 1.9 'income transaction balances'.

The money in what I call 'capital transaction balances' also goes round and round, for buying existing assets, both physical and financial, and for making and repaying loans. Whereas the amounts that most people hold on income account are probably fairly small but fairly steady, much of the money in the capital account is held only intermittently and for short periods, but as the amounts held are relatively large, the aggregate amount is certainly substantial.

Probably the great bulk of notes and coin is normally in the income circulation; there is probably a certain amount in idle balances, but probably very little in the capital circulation. The deposit accounts with the banks are presumably all in idle balances, though it is probable that a good deal of current-account money is also held idle. How much depends, I suppose, on the rate of interest paid on deposits; the higher these are, the more trouble people will be prepared to take to shift money on to deposit for short periods.

We find that the amount of cash and coin in the hands of the public normally moves very closely in proportion to the national

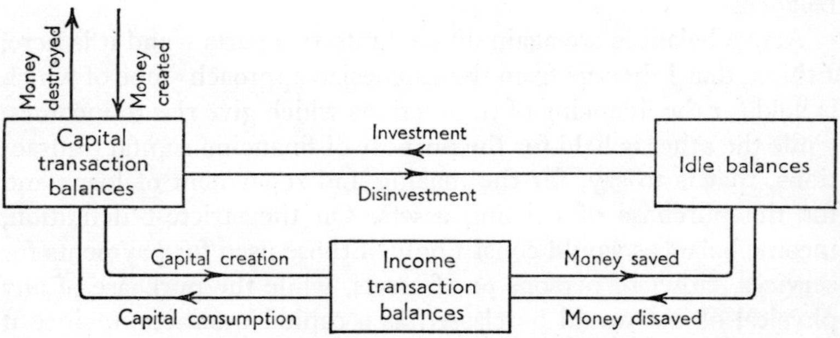

Fig. 1.9 Monetary stocks and flows

money income and that this proportion does not change perceptibly with changes in interest rates. Such variations in the ratio as we have seen have come mainly from the effects of war, when, as can be seen from Table 1.5, people seem to have kept an unusually high proportion of their assets in cash, either because of the need for extra liquidity, or in order to avoid awkward questions about black-market operations or tax evasion. It is possible that some such considerations continued for a long time after the war, for whenever an issue of notes was called in for replacement there was quite a sharp drop in the ratio of notes held by the public to national income. Apart from these exceptional movements, the remarkable stability of the ratio of cash to income, which is now the same as before the war, suggests that, since cash is probably held almost entirely in the income circulation, the quantity of all money in the income circulation also constitutes an almost constant proportion of national income, a proportion which is independent of the rate of interest.

The total quantity of money, on the other hand, and *a fortiori* the quantity in the capital circulation and idle balances, has shown very wide variations in its ratio to national money income. We have no means of estimating the total quantity of money in the income circulation, but we shall get a closer approximation to the quantity in the capital circulation and idle balances combined if we take only bank deposits than if we take the total of all money. I therefore propose to investigate the relationship to the rate of interest, not of all money, but of bank deposits only.

Fig. 1.9 shows, in the simplest possible form, my picture of the stocks and flows of money in a closed system. It assumes that money lent by the banks either to the private or the public sector is initially used for capital expenditure. It is therefore shown as entering the capital circulation. The capital circulation is also fed by money, whether newly saved or not, which is transferred from idle balances; or, more rarely, from the income circulation by not replacing physical capital for the replacement of which money has been set aside out of income. (If fixed investment is calculated gross, there cannot be negative fixed investment; but it is always possible to run down stocks.) In all cases, money can enter the capital circulation only by being lent or repaid, or by being used for the purchase of an existing capital asset. Whenever this happens, it increases the aggregate demand for assets and tends to raise their aggregate price. If we can assume that fixed-interest securities are representative of all non-monetary assets and that their prices move similarly to those of all assets, an inflow of money into the capital circulation will also tend to lower the rate of interest.

Money leaves the capital circulation either to finance the creation of new capital assets or to be held idle. (If it is withdrawn in order to be consumed, it is assumed that it is held idle first.) Whatever the reason, its withdrawal from the capital circulation means that some asset is sold, or some money borrowed or repaid without the proceeds being reused inside the capital circulation. It therefore tends to lower aggregate asset prices and, if prices of fixed-interest securities move similarly to prices of all assets, to raise the rate of interest.

Money enters the income circulation either from the capital circulation to finance the creation of new physical capital assets or from idle balances to finance the consumption of past savings. In either case aggregate incomes tend to rise. It leaves the income circulation either because consumption is less than income or, more rarely, because money set aside for replacing stocks is lent or repaid, or used to buy an existing capital asset. In either case aggregate incomes tend to fall. If we assume that changes in aggregate incomes are proportionate to the quantity of money in the income circulation, aggregate incomes can rise only if more money enters the income circulation than leaves it. In this model, money is not regarded as saved until it leaves the income circulation, and investment therefore exceeds saving by the amount of the increase in income transactions balances.

Idle balances are fed from the income circulation by money newly saved, and from the capital circulation by money disinvested, and are depleted by being transferred to the capital circulation, for the making or repayment of a loan or for the purchase of an existing capital asset, or, more rarely, to the income circulation to finance consumption in excess of income. The net flow from idle balances to the capital circulation depends on three factors: on the amount of new saving, which is continually tending to raise the amount of idle money above the proportion of assets which it is desired to hold in this form at the existing rate of interest; on changes in the yield offered on investments, which, if the yield on fixed-interest securities is assumed to be typical of that on all investments, are the same as changes in the rate of interest; and on changes in the liquidity preference schedule, which determines the proportion of total assets which it is desired to hold as idle balances at each level of interest rates.

In the light of this model, and of our discussion in the first two lectures of the relationship between long-term and short-term interest rates, I have attempted to construct, from historical data, liquidity preference schedules for the United Kingdom, and shall try to decide how far the various changes in interest rates have been movements along the functions, temporary departures from the functions, or actual shifts in the functions, and why.

In Table 1.5 I show, for each year from 1921 to 1965, the U.K. net national income, the average total of clearing-bank deposits, the percentage ratio of clearing-bank deposits to national income, and the average yield on 2½ per cent Consols, representing the

TABLE 1.5

NATIONAL INCOME, QUANTITY OF MONEY AND YIELD ON CONSOLS, 1921–65

Year	*Net national money income (£m.)*	*Net clearing-bank deposits (£m.)*	*Currency circulation in hands of public (£m.)*	*Currency circulation as percentage of national income*	*Bank deposits as percentage of national income*	*Av. yield on 2½% Consols (%)*
1921	4,662	1,764	392	8·4	37·8	5·21
1922	3,766	1,730	355	9·4	45·8	4·42
1923	3,643	1,629	343	9·4	44·7	4·31
1924	3,757	1,622	346	9·2	43·1	4·39
1925	3,979	1,610	340	8·5	40·4	4·44
1926	3,764	1,615	336	8·9	42·9	4·55
1927	3,981	1,661	333	8·4	41·8	4·56
1928	4,006	1,709	331	8·3	42·6	4·47
1929	4,147	1,743	324	7·8	42·0	4·60
1930	4,149	1,747	321	7·7	42·1	4·48
1931	3,763	1,711	324	8·6	45·5	4·39
1932	3,614	1,745	331	9·1	48·3	3·74
1933	3,704	1,906	337	9·1	51·5	3·39
1934	3,975	1,830	344	8·7	46·0	3·10
1935	4,146	1,947	358	8·6	46·9	2·89
1936	4,355	2,156	390	9·0	49·5	2·93
1937	4,599	2,220	437	9·5	48·3	3·28
1938	4,816	2,213	442	9·2	46·0	3·38
1939	5,160	2,175	454	8·8	42·1	3·72
1940	6,120	2,408	519	8·5	39·4	3·40
1941	7,080	2,849	603	8·5	40·2	3·13
1942	7,800	3,145	763	9·8	40·3	3·03
1943	8,300	3,544	928	11·2	42·7	3·10
1944	8,500	4,012	1,098	12·9	47·2	3·14
1945	8,480	4,541	1,255	14·8	53·5	2·92
1946	8,100	4,922	1,332	16·4	60·7	2·60
1947	8,650	5,454	1,351	15·6	63·0	2·76
1948	9,678	5,703	1,229	12·7	59·0	3·21
1949	10,249	5,761	1,238	12·1	56·2	3·30
1950	10,792	5,800	1,244	11·6	53·7	3·54
1951	11,873	5,918	1,291	10·9	49·8	3·78
1952	12,790	5,844	1,370	10·7	45·7	4·23
1953	13,791	6,012	1,462	10·6	43·6	4·05
1954	14,597	6,225	1,551	10·6	42·7	3·75
1955	15,484	6,171	1,657	10·7	39·8	4·17

TABLE 1.5—*continued*

Year	*Net national money income (£m.)*	*Net clearing bank deposits (£m.)*	*Currency circulation in hands of public (£m.)*	*Currency circulation as percentage of national income*	*Bank deposits as percentage of national income*	*Av. yield on 2½% Consols (%)*
1956	16,837	5,998	1,765	10·5	35·6	4·73
1957	17,825	6,122	1,842	10·3	34·3	4·98
1958	18,584	6,319	1,905	10·2	33·9	4·98
1959	19,532	6,661	1,969	10·1	34·5	4·82
1960	20,823	6,900	2,062	9·9	33·1	5·42
1961	22,277	7,035	2,151	9·7	31·6	6·20
1962	23,221	7,228	2,160	9·3	31·1	5·98
1963	24,656	7,560	2,218	9·0	30·6	5·58
1964	26,496	8,069	2,341	8·8	30·4	6·03
(1965)	28,159	8,498	2,493	8·8	30·2	6·42

Sources: National income: London and Cambridge, 'Key Statistics', Official National Income Statistics.
Quantity of money: 'Key Statistics', Clearing Bank Statements, Official Statistics.
Yield on Consols: 'Key Statistics', Official Statistics.

long-term rate of interest. I use clearing-bank deposits, rather than the total deposits of all banks in the United Kingdom, merely because they are the only figures conveniently available for the whole period. I do not think it likely that the differences between the movements of the two series are large enough to invalidate my conclusions.

In Fig. 1.10 the annual average yields on Consols are plotted as a scatter diagram against the annual ratios of average clearing-bank deposits to national income. Different symbols are used for the three periods, 1921 to 1933, 1934 to 1946 and 1947 to 1965. It will be seen that the years from 1947 to 1965 form a markedly continuous series, with the yield on Consols rising as the ratio of deposits to national income falls, from 2¾ per cent with a 63 per cent ratio in 1947 to 6·4 per cent with a 30 per cent ratio in 1965. In 1963, when the ratio was 31 per cent, or just under half what it was in 1947, the yield on Consols was 5·6 per cent, or just over twice its 1947 level. In fact a curve, passing through 2½ per cent at a ratio of 70, and showing the yield on Consols as doubling every time the ratio halves, provides a remarkably good fit for the series as a whole. This curve passes slightly below the rates for the period 1921 to 1933, which, except for the years 1925, 1932 and 1933, are about 0·5 per cent above it. But the rates for the years 1934 to 1946 are all well below the curve and seem to be on a

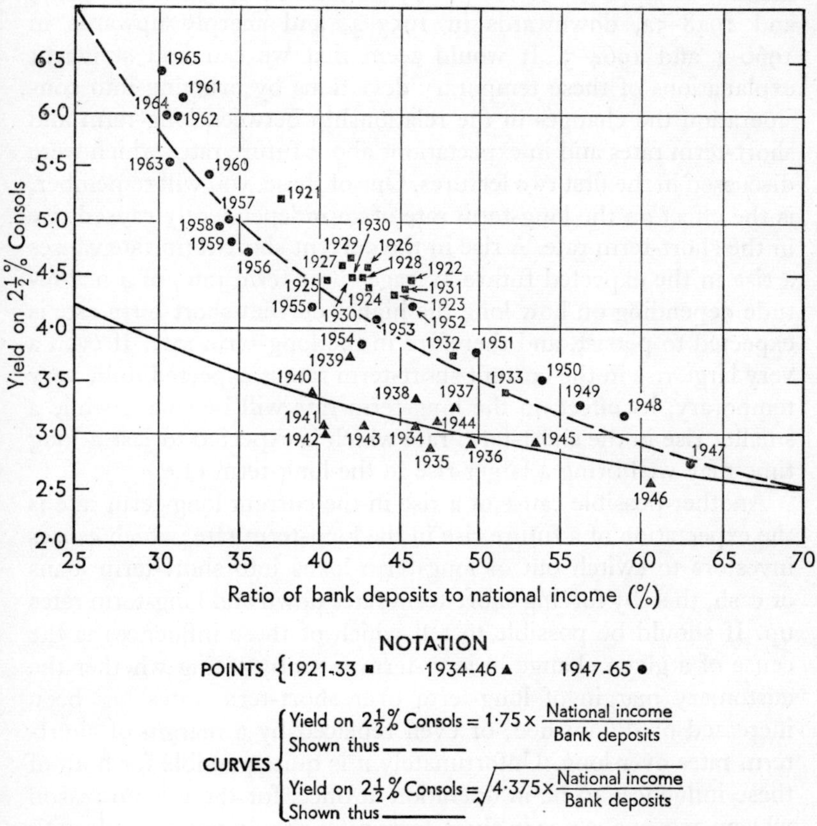

Fig. 1.10 U.K. bank deposits and long-term interest rates, 1921–65

different schedule altogether. This seems (surely by a coincidence) to be well described by a curve which also passes through 2½ per cent with a ratio of 70, but which shows the rate as doubling only when the ratio falls by three-quarters. It looks as if, between 1933 and 1934, there was a large downward shift and flattening of the whole liquidity preference function, and that this persisted, with a temporary upward deviation in 1937–9, until 1946, after which year there was an upward shift back to something very like the function which had existed in 1921–33.

In addition to these major shifts in the function, there are a number of smaller and temporary deviations, upwards in 1937–9 and 1948–52, downwards in 1953–4, and sharply upwards in 1960–1 and 1964–5. It would seem that we can find sufficient explanations of these temporary deviations by bringing into consideration the changes in the relationship between long-term and short-term rates and in expectations about future rates which were discussed in the first two lectures. One of these, you will remember, is the effect on the long-term rate of an independently caused rise in the short-term rate. A rise in the current short-term rate causes a rise in the expected future average short-term rate, of a magnitude depending on how long the higher current short-term rate is expected to persist, and therefore in the long-term rate. If even a very large rise in the current short-term rate is expected to be very temporary, its effect on the long-term rate will be small; while a smaller rise in the short-term rate which is expected to last a long time may well bring a larger rise in the long-term rate.

Another possible cause of a rise in the current long-term rate is the expectation of a future rise in the long-term rate, which causes investors to switch out of long-term loans into short-term loans or cash, thereby forcing short-term rates down and long-term rates up. If should be possible to tell which of these influences is the cause of a given change in long-term rates by seeing whether the customary margin of long-term over short-term rates has been increased or diminished, or even replaced by a margin of short-term rates over long. Unfortunately it is quite possible for both of these influences to be in operation at once, for there is no reason why an exogenous rise in short-term rates should not coincide with fears of a future rise in long-term rates. In this case, it is possible for both rates to rise together, leaving the margin unchanged.

This is in fact what seems to have happened in 1936–9. (See Table 1.6.)

Of the rise of 0·79 per cent in the long-term rate between 1936 and 1939 about 0·25 per cent can be accounted for by a drop in the deposits–national income ratio from 49·5 per cent to 42·1 per cent. The remainder can well be accounted for by growing fears of war,

TABLE 1.6

LONG-TERM AND SHORT-TERM INTEREST RATES, 1935–40

Year	*Short bonds*	*Consols*	*Margin*
1935	2·06	2·89	0·83
1936	2·15	2·93	0·78
1937	2·48	3·28	0·80
1938	2·58	3·38	0·80
1939	2·89	3·72	0·83
1940	2·52	3·40	0·88

which in all past experience had been accompanied by rising interest rates. Why this was not accompanied by the normal fall in short-term rates and a widening of the margin can be explained by an accidental and wholly extraneous circumstance. This was the 'Treasury bill famine', caused by the methods used to finance the fluctuating requirements of the exchange equalisation account, and resulting in a fall in the clearing banks' liquid assets ratio from 32·2 per cent in 1936 to 28·8 per cent in 1939, which forced the banks to sell short-dated government bonds in order to finance their customers' loan requirements. That the rise in the yields on short bonds was not due to any balance-of-payments considerations is shown by the fact that the Treasury bill rate remained at an extremely low level throughout.

Of the rise in the yield on Consols from 2·76 per cent in 1947 to 3·78 per cent in 1951, about three-quarters can be accounted for by the fall in the deposits–national income ratio from 63 per cent to 50 per cent. The remainder was almost certainly due to fears about future prices of long-dated securities, for the yield on short bonds fell from 2·22 per cent in 1947 to 1·86 per cent in 1951, so that the margin of the Consols' yield over that of short bonds widened from 0·54 per cent in 1947 and 1·20 per cent in 1948 to 1·92 per cent in 1951. (See Table 1.7.)

While the rise in the yield on Consols up to 1951 can be explained on the grounds of fears about the future level of prices of long-dated government securities, the further rise to 1952 seems to have been caused, at least in part, by the sharp

TABLE 1.7

LONG-TERM AND SHORT-TERM INTEREST RATES, 1947–54

Year	*Short bonds*	*Consols*	*Margin*
1947	2·22	2·76	0·54
1948	2·01	3·21	1·20
1949	1·95	3·30	1·35
1950	2·01	3·54	1·53
1951	1·86	3·78	1·92
1952	2·98	4·23	1·25
1953	3·03	4·08	1·05
1954	2·41	3·75	1·34

rise in short-term rates. The fall in the long-term rate in 1953 seems to have been due wholly to a more optimistic view about future prices, but the further fall in 1954 seems to have been due both to expectations of a further fall in long-term rates and to an actual fall the current short-term rate.

Of the rise in the Consols' yield from 4·82 per cent in 1959 to 6·20 per cent in 1961, less than 0·5 per cent can be attributed to the fall in the deposits–national income ratio from 34·5 per cent to 31·6 per cent, while of the rise in the yield from 5·58 per cent in 1963 to 6·42 per cent in 1965, hardly any can be attributed to the fall in the ratio. The most important of the other factors at work seems to have been the rise in the short-term rate, due to the two balance-of-payments crises, which caused the margin between the rates to become negative in 1960 and again in 1963. It may be noted that a negative margin in 1957 was accompanied by only a relatively small rise in the yield on Consols, presumably because the rise in the short-term rate was not expected to be of long duration.

It is possible that similar pressure from the current short-term rate may have caused the yields on Consols in the 1920s to lie above their normal liquidity preference curve, so that this may have been closer to that of 1947–65 than is suggested by the actual yields recorded. The strain first of forcing the pound to appreciate to its pre-war gold parity and then of maintaining it there made it necessary to keep short-term rates consistently high. As a result,

TABLE 1.8

LONG-TERM AND SHORT-TERM INTEREST RATES, 1959–65

Year	*Short bonds*	*Consols*	*Margin*
1959	4·16	4·82	0·66
1960	5·49	5·42	−0·07
1961	5·71	6·20	0·49
1962	5·24	5·98	0·74
1963	4·74	5·58	0·84
1964	5·24	6·03	0·79
1965	6·70	6·42	−0·28

the short-bond rate for the eleven years from 1921 to 1931 averaged 4·6 per cent, or 0·1 per cent more than the average yield on Consols.

While changes in expectations about future interest rates and in the relationship between the long-term and the short-term rate may be sufficient to explain the various temporary deviations from the liquidity preference curve, they certainly cannot by themselves explain the prolonged shifts in the whole curve. The customary explanation of such a shift is a change in the quantity of money which the public wishes to hold idle at a given level of interest rates. There are, however, two other possible explanations of such a shift, which seem more applicable to the shifts which have actually occurred. The first of these is a sudden change, not in the quantity of money transferred between idle balances and the capital circulation, but in the quantity of assets in the capital circulation in which a market has to be maintained with an unchanged quantity of capital transactions balances. In normal circumstances one would expect the volume of marketable capital assets to move in fairly close proportion to the national income, or at least that the proportion would change slowly and persistently over time. If, however, as is possible in certain circumstances, there were a large and rapid change in the quantity of marketable assets, the maintenance of an unchanged rate of interest would require a corresponding percentage change in the quantity of money held in capital transactions balances. If the rise in marketable assets were caused merely by previously non-marketable assets becoming marketable, the fact that they had become better substitutes for money would reduce the demand for money to hold idle. The consequent release of idle money would probably provide much or all of the additional capital transactions balances needed, with little or no rise in the rate of interest; indeed, the volume of idle balances released might well exceed the increase in capital transactions balances required to keep the rate of interest unchanged, so that interest rates would fall, not only on the assets newly made marketable, but also on already marketable assets.

If, however, the increase in marketable assets were due, not to making existing assets marketable, but to the sudden creation of a large quantity of new (presumably financial) marketable assets, it is unlikely that, unless the new assets were very close substitutes for money, sufficient idle balances would be released to provide the additional transactions balances needed to prevent interest rates from rising. Indeed, if the new assets were poor substitutes for money, the public might need to hold, at existing rates of interest, not only more capital transactions balances but more idle balances too. In this case, at unchanged deposits–national income ratios, the rate of interest might rise quite sharply.

The second explanation involves the abandonment of our assumption that changes in the yields of long-dated government securities are representative of the changes in the yields of all non-monetary assets. A liquidity preference function, showing the proportion of its total assets which the public wants to hold in the form of money at each rate of interest is also, in its obverse aspect, a function showing the proportion it wants to hold in non-monetary assets. So long as government securities can be assumed to be representative of all non-monetary assets, a liquidity preference function is the equivalent, on its obverse side, of a government securities preference function. But as soon as we abandon this assumption, our function is no longer one showing the distribution of demand between money and non-monetary assets at each rate of interest, but one showing the distribution of demand between government securities and all other assets, both monetary and non-monetary. It thus ceases to be a liquidity preference function, and becomes merely a government securities preference function. It is thus liable to be shifted, perhaps widely, by any change in the relative demands for government securities and for other non-monetary assets.

If, after such a shift, government securities again become representative of all non-monetary assets, we shall have a new liquidity preference function, perhaps widely different from our old one, at a different level and very possibly with a different slope. It seems likely that it was this sort of shift, in the demand to hold safe fixed-interest securities as compared with other non-monetary assets, which took place in 1933–4. An acute trade depression, with heavy falls in the profits and dividends both of British and of overseas companies, had made ordinary shares less attractive investments. Frequent defaults had reduced the attractiveness of many foreign fixed-interest securities; and a heavy fall in prices of commodities had discouraged the holding of stocks. At the same time, the abandonment of the gold standard had removed the necessity for, and the fear of, high short-term interest rates. In addition to these factors there had been an intense publicity campaign, combined with a period of monetary expansion, to induce investors to convert their 5 per cent War Loan into a new 3½ per cent stock. In the circumstances, it is not surprising that the public was persuaded to revise its whole scale of preferences for safe fixed-interest securities as compared with other non-monetary assets, and that the liquidity preference function, as reflected by the relationship between the yield on Consols and the deposits–national income ratio, should have been shifted sharply downwards.

The new function, apart from the upward deviation which we have noted in 1937–9, persisted not only during the pre-war period but also throughout the war. That the Government was able to persuade the public to retain it for so long must be attributed to the unprecedented effectiveness of its war-time controls on expenditure, which left the public with large unspent balances which they had little opportunity to use for any purpose except to hoard or to lend to the Government. The return of the function in 1947 to approximately its 1921–33 level is also quite understandable. The basic cause seems to have been the obvious and growing ineffectiveness, in peace-time conditions, of the controls in preventing money from leaking rapidly out of idle balances into the income circulation and raising incomes more rapidly than output. The consequences were seen in extremely full employment, rapidly rising prices and profits and, after the premature attempt to return to the gold standard at a fixed parity, an acute balance-of-payments crisis. All these circumstances are so completely the reverse both

TABLE 1.9

NATIONAL INCOME, THE QUANTITY OF MONEY AND THE YIELD ON CONSOLS, 1875–1913

Year	*National income* (£m.)	*Quantity of money* (£m.)	*Ratio of quantity of money to national income* (%)	*Yield on Consols* (%)
1875	1,124	463	41·2	3·20
1876	1,125	470	41·8	3·16
1877	1,130	469	41·5	3·15
1878	1,106	456	41·2	3·15
1879	1,051	452	43·0	3·08
1880	1,104	461	41·8	3·05
1881	1,144	473	41·3	3·00
1882	1,188	490	41·2	2·98
1883	1,216	507	41·7	2·97
1884	1,169	517	44·2	2·97
1885	1,149	514	44·7	3·02
1886	1,164	507	43·5	2·98
1887	1,193	512	42·9	2·95
1888	1,276	530	41·5	2·85
1889	1,364	561	41·1	2·69
1890	1,431	589	41·2	1·67
1891	1,419	612	43·1	2·68
1892	1,393	628	45·1	2·65
1893	1,360	628	46·2	2·60
1894	1,406	640	45·5	2·52
1895	1,472	694	47·2	2·40
1896	1,500	737	49·1	2·30
1897	1,551	750	48·3	2·26
1898	1,633	768	47·0	2·28
1899	1,706	793	46·4	2·35
1900	1,791	817	45·6	2·52
1901	1,759	827	47·0	2·66
1902	1,775	843	47·5	2·65
1903	1,751	843	48·1	2·76
1904	1,779	833	46·8	2·83
1905	1,857	850	45·8	2·78
1906	1,978	874	44·2	2·83
1907	2,076	888	42·8	2·93
1908	1,967	910	46·3	2·90
1909	2,016	936	46·4	2·97
1910	2,108	959	45·5	3·08
1911	2,185	997	45·6	3·15
1912	2,318	1,038	44·8	3·28
1913	2,424	1,085	44·8	3·40

SOURCES: National income: J. B. Jefferys and Dorothy Walters, 'National Income and Expenditure in the United Kingdom, 1870–1952', *Income and Wealth*, series V. Quantity of money: from J. Tinbergen, *Business Cycles in the U.K., 1870–1914*. Yield on Consols: 1872–1888, from J. Tinbergen, *Business Cycles in the U.K., 1870–1914*. 1888–1913, *The Economist*.

of the trade depression of the early 1930s and of the effectively controlled war-time economy that a reversion of the public's scale of preference for government securities to its former level is only too easily explicable.

The downward shift of the liquidity preference curve in 1934, after the War Loan conversion of 1932, has an interesting parallel in the Goschen conversion of 1888, when 3 per cent Consols were converted to a rate which was to be $2\frac{3}{4}$ per cent until 1903 and then $2\frac{1}{2}$ per cent. In Table 1.9 and Fig. 1.11 I show the relationship between the yield on Consols (adjusted between 1888 and 1903 for the prospective change in the rate) and the money–national income ratio for the years 1875 to 1913. The estimates both for the quantity of money (which I have had to use instead of bank deposits) and for the national income have wide margins of error; but it is difficult to believe that the errors would have taken the systematic form which would have been needed to give the results shown in Fig. 1.11.

It will be seen that, especially if we allow for the shift to the right caused by using total money instead of bank deposits, the general level in interest rates is much lower in Fig. 1.11 than in Fig. 1.10. Only at the very end of the period, in 1912 and 1913, does the long-term rate reach anywhere near the 1934–46 curve, while the 1947–65 curve is, of course, much higher still. The most obvious cause of this great disparity, at similar money–national income ratios, between the levels of interest rates before and after the 1914–18 war is the great increase in the quantity of government securities during the war. During the greater part of the nineteenth century the national debt had been reduced while the national income had risen greatly, so that by the end of the century there was a great shortage of safe fixed-interest securities and Consols were fetching famine prices. The war-time increase in the national debt completely changed this situation, for the national debt increased nearly tenfold while the national income less than doubled. This sudden leap in the total volume of marketable assets must have tended to force up the whole range of assets yields, while the greater increase in the quantity of government securities than in that of other assets must have tended to increase their yields relatively to the total of all assets. No similar explanation can be used for the rise in interest rates after the 1939–45 war, for the ratio of public authorities' securities in the hands of the public to national income has been, if anything, lower than in the inter-war period.

As well as being generally lower, the pre-1914 figures show a much smaller range of movement than those since 1921. The ratio of money to national income ranges only from 41 per cent to 49 per cent and the yield on Consols only from 2¼ per cent to under

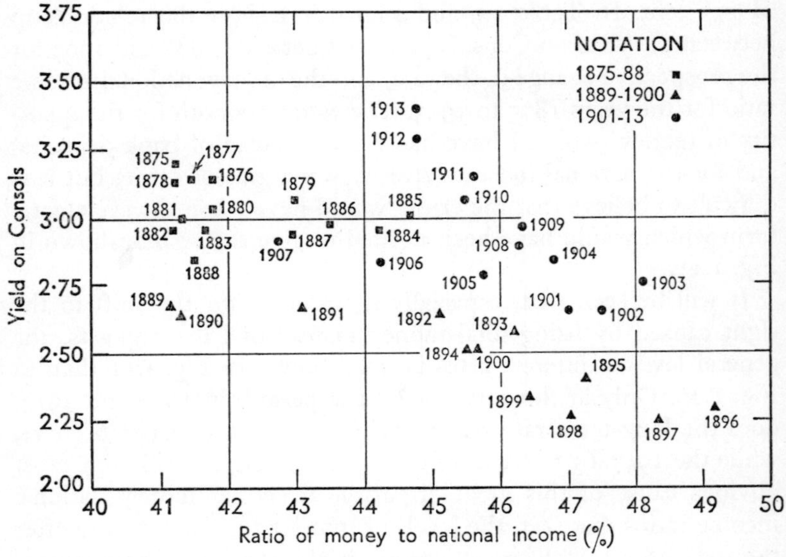

Fig. 1.11 U.K. quantity of money and long-term interest rates, 1875–1913

3½ per cent. Fig. 1.11 is therefore drawn on a larger scale than Fig. 1.10. In spite, however, of the lower level and narrower movements, the pattern shown in Fig. 1.11 resembles in many ways that in Fig. 1.10. The points for the years from 1875 to 1887, together with those from 1901 to 1907, form a series with a yield falling from just under 3¼ per cent with a money–national income ratio of 41 per cent to about 2¾ per cent with a ratio of 48 per cent. This gives a 14 per cent fall in yield with a rise of 17 per cent in the ratio, which is remarkably close to the relationship between changes in yield and changes in ratio shown in the 1947–65 curve in Fig. 1.10. The points for the years 1889 to 1900 clearly form another and appreciably lower series, with the rate of interest falling from about 2·7 per cent with a 41 per cent ratio to about 2¼ per cent with a 49 per cent ratio, giving a 17 per cent fall in the rate with a 19½ per cent rise in the ratio. This shows a slope as steep as that for 1947–65, and much steeper than that for 1934–46. It seems possible, however, that the years 1895–9, which form a separate group with the highest money–national income ratios, may be showing a deviation below the schedule established in 1889, perhaps as the result of the trade depression and the exceptionally low short-term interest rates of the mid-1890s. If we take only the years from 1889 to 1894, we get a fall in the rate from about 2·7 per cent to about 2·55 per cent, or 5½ per cent, with a rise in the ratio from 41 per cent to 46 per cent, or by 12 per cent. This gives a curve with a slope very similar to that of 1934–46.

In 1908 there begins a new development. Although the ratio of money to national income rises sharply from 42·8 per cent in 1907 to 46·3 per cent in 1908, the yield on Consols remains almost unchanged at 2·9 per cent. Then from 1908 to 1913, with only a small fall in the money–national income ratio, the rate breaks sharply upwards, reaching 3·4 per cent in 1913. This may be compared with a rate of 2·5 per cent in 1900, when the money–national income ratio was very little higher.

One reason for this upward break may well be the change in expectations about the long-term rate which we deduced in Lecture II from the change in the relationship between the yield on Consols and the short-bond rate. But it seems likely that there was also a second and more important reason, which may also help to explain the change in expectations. Between 1908 and 1913 there developed the greatest foreign investment boom in British history, with net exports of long-term capital, mainly in the form of new issues on the London market, reaching some £200 million, or 8 per cent of national income, in 1913. This enormous inflow of new overseas securities on to the London capital market must have had a double effect. While it was happening, it must have attracted money out of government securities; and it must have left behind it a large and permanent increase in the volume of marketable assets, necessitating the attraction of an increased volume of capital transactions balances out of a stationary or falling total quantity of money. Thus it seems likely that, even if the 1914–18 war had never begun and in spite of the trade recession which had already begun to bring down interest rates in the early months of 1914, the general level of interest rates would have remained permanently higher, at similar money–national income ratios, than they had been before 1908.

POSTSCRIPT (JUNE 1969)

Since 1965, long-term interest rates in the United Kingdom, apart from a slight reaction in 1967, have continued to rise rapidly, with the average yield on 2½ per cent Consols reaching the unprecedented levels of 7·4 per cent in 1968, nearly 8½ per cent in the first quarter of 1969, and over 9 per cent in the second quarter. This rise in yields, which is shown in Table 1.10 (a revision and continuation of Table 1.5 on p. 39), has occurred without much change in either the ratio of clearing-bank deposits to national income or, as Table 1.11 shows, in the yield calculated on the formula used for drawing the upper curve in Fig. 1.10 on p. 41. In consequence, the actual yield on Consols, which in 1963 and 1964 was close to the calculated yield, has in recent years risen far above it, by 0·5 per cent in 1965, 0·9 per cent in 1966 and 1·6 per cent in 1968. The calculated yield for the first half of 1969

TABLE 1.10

NATIONAL INCOME, QUANTITY OF MONEY AND YIELD ON CONSOLS, 1961–9

Year	*Net national money income* (£m.)	*Net Clearing-bank deposits* (£m.)	*Currency circulation in hands of public* (£m.)	*Currency circulation as percentage of national income*	*Bank deposits as percentage of national income*	*Average yield on 2½% Consols* (%)
1961	22,327	7,035	2,151	9·6	31·5	6·2
1962	23,353	7,228	2,161	9·2	30·9	6·0
1963	24,845	7,560	2,210	8·9	30·2	5·6
1964	26,821	8,069	2,332	8·7	30·0	6·0
1965	28,613	8,498	2,483	8·7	29·7	6·4
1966	29,921	8,863	2,637	8·8	29·6	6·8
1967	31,148	9,224	2,700	8·7	29·6	6·7
1968	32,978	9,804	2,838	8·7	29·8	7·4
1969 (1st half – provisional annual rate)	(34,600)	10,040	2,895	8·4	28·9	8·8

TABLE 1·11

CALCULATED AND ACTUAL ANNUAL AVERAGE PERCENTAGE YIELDS ON 2½ PER CENT CONSOLS

Year	*Calculated yield* $\left(1{\cdot}75 \times \frac{\text{national income}}{\text{bank deposits}}\right)$	*Actual yield*	*Excess of actual over calculated yield*
1961	5·6	6·2	0·6
1962	5·7	6·0	0·3
1963	5·7	5·6	−0·1
1964	5·8	6·0	0·2
1965	5·9	6·4	0·5
1966	5·9	6·8	0·9
1967	5·9	6·7	0·8
1968	5·8	7·4	1·6
1969 (1st half—provisional)	6·1	8·8	2·7

does not seem to have been much higher than the average for 1968, so that the actual yield may have been something over 2½ per cent above that which might have been expected on the basis of the earlier relationship between the yield on Consols and the ratio of bank deposits to national income.

The great excess in 1968 and 1969 in the yield on Consols over what might have been expected, on the basis of previous experience, from the relationship between the volume of bank deposits and the national money income is probably due to a combination of causes. A small part of the discrepancy may be due to the fact that in recent years changes in national money income, at factor cost prices, may not have been as good an indication of changes in the demand for income transaction balances as changes in final expenditure on goods and services at market prices. Normally, the annual percentage increases in national income at factor cost do not differ greatly from those in final expenditure at market prices: from 1961 to 1965 national income rose by 27 per cent while final expenditure rose by 29 per cent. But between 1965 and 1968 the rapid rises in the sterling value of imports and in taxes on expenditure caused final expenditure to rise much faster than national income, by about 21 per cent, as compared with a rise of about 14 per cent in national income. If national income had risen as fast as final expenditure, the calculated yield on Consols in 1968 would have been nearly 6·2 per cent, instead of 5·8 per cent – still 1·2 per cent below the actual yield in 1968 and over 2 per cent below the actual yield in the first quarter of 1969.

The most obvious reason for this remaining large discrepancy between the calculated and actual yields on Consols is the high level of short-term rates, caused partly by the weakness of the U.K. balance of payments and of sterling and partly by the rise in interest rates throughout the world. This is reflected in the rise in the yield to maturity of short bonds, as shown in Table 1.12 (a revision and continuation of Table 1.8 on p. 45).

TABLE 1.12

LONG-TERM AND SHORT-TERM INTEREST RATES, 1961–9

Year	*Short bonds*	*Consols*	*Margin*
1961	5·7	6·2	0·5
1962	5·2	6·0	0·8
1963	4·8	5·6	0·8
1964	5·5	6·0	0·5
1965	6·6	6·4	−0·2
1966	6·8	6·8	—
1967	6·7	6·7	—
1968	7·6	7·4	−0·2
1969 (1st half)	8·6	8·8	0·2

If we take as normal the margin of the yield of Consols over that of short bonds in 1963 (a year in which the actual yield on Consols was about the same as the calculated yield), it is clear that from 1965 onwards the yield on short bonds has been abnormally high in relation to that on Consols. As argued earlier (see pp. 14–17), this is a prima facie indication that the market did not expect the current yields to be maintained indefinitely. The amount by which a high short-term rate can force up the long-term rate is uncertain, since it depends upon how long the short-term rate is expected to stay high and how far it can then be expected to fall. It is, however, probably safe to say that, while it cannot be doubted that the high short-term rate is exercising a considerable effect on the long-term rate, it is unlikely to provide the whole of the explanation of the discrepancy between the actual and the (adjusted) calculated rate. Even with a marked fall in short-term rates, other factors would probably prevent the fall in long-term rates from going very far.

To account for the remaining discrepancy we probably have to look to the reverse of the process suggested on p. 47 to account for the downward shift of long-term interest rates in 1933–4. At that time the acute trade depression and the accompanying heavy fall in business profits throughout the world seem to have caused a shift out of ordinary shares and foreign investments into the safety of British government securities. In recent years, on the other hand, and especially since 1965, increasing fears of inflation have intensified the desire to shift out of fixed-interest securities into assets which can be expected to rise in value as the inflation proceeds – into physical assets of all kinds and claims to the ownership of physical assets in the form of ordinary shares.

The effects of inflation have been intensified by those of the introduction in 1965 (with effect from 1966) of corporation tax. This tax is borne by dividends, both on ordinary and on preference shares, which are distributions of profits, but not by interest paid on loans or debentures, which is a cost. The result was greatly to discourage issues of ordinary, and still more of preference, shares and to stimulate the issue of loans and debentures. At the same time, those investment institutions which were themselves subject to corporation tax preferred to hold investments, including both ordinary and preference shares, dividends on which had already borne tax, rather than loans and debentures, interest on which was subject to corporation tax in their hands. The consequent increase in the supply of and fall in the demand for bonds reinforced the fall in their prices and the rise in their yields; while the decrease in the supply of and increase in the demand for ordinary shares reinforced the rise in their prices and the fall in their yields. The 'reverse yield gap' between yields on ordinary shares and on bonds was thus widened further.

Some idea of how much of the widening of the 'reverse yield gap' was due to fears of continued inflation and how much to the effects of corporation tax can be obtained by comparing both yields with that on preference shares, which fears of inflation tended to increase and the effects of corporation tax to reduce.

TABLE 1.13

YIELDS ON DEBENTURES, ORDINARY SHARES AND PREFERENCE SHARES, 1963–8

Years	*Debentures and loan stocks (redemption yield)*	*Industrial ordinary shares*	*Reverse yield gap*	*Commercial and industrial preference shares*
1963		4·4		6·5
1964		4·6		6·9
1965	7·1	5·5	1·6	6·9
1966	7·7	5·7	2·0	7·1
1967	7·6	5·2	2·4	6·9
1968	8·2	3·7	4·5	7·2
1969	10·3	3·9	6·4	9·0

Source: *Financial Times* Actuaries Indices, quoted in *Digest of Statistics.*

It will be seen that, whereas the average yield on debentures rose from 7·1 per cent in 1965 to 10·3 per cent in 1969, and that on ordinary shares fell from 5·5 per cent to 3·9 per cent, thus widening the reverse yield gap from 1·6 per cent to 6·4 per cent, the yield on preference shares rose much less, from 6·9 per cent to 9·0 per cent. These results suggest that, while the fears of inflation were the more important factor, the effects of corporation tax were quite substantial.

Of the factors which in recent years have combined to drive up the rate of interest, some may be expected to intensify in future, while others seem likely to operate in the opposite direction. Among those tending to raise interest rates further, the most important seems to be the increased use of monetary policy to check inflation both in the United Kingdom and in the United States; while among those tending to lower them in the United Kingdom are (it may be hoped) a continued improvement in the balance of payments and a considerably slower rate of inflation than in the recent past. The former factors are likely to be more important in the near future, the latter in the long run. While the

United Kingdom will be forced, until it has not only achieved a large favourable balance of payments but has maintained it for long enough to repay the enormous foreign short-term debts it has incurred in recent years, to keep its rate of inflation below that of most other industrial countries, it may take the public a considerable time to realise what is happening. Not until then is there likely to be any substantial fall in long-term interest rates – unless, indeed, some future government repeals or modifies corporation tax.

2

Deposit Rates after Mr Jones[1]

THE National Board for Prices and Incomes, in its Report No. 34 on Bank Charges, makes four proposals about the interest rates paid and charged by the London clearing banks: (1) that they should abandon their present convention of fixing the rate paid on deposits at seven days' notice at 2 per cent below Bank Rate, and compete for deposits on interest rates, both with each other and with outside institutions; (2) that they should introduce and compete for deposits fixed for longer periods; (3) that they should abandon any agreement on the minimum rate for overdrafts, and compete on interest for these; and (4) that they should introduce and compete on interest for loans fixed for longer periods.

The main reason adduced by the Board for these recommendations does not seem to be that the banks, by means of a price cartel, have been making excessive profits, but that, by restricting the types of business they undertake and the rates of interest they offer, they have been progressively losing business to non-clearing banks and other financial intermediaries. The Board seems to think that the public interest has thereby suffered, apparently on the ground that, if the banks were doing a larger business, they would be able to operate on a smaller margin between borrowing and lending rates than either they or other financial intermediaries are now able to afford.

The orthodox reply to the Board's proposals on deposit rates is that the faster growth of deposits with the non-clearing financial intermediaries than with the clearing banks is the result of the Government's monetary measures to check inflation, which have prevented the clearing banks' deposits from rising as fast as the national money income. The economy in their use thus necessitated, and the rise in their velocity of circulation, have been achieved largely by the growth of financial intermediaries, stimu-

[1] First published in *The Banker*, Oct. 1967.

lated by the rise in interest rates. A successful attempt by the clearing banks to attract deposits from these institutions would result, not in an increase in the banks' total deposits but merely in a transfer from current account to deposit account, thus slowing down the average velocity of circulation, raising interest rates throughout the system, and imposing an undesired check on business activity. For instance, if depositors with building societies were induced to transfer their deposits to the clearing banks, the building societies would have to repay them with cheques drawn on the societies' current accounts with the clearing banks. The consequent debits to their current accounts would be equal to the amounts placed on deposit account with the clearing banks by their former depositors. The clearing banks' total deposits would remain unchanged, while the ability of the building societies to finance house purchases would be reduced.

The Board accept this argument, as far as it goes, but reply that government monetary policy is not an independent variable, but is framed in accordance with the economic situation as it exists. If, by attracting deposits from other institutions, the clearing banks do in fact bring about a general rise in interest rates and a check to demand, the Government will have to take steps to prevent the undesired business recession. It might, for instance, issue fewer long-dated securities on the stock market and more Treasury bills to the discount market and, indirectly, to the banks, thereby checking the rise in interest rates and expanding bank deposits. A similar result would be achieved if the deposits were attracted, not from financial institutions in the private sector but from the Government itself. If, for instance, the banks were able to attract deposits away from the Post Office Savings Bank, the Government would be obliged, if it did not wish to raise interest rates by increasing its borrowings on the stock market, to borrow more from the banks on Treasury bills, thus raising the total of bank deposits.

EFFECTIVE COMPETITION?

The proposals of the National Board for Prices and Incomes can be discussed from two aspects: their probable effectiveness, and the results which might be expected to follow if they could, in fact, be made effective. From the first point of view, it is doubtful if, even if the agreement on bank deposit rates were abandoned, the banks could be expected to compete with each other for deposits by offering higher rates. In any industry with only five major firms of roughly equal size and efficiency, no firm can afford to act as if it were in a perfectly competitive market, for each will have to take account of what the others will do if it starts cutting prices. Within the banking system, the reaction of the other banks to any attempt by one of them to attract more deposits by raising the rate of interest will be even more rapid than in most industries. The keeping of money on deposit account does not necessitate the sort of confidential relationship between banker and customer which is essential for a loan transaction, or even, to some extent, for the keeping of a current account. Even a small difference in the rates offered on deposit accounts would probably result in rapid and substantial transfers, which would quickly deplete the cash reserves of the banks offering the lower rates. Faced with the alternative of calling from the discount market and so depleting their other liquid assets, these banks would almost certainly feel obliged to raise their deposit rates in turn. Thus, so long as bank lending rates remain unchanged, all that the bank which initiates the rise in the deposit rate will have achieved is a narrowing of the margin between its deposit and lending rates and a fall in its profits. It is conceivable that small and temporary differences in deposit rates might be used to supplement calling from the discount market as a means of adjusting cash reserves between banks; apart from this, no bank is likely to be able to afford to quote a rate for deposits, on otherwise identical terms, lower than that offered by any other clearing bank.

There remains the possibility that the initiating bank might think it worth its while to trigger off a rise in the general level of bank deposit rates in the hope that this might attract deposits from outside institutions to the clearing banks as a whole. Such a bank would, of course, have to rely on the argument put forward by the National Board for Prices and Incomes, that the banks, by reducing the lending power of outside institutions and inducing an unwanted business recession, would be able to blackmail the Government into taking steps to expand the total of bank deposits. Even, however, if it were able to foresee success in this, there is another factor (which the Board does not mention) which might well make a bank hesitate before raising its deposit rate. To attract deposits away from outside institutions requires a differential rise in the rate, and probably a larger absolute rise. But the higher the absolute level of the deposit rate, the smaller the amount and the shorter the period which justify the trouble of shifting temporarily idle current account balances to deposit account. The historical relationship between the deposit rate and the proportion of total balances held on deposit account is clearly brought out in the following table:

TABLE 2.1

LONDON CLEARING BANKS, 1951–67

Yearly averages	*Deposit rate*	*Current accounts* (£m.)	*Deposit accounts* (£m.)	*Total* (£m.)	*Percentage of total on deposit account*
1951 (Apr–Dec)	0·5	4,027	1,844	5,871	31·4
1952	1·7	3,907	1,938	5,845	31·1
1953	1·8	3,938	2,051	5,989	34·2
1954	1·2	4,078	2,094	6,172	33·9
1955	2·3	4,054	2,070	6,124	33·8
1956	3·4	3,932	2,008	5,940	33·8
1957	4·2	3,905	2,139	6,044	35·4
1958	3·4	3,769	2,442	6,211	39·3
1959	2·0	4,064	2,431	6,495	37·4
1960	3·3	4,207	2,515	6,722	37·4
1961	3·7	4,157	2,638	6,795	38·8
1962	2·9	4,186	2,747	6,933	39·6
1963	2·0	4,486	2,781	7,267	38·3
1964	3·0	4,836	2,922	7,758	37·7
1965	4·4	4,869	3,292	8,161	40·3
1966	4·5	4,955	3,536	8,491	41·6
1967 (Jan–June)	4·1	4,945	3,692	8,637	42·7

Since a current account balance shifted to the same customer's deposit account as the result of a rise in the deposit rate would have been idle in any case, the move has no effect on the economy and does not necessitate any expansion of total deposits by the Government, over and above what is needed to offset the shift from current to deposit accounts caused by the transfer to deposit account of balances from outside institutions. There will therefore be a net fall in bank profits, for they will be paying out more in interest, while, since the deposits would have been idle if they had remained on current account, there is no saving in expenses. The only possibly offsetting item is a rise in bank charges on current accounts with smaller average credit balances, but this is unlikely to make up for the higher interest payments.

The effect of changes in the deposit rate on the distribution of balances between current and deposit accounts makes quite arguable the proposition, put forward by the Board as a *reductio ad absurdum*, that, if it does not pay the banks to raise their deposit rates, it should pay them to reduce them, or even to abolish them altogether. If the banks were, in fact, to cease to accept money on deposit account, part of the balances previously so held would be transferred to outside institutions, thus increasing their lending power, bringing down interest rates and expanding demand. Let us accept the Board's contention that this expansion of demand would be offset by monetary policy, leading to a fall in the banks' total deposits. But not all deposit accounts would be transferred to outside institutions; some would merely revert to current account This type of shift has no effect on demand, and would not need to be offset by a reduction of deposits. While, therefore, the total of bank deposits would fall, the fall would be smaller than that of deposit accounts and the total of current accounts would rise. Thus on the one side the banks would lose by a fall in the size of their total business, and on the other they would gain by an increase in their interest-free deposits. Whether or not the gain would exceed the loss would depend on the proportions transferred, on the one hand to outside institutions and on the other to current account. If the proportion transferred to current account was large, it might well pay the banks to cease to accept money on deposit account and to restrict themselves to current accounts only (although they would, of course, have to make allowance for the transitional costs of reducing their scale of business and for some loss of customer goodwill), transferring the function of accepting interest-bearing deposits to specialist subsidiaries.

LENDING RATES

While it seems unlikely that it would pay any bank to take the initiative, by raising its deposit rate, in narrowing the margin between its borrowing and lending rates, the position might well be altered if the banks were free to vary their lending rates in response to changes in the demand for bank advances. Such a change might perhaps be compatible with a general directive to the banks to keep the total of their advances within a given limit; but it would be difficult to operate a system of selective controls by means of interest rates (which might, for instance, involve charging exporters 5 per cent, other manufacturers 7 per cent, retailers 10 per cent, hire-purchase companies 15 per cent, and casinos 20 per cent). Further, even if the banks were completely at liberty to charge whatever they found necessary to equate the demand for loans with the supply, it is most unlikely that they would, in fact, abandon quantitative restrictions altogether. No business in oligopolistic competition can afford to maximise its short-run profits; it must attempt to maximise its long-run profits by giving preference to customers whose business is expected to be remunerative later on, while refusing some who, while willing to pay more at the moment, are less likely to be valuable customers in the future. Nevertheless, it is likely that, if individual banks had a completely free hand, lending rates would fluctuate a good deal more widely than they have done in the past, rising higher in periods of credit shortage and falling lower in periods of easy money; if so, deposit rates would probably fluctuate with them. In this case, if recent history repeats itself and periods of credit shortage continue to last longer than those of easy money, the average levels of both deposit and lending rates would tend to be higher than in the past.

While the probability of a complete freeing of bank interest rates cannot be put very high, it is perhaps worth considering what would happen if a higher average level of deposit rates were successful in diverting deposits from outside institutions. Let us assume, for instance, that the clearing banks are able to attract £100 millions of deposits from the building societies. The building societies will have to draw cheques for £100 millions on their current accounts with the clearing banks, which their former depositors will put to their credit in deposit accounts with the same banks. The result is a fall of £100 millions in the banks' current accounts and a rise of £100 millions in their deposit accounts (in addition to any transfers directly from current to deposit accounts by the banks' own customers). The building societies have £100 millions less to lend to house-buyers, while the lending power of the banks will not increase. The counterpart to the reduced loans of the building societies is the transfer of formerly active current account balances to idle deposit account balances, with a consequent fall in the average velocity of circulation of bank deposits, a rise in interest rates, and a check to demand.

According to the Board's argument, the Government will now intervene to increase the supply of liquid assets, thus enabling the banks to expand their other assets and their current accounts, until the £100 millions withdrawn from current accounts is replaced. But this will not restore the original position. Let us suppose that the banks' assets are distributed as follows: Items in transit, 5 per cent (of gross deposits); cash, 8 per cent; other liquid assets, 22 per cent; securities, 15 per cent; and advances, 50 per cent. To enable the banks to expand their deposits by £100 millions, the Government and the Bank of England must take steps to expand the banks' holdings of cash by £8 millions and of other liquid assets by £22 millions. This will enable the banks (if they wish to maintain their existing asset structure) to increase their advances by £50 millions and their holdings of securities by £15 millions. But this will not replace the £100 millions of loans which the building societies can no longer provide for the housing market. Even if the banks, following the proposals of the Board, are themselves willing to provide long-term finance for house purchase, this will supply only half the gap. To fill the rest, the Government would itself have to use the proceeds of the additional bonds and bills sold to the Bank of England and the clearing banks to provide finance for private-sector house purchase. It is, perhaps, the idea of avoiding difficulties of this sort which lies behind the Board's recommendations, not only that the banks should undertake the sort of business now carried on by outside undertakings, but that the assets structures of these undertakings should be made to approximate more closely to those of the banks.

3

The Two Britains[1]

In December 1963 the total number of unemployed in Great Britain was 460,000, or about 2 per cent of the labour force. After adjustment for season, this was if anything below the level which post-war experience suggests to be the minimum consistent with a non-inflationary rise in money incomes – that is, a rise in incomes no greater than the sustainable increase in total national output. As Table 3.1 on p. 66 and Fig. 3.1 on p. 67 indicate, the only years since the war in which gross domestic income per head of population has shown an increase in money terms of less than 4 per cent over the previous year have been 1952, 1958 and 1962 – all of which were years with a relatively high unemployment average of around 2 per cent. Fluctuations in the rate of increase of wages and salaries per employee have been rather narrower than those in gross domestic income, and have usually followed them with an appreciable time-lag.

The average percentage of unemployment for Great Britain as a whole conceals wide differences between regions. In December 1963 the percentages varied from 1·2 in London and South-East England to 4·2 in Scotland and 4·4 in Northern England. In terms of unemployment percentages, the country is divided into two clearly distinguishable areas. In one of these, comprising the whole of the Midlands and South of England, the highest unemployment percentage for any region was 2·0 (in the South-West), with an average for the whole area of 1·4. In the other, comprising Northern and North-Western England, Scotland and Wales, the lowest

[1] First published in *The Banker*, Feb. 1964. My thanks are due to the Statistics Department of the Ministry of Labour, for allowing me to use unpublished statistics of the regional distribution of employees; to the Economic Research Division of the London School of Economics, for help with the extraction and compilation of the figures; and to Dr Bernard Corry, for allowing me to use some of the results of his own much wider programme of research in a similar field.

TABLE 3.1

INCOMES AND UNEMPLOYMENT, 1949–62

	Money incomes (percentage increase over previous year)		*Average number unemployed ('000)*				*Average percentage unemployed*			
	Gross domestic income per head of population	*Wages and salaries per employee*	*Midlands and South*	*North and Wales*	*Great Britain*	*North and Wales as percentage of Great Britain*	*Midlands and South*	*North and Wales*	*Great Britain*	*North and Wales as percentage of Great Britain*
1949	5·3	6·1	128	180	308	58·4	0·97	2·53	1·51	167
1950	6·7	3·8	133	181	314	57·6	0·99	2·53	1·53	165
1951	10·5	10·0	110	142	252	56·4	0·82	1·97	1·22	161
1952	2·4	8·6	178	236	414	57·0	1·31	3·28	1·99	165
1953	5·7	3·8	160	182	342	53·2	1·17	2·52	1·64	154
1954	7·2	5·7	130	155	285	54·5	0·94	2·12	1·34	158
1955	8·5	7·8	101	132	232	56·9	0·72	1·79	1·09	164
1956	6·9	7·9	126	131	257	51·0	0·88	1·78	1·18	151
1957	4·7	5·3	163	150	313	47·9	1·13	2·03	1·43	142
1958	2·6	4·1	228	229	457	50·1	1·58	3·11	2·10	148
1959	5·4	4·8	218	256	474	54·0	1·50	3·48	2·17	160
1960	8·0	5·6	161	200	361	55·4	1·09	2·71	1·63	166
1961	4·4	6·5	166	175	341	51·3	1·10	2·36	1·51	156
1962	3·3	3·8	223	240	463	51·9	1·46	3·21	2·03	158

percentage for any was 2·5 (in the North-West), with an average for the whole area of 3·4. The difference in the unemployment percentages means that, with less than one-third of the employees, the North and Wales had 55 per cent of the total number unemployed in Great Britain.

It is largely this unequal distribution of unemployment, and the high levels recorded in the North and Wales, rather than the general average throughout the country, which for many people have constituted a main objection to the policy of maintaining a margin of unused resources sufficient to prevent an over-rapid rise in money incomes. It has therefore been one of the main causes of the inability to check the general tendency towards inflation. This provides an additional reason for seeking to bring the level of unemployment in the North and Wales nearer to the national average.

That this has not so far been achieved has not been for want of trying. To achieve a substantial reduction of unemployment in the high unemployment areas has been the declared policy of every government since the war. Until recently, the methods used have

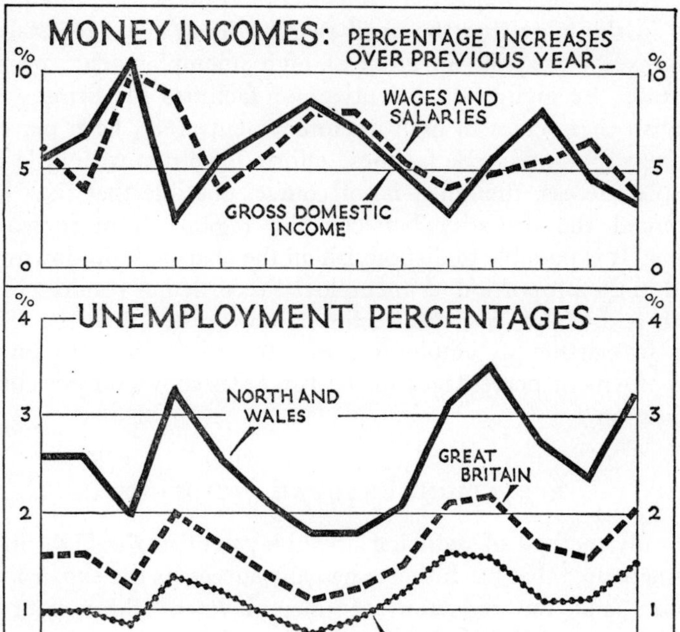

Fig. 3.1 Incomes and unemployment

been largely negative, by preventing or discouraging firms from undertaking new industrial construction in low unemployment areas in the hope that they will thereby be induced to establish themselves or expand in areas of high unemployment; positive measures, by giving tax incentives or facilities for firms which establish themselves in high unemployment areas, have played a relatively minor part. So far these efforts have met with little perceptible success, though it is, of course, possible that they have prevented the disparity between the regions from increasing further. It is possible to distinguish on the chart a slight downward trend in the proportion of unemployed recorded as resident in the North and Wales, but this decline is not greater than the fall in their proportion of employees, and the disparity between the unemployment percentages in the two areas shows no perceptible diminution.

REFLATION: UNEQUAL INCIDENCE

The only method of reducing unemployment in the high unemployment area that has hitherto had any success is the expansion of demand and the reduction of unemployment throughout the country as a whole. Unfortunately, the effect of such measures is usually to reduce unemployment in the low unemployment area faster than in the high unemployment area, bringing a speed return to conditions of excess demand and over-rapid rises of money incomes. In consequence, successive governments have been forced, usually by the effects of excess demand on the balance of payments, to reverse their policies before unemployment in the high unemployment area has had time for fall very far.

Just as unemployment usually falls faster in the low unemployment area when demand is first expanded, so it also rises faster in the low unemployment area when demand is first checked. Thus the proportionate disparity between the unemployment percentages in the high and low unemployment areas tends to rise as unemployment falls (1953–5, 1958–60), and to fall as unemployment rises (1955–7, 1960–1). The explanation of this seems to be that both expansions and contractions of demand and output have since the war started in the consumption goods industries, concentrated mainly in the Midlands and South, and have spread only later to the production goods industries, concentrated mainly in the North and Wales.

This explanation is confirmed by the one apparent exception to the normal movement. In 1951–2 unemployment rose faster, and in 1952–3 it fell faster, in the North and Wales than in the Midlands and South. This was because both the 1951–2 recession and the 1952–3 recovery particularly affected the Lancashire textile industry, one of the few consumption goods industries concentrated in the North; whereas in both 1955–7 and in 1960–1 the main initial sufferers were the durable consumption goods industries, particularly the car industry, concentrated mainly in the Midlands and South. If we omit the North-West region from the 1951–2 and 1952–3 unemployment changes, as in Table 3.2, we find that the figures for the rest of the high unemployment area move as in the other cycles.

TABLE 3.2

UNEMPLOYMENT 1951–3

('000)

	Great Britain	*North-West*	*Great Britain less North-West*	*Northern England, Scotland and Wales*	
					Percentage of Great Britain less North-West
Average 1951	252	36	216	106	49·0
,, 1952	414	107	307	128	41·7
,, 1953	342	60	282	122	43·2

The disappointing results of earlier efforts to reduce unemployment in the high unemployment area, either by restraints on new investment in the low unemployment area or by measures to expand general demand, have recently led the Government to adopt more vigorous direct measures to increase the demand for labour in the North. These have taken the form partly of greatly increased tax incentives for capital construction in certain parts of the area, and partly of government-financed measures to improve and develop its economic and social infrastructure. It is hoped by these means to create conditions in which firms will desire to expand or establish businesses in the area without the need of other special inducements. It is still far too early to make any estimate of how far, if at all, these measures will be any more successful than those of earlier years; but the scale of the present effort is so much greater than that of earlier ones that it is perhaps worth while to look at some of the possible consequences that its success might have for the Midlands and South.

There have been only five years since the war – 1952, 1958, 1959, 1962 and 1963 – in which the average level of unemployment in Great Britain has reached or exceeded the level of 2 per cent, which appears, with the present distribution of unemployment, to be the minimum consistent with the absence of an excessively rapid rise in money incomes. In these five years (excluding the first quarter of 1963), while unemployment in Great Britain averaged 2·1 per cent, that in the Midlands and South averaged 1·5 per cent and in the North and Wales 3·3 per cent. If unemployment in the North and Wales could be reduced to the national average, the question arises what would be the effect on the critical level, in Great Britain as a whole and therefore in the Midlands and South, below which an inflationary rise in incomes would begin.

In attempting to answer this question, the first step is to examine the effect that the existence of relatively high rates of unemployment in one part of the country has upon the rate of rise in incomes in the rest of the country, where unemployment rates are much lower.

MOBILITY: BUILDING A 'BERLIN WALL'?

If the unemployed labour in the high unemployment area were wholly immobile, it is difficult to see why its existence should have any effect at all on the rest of the country. In this case, the absorption of the excess unemployment locally (unless achieved by measures that had a generally inflationary effect on the country as a whole) would not raise the critical unemployment level in the rest of the country; the level for the country as a whole, and for the North and Wales, would fall to the present Midlands and South level of 1·5 per cent. But if the unemployed labour of the North and Wales is at least partly mobile, so that workers can move to the low unemployment area to help to relieve the labour shortage there, the low unemployment area is in effect keeping part of its reserves of labour outside its own boundaries. It can thus avoid an excess demand for labour with a lower level of unemployment than would have been necessary in the absence of the inflow from outside. This is true of any area, whether a separate country or not, which is attracting an inflow of immigrant labour. Such an area can (and indeed, if it is to absorb immigrants, must) maintain a potential excess of demand for labour over supply, an excess which is prevented from becoming actual by the inflow from outside. Until 1961 an extreme instance of this phenomenon could be seen in West Germany, which was able to reduce its own unemployment to an extremely low figure, without inducing an excess demand for labour, because the potential excess demand was continually prevented from becoming actual by the very large annual inflow of labour from East Germany. With the erection of the Berlin Wall, however, this inflow was almost entirely cut off, the potential excess demand for labour became actual, and the rate of rise in wages began to accelerate. A similar effect in the Midlands and South could be expected to result from a cessation of the inflow of labour from the North and Wales, reflecting the success of measures to induce the absorption of the excess labour locally. The Midlands and South could no longer keep part of their reserves of labour outside their own boundaries, and their critical unemployment percentage would rise.

How much it would rise would depend largely on how important this movement of labour had been in the recent past for both areas. Fortunately, some idea of this can be obtained from the Ministry of Labour's estimates, based on a series of mid-year 1 per cent samples of registration books, of inter-regional movements of employees. From these it is possible to compile annual estimates of the movement of labour out of the North and Wales into the Midlands and South. These are shown in Table 3.3.

For the whole eleven years the total net number of migrants was 273,000, of whom 185,000 were men and 88,000 women. There is some sign of cyclical variation, especially in the estimates for men, for whom the migration peaks of 18,000 in 1954–5 and 33,000 in 1959–60 coincide with peaks in the percentage of total unemployment accounted for by the North and Wales – 56·9 in 1955 and 55·4 in 1960. There is a much more marked indication of an upward trend in the figures. Total net migration in the four years from 1958–9 to 1961–2 averaged 36,000 a year, or nearly twice the annual average of the previous four years. An obvious explanation of this increase is that the average percentage of unemployment in the North and Wales rose from 2·2 in 1955–8 to 2·9 in 1959–62; but a contributory factor may have been the greater rise in unemployment in the North and Wales than in the Midlands and South, so that the unemployment percentage in the North and Wales increased from an average of 151 per cent of that for Great Britain as a whole in 1955–8 to one of 160 per cent in 1959–62.

These estimates of inter-area migration help us to form a view, both about how mobile the unemployed labour of the North and Wales in fact is and about how important the flow in inter-area

TABLE 3.3

MIGRATION OF EMPLOYEES FROM THE NORTH AND WALES TO MIDLANDS AND SOUTH, 1951–2 TO 1961–2

('000)

Year	*Men*	*Women*	*Total*	*Year*	*Men*	*Women*	*Total*
1951–2	9	7	16	1957–8	7	6	13
1952–3	14	6	20	1958–9	20	6	26
1953–4	13	6	19	1959–60	33	17	50
1954–5	18	3	21	1960–1	23	11	34
1955–6	14	4	18	1961–2	23	10	33
1956–7	11	12	23				

immigrants is to the Midlands and South. During the period 1959–62, when the number of migrants averaged about 36,000 a year, the average number of unemployed in the North and Wales was 218,000, so that the annual emigration was equivalent to only about one-sixth of the total of unemployed. Even if we include only the number by which the unemployed in the North and Wales exceeded what they would have been if the unemployment rate had averaged 1·3 per cent, as in the Midlands and South, the excess is still well over three times the average annual migration. It is clear, therefore, that the unemployed in the North and Wales are very far from being completely mobile. A reduction in unemployment there could thus be expected to reduce the critical level of the national average to something less than the present 2 per cent, and to require a rise in the critical level in the Midlands and South by something less than 0·5 per cent above the present 1·5 per cent.

Some support for this conclusion can be drawn from the figure for the Midlands and South. Between 1958 and 1962 inter-area migration totalled about 143,000. During the same period the number of employees in the Midlands and South is estimated to have increased from 14,443,000 to 15,323,000, or by 880,000. Thus, out of the total increase in the Midlands and South, less than one-sixth was contributed by migration from the North and Wales. With so large a part of the increase derived from other sources, it seems unlikely that the cessation of immigration from the North and Wales would raise the critical percentage of unemployment by as much as third. If, therefore, we assume that the other causes of the rise in the number of employees in the Midlands and South continue to operate unchanged, a reasonable guess might be that a reduction in the rate of unemployment in the North and Wales to the national average would reduce the critical level of unemployment for the country as a whole (and, by definition, for both parts of it), to around 1·7 or 1·8 per cent.

This guess, however, cannot be converted into a forecast unless we can be assured that the condition is fulfilled that the other factors in the expansion of the number of employees in the Midlands and South continue to operate unchanged. These other factors can be grouped under three main heads: the natural growth of the population of working age; the changes in the proportion of the population of working age in, or seeking, civil employment; and the net migration of workers to or from overseas. The factors affecting the proportion of the population in civil employment can again be broken down under three heads: changes in the number of the armed forces; changes in the number of self-employed; and changes in the proportion not recorded as working at all (though many of them, particularly women, work harder than most of those recorded as employed). Since the number of employees and self-employed includes a certain number who continue to work after the age of 65, the combined total of male employees, self-employed and members of the armed forces may exceed (and at times has exceeded) the number of men between the ages of 15 and 65.

For each of these factors we can make estimates of greater or less reliability. With the help of life tables we can calculate the natural growth of the total population of working age; and from this we can calculate the natural growth in the number of employees, that is to say, the increase that would have taken place in their number if the population of working age had shown only its natural increase and if the ratio of employees to population of working age had remained unchanged. (Since the age distribution of the population is available conveniently only in five-year groups, we can calculate the natural rate of increase only over five-year periods.) Similarly, we can calculate the effects of changes in the ratio of employees to total population of working age.[1]

Firm figures are available for the changes in the numbers in the armed forces, and we can calculate the changes in the number of the self-employed by subtracting from the number in civil employment the number of employees, less the wholly unemployed. As there are no figures for the distribution of these between areas, it is assumed that they are distributed in proportion to the number of employees. Since the releases from the armed forces during this period were presumably mainly of national servicemen, for these this assumption may not be unrealistic. The same cannot be said of servicewomen or of the self-employed, but the numbers involved here are small. After accounting under these two headings for part of the change in numbers resulting from the change in the ratio of employees to population of working age, we are left with a balance that may be regarded as resulting from the change in the proportion that does any kind of remunerated work.

For the final figure – of changes in the number of employees caused by net overseas migration – no direct estimates are possible. We can, however, obtain some rough idea by subtracting the total of all the above changes from the total change in the number

[1] Since life tables and figures of age distribution are not available for separate regions, we have to apply to the number of employees in the Midlands and South the result of calculations for the whole of England. As the Midlands and South contain four-fifths of all the employees in England, it may be hoped that the consequent error will not be too serious, although it will be proportionally more serious in the results for the North and Wales, which are obtained by difference.

Another difficulty has been that the two life tables available are based on the years 1950–2 and 1959–61 respectively. The first of these is too early and the second too late for the period 1952–7. Calculations were therefore made with the help of both tables, and the results averaged. For the period 1957–62 the 1959–61 life table was appropriate.

of employees over the period, though since the resultant figure includes all the errors and omissions of the whole series of calculations, the results must be regarded with the greatest reserve.

The resulting estimates of the causes of the changes in the number of employees in the Midlands and South, the North and

TABLE 3.4

CHANGES IN NUMBER OF CIVIL EMPLOYEES (EMPLOYED AND UNEMPLOYED) ('000)

	1952 to 1957			*1957 to 1962*		
	Men	*Women*	*Total*	*Men*	*Women*	*Total*
MIDLANDS AND SOUTH						
Number of employees in first year of quinquennium	8,902	4,675	13,577	9,330	5,116	14,446
Natural increase	+85	−29	+56	+265	+60	+325
Releases from armed forces	+100	+6	+106	+165	−1	+164
Reduction in self-employed	−9	+8	−1	−23	−3	−26
Change in proportion employed of population aged 15–64	+183	+400	+583	−236	+184	−52
Inter-area migrants	+70	+31	+101	+106	+50	+156
Overseas migrants, errors and omissions	−1	+25	+24	+214	+96	+310
Number of employees in last year of quinquennium	9,330	5,116	14,446	9,821	5,502	15,323
NORTH AND WALES						
Number of employees in first year of quinquennium	4,798	2,425	7,223	4,870	2,534	7,404
Natural increase	+40	+14	+54	+135	+35	+170
Releases from armed forces	+61	+3	+64	+97	−1	+96
Reduction in self-employed	−4	+3	−1	−12	−2	−14
Change in proportion employed of population aged 15–64	+40	+152	+192	−129	+129	—
Inter-area migrants	−70	−31	−101	−106	−50	−156
Overseas migrants, errors and omissions	+5	−32	−27	+4	−27	−23
Number of employees in last year of quinquennium	4,870	2,534	7,404	4,859	2,618	7,477
GREAT BRITAIN						
Number of employees in first year of quinquennium	13,700	7,100	20,800	14,200	7,650	21,850
Natural increase	+125	−15	+110	+400	+95	+495
Releases from armed forces	+161	+9	+170	+262	−2	+260
Reduction in self-employed	−13	+11	−2	−35	−5	−40
Change in proportion employed of population aged 15–64	+223	+552	+775	−365	+313	−52
Inter-area migrants	—	—	—	—	—	—
Overseas migrants, errors and omissions	+4	−7	−3	+218	+69	+287
Number of employees in last year of quinquennium	14,200	7,650	21,850	14,680	8,120	22,800

Wales, and Great Britain as a whole, are set out in Table 3.4. It will be seen that, while the increases in the total number of employees in the Midlands and South are very similar in the two periods – 869,000 (428,000 men and 441,000 women) in 1952–7 and 877,000 (491,000 men and 386,000 women) in 1957–62, the causes of the increases are very different. Between 1952 and 1957 the natural increase was small but the increases in the proportions employed were large, especially for women. Between 1957 and 1962, on the other hand, the natural increases were much larger, especially for men,[1] but the proportion of men employed fell sharply, while the rise for women was much smaller than in 1952–7. A large part of this last change seems to have been attributable to the fact that most of the natural increase occurred in the 15 to 19 age group, which for Great Britain increased from about 3¼ millions in 1957 to nearly 4 millions in 1962. This, together with a rise in the proportion of the age group receiving education, brought an increase of more than 300,000 in the number of persons over 15 receiving secondary or further education.

A considerable part of the decline in the proportion of the population at work was offset by a marked increase in the number released from the forces, and for the South and Midlands by the increased flow of inter-area migrants. Still more important was the inflow of immigrants from overseas. While the estimates for this cannot be relied on to give more than the very roughest idea of the real position, it seems safe to say that the very large increase in net immigration which is known to have taken place in 1959–62 has been concentrated almost entirely on the Midlands and South.

When we attempt to look forward, as we do in Table 3.5, to the probable future changes in the labour supply of the Midlands and South, it is clear that its rate of expansion, especially in the second half of the next decade, is likely to be much slower than in the past decade. According to the projection made by the Registrar-General, the rise in the number of men in the United Kingdom between the ages of 15 and 64, which was 730,000 between 1957

[1] The differences between the natural rates of increase for men and women are largely due to the small number of men reaching retiring age during both periods – an after-effect of the heavy casualties of the First World War.

and 1962, is expected to be 526,000 from 1962 to 1967, and only 233,000 from 1967 to 1972. For women, the increase is expected to slow down from 355,000 in 1957–62 to 180,000 in 1962–7 and to be replaced by a small decrease in 1967–72. On the basis of this projection, the natural increase in the number of employees in the Midlands and South is expected to decline from 325,000 in 1957–62 to 300,000 in 1962–7 and to only 40,000 in 1967–72. The impact of these declines in the rate of growth of the labour force will be greatly reinforced by the future absence of net reductions in the armed forces, which added something like 270,000 to the civilian

TABLE 3.5

PROJECTION OF FUTURE CHANGES IN NUMBER OF CIVIL EMPLOYEES IN THE MIDLANDS AND SOUTH

('000)

	1962 to 1967			*1967 to 1972*		
	Men	*Women*	*Total*	*Men*	*Women*	*Total*
Number of employees in first year of quinquennium	9,821	5,502	15,323	10,121	5,722	15,843
Natural increase	+250	+50	+300	+50	−10	+40
Releases from armed forces	+10	—	+10	—	—	—
Reduction in self-employed	—	—	—	—	—	—
Change in proportion employed of population aged 15–64	−100	+120	+20	−100	+60	−40
Inter-area migrants	+70	+30	+100	—	—	—
Overseas migrants	+70	+20	+90	+50	+15	+65
Number of employees in last year of quinquennium	10,121	5,722	15,843	10,121	5,787	15,908

labour force in the Midlands and South between 1952 and 1962, and which in future are likely to be very small or possibly negative.

The main uncertainty is about the changes to be expected in the proportion of the population of working age in employment. For men, this proportion seems certain to continue its fall. Apart from those receiving full-time education, practically all men between the ages of 15 and 65 are already working. The only possible offset, therefore, to the foreseen rapid rise both in the proportion of the 15–18 age group staying on at school, and in the proportion of the 18–25 age group receiving university or other further education, is a rise in the number of those remaining at work after 65.

While every effort should be made to encourage this, it is unlikely to offset more than a small part of the number withdrawn for education. To put the fall from this cause at 100,000 for each quinquennium may be an underestimate.

For women, prediction is even more difficult. It is assumed here that the loss to the labour force of more girls staying on at school or receiving further education will be more than offset by the increase in the number of married women returning to employment, but that the net increases will probably tend to get progressively smaller. The estimated net increases of 120,000 in 1962–7 and 60,000 in 1967–72 may prove to be too large.

These decreases in the rate of rise in the number of employees in the Midlands and South will be accentuated if the Government's measures for stimulating the demand for labour in the North and Wales are, in fact, successful. Table 3.5 reflects the assumption that the inter-area movement of labour will decrease progressively between 1962 and 1967, and cease altogether after 1967. One consequence of this success would presumably be that in future immigrants from overseas would spread themselves more evenly throughout the country, instead of remaining concentrated in the Midlands and South. This effect is allowed for in Table 3.5, where the estimates for the increase in employees from overseas are based on the Registrar-General's assumption of a net inflow of 60,000 in 1962–3, declining to 20,000 a year in later years.

The combined results of these various estimates give increases in the total labour force in the Midlands and South of 520,000 in 1962–7 and of only 65,000 in 1967–72, as compared with increases of 869,000 in 1952–7 and 877,000 in 1957–62. On the basis of the arguments raised earlier in this article, we should expect that the minimum reserves of labour which the area would need to hold within its own boundaries in order to prevent inflation would be more than the 1·7 or 1·8 per cent which we thought might be possible in the absence of changes in factors other than the equalisation of unemployment rates throughout the country. Thus the cost to the Midlands and South of a reduction in the level of unemployment in the North and Wales to the average of the country as a whole may be a rise in its own critical unemployment level from the present 1·5 per cent to something like 2 per cent, or even more.

POSTSCRIPT (JULY 1969)
RECENT CHANGES IN UNEMPLOYMENT AND NUMBER OF EMPLOYEES

Unemployment

The measures to restrain internal demand, forced on the Government in 1966 and subsequent years by the continued balance-of-payments deficit, have resulted in the maintenance in Great Britain for two and a half years of an average unemployment percentage of about 2·4 per cent. It would seem, therefore, that the cyclical process is, at least temporarily, in abeyance. Attempts have been made to render the higher unemployment level more acceptable socially and politically, both by redundancy payments and higher unemployment benefits and by intensified efforts to reduce the disparity between the unemployment percentages in different parts of the country. The measures used include a more vigorous restriction of industrial development certificates in low unemployment areas; higher investment grants in the development areas for all firms and selective employment tax premiums for firms

TABLE 3.6

NUMBERS AND PERCENTAGES OF UNEMPLOYED, 1963–9

('000)

	Average number unemployed				*Average percentage unemployed*			
	Midlands and South	*North, Scotland and Wales*	*Great Britain*	*North, Scotland and Wales as percentage of Great Britain*	*Midlands and South*	*North, Scotland and Wales*	*Great Britain*	*North Scotland and Wales as percentage of Great Britain*
1963	273	300	573	52·3	1·75	3·96	2·47	166
1964	168	213	381	55·9	1·07	2·81	1·64	171
1965	155	174	329	52·8	0·98	2·30	1·40	164
1966	186	174	360	48·4	1·16	2·28	1·52	150
1967	306	253	559	45·2	1·93	3·37	2·39	141
1968	308	256	564	45·4	1·96	3·43	2·43	141
1969 (1st half – seasonally corrected)	294	245	539	45·5	1·87	3·31	2·33	142

in manufacturing industries; and financial assistance from the Board of Trade for small firms trying to expand in development areas. As Table 3.6 (a continuation of Table 3.1 on p. 66) suggests, these measures seem to have had an appreciable effect, since in 1967, 1968 and the first half of 1969 the proportion of unemployed in the North-West and North of England, Scotland and Wales, at 45 per cent of the total in Great Britain, was the lowest for twenty years, while the unemployment percentage was not much more than 40 per cent above the average for Great Britain, a proportion previously achieved only in 1957.

TABLE 3.7

REGIONAL UNEMPLOYMENT, 1957–69

	Unemployment in Great Britain (%)	*Regional unemployment percentages as percentages of Great Britain*						
		South-East, East and South	*Midlands, Yorks. and Humberside*	*South-West*	*North-West*	*North*	*Scotland*	*Wales*
1957	1·43	72	71	116	110	118	181	180
1958	2·10	67	80	103	128	114	148	178
1959	2·17	61	74	98	127	152	179	172
1960	1·63	62	64	101	118	175	222	164
1961	1·51	66	76	93	108	163	206	167
1962	2·03	64	79	87	125	186	184	164
1963	2·47	63	79	85	124	198	191	145
1964	1·64	61	64	95	124	202	217	155
1965	1·40	64	69	111	113	182	213	182
1966	1·52	67	80	118	97	170	188	187
1967	2·39	70	91	104	104	166	161	168
1968	2·43	69	93	103	101	193	158	164
1969 1st (half)	2·33							

The effects of the reduction in the difference between the average unemployment percentages in Scotland, the North of England and Wales on the one hand and in the Midlands and South of England on the other have varied considerably between regions (see Table 3.7). Boundary changes make it impossible to separate London and the South-East from the East and South of England, or the Midlands from Yorkshire and Humberside, but comparisons between these areas and the other regions are possible over time. These show that the main improvements have been in North-West England, wherein 1966–8 the unemployment percentage was very little higher than the national average, and to a smaller extent in Scotland, where the percentage in 1966–8 was about 70 per cent above that for Great Britain, as compared with nearly double in 1958–65. Of the low unemployment regions, the South-West, after rising well above the national average in 1965 and 1966, fell back almost to equality with it in 1967–8, and is now very similar to the North-West. In the South-East, East and South unemployment, while still low, has risen from about 65 per cent to nearly 70 per cent of the national average. The main worsening has been in the Midlands, Yorkshire and Humberside, where the unemployment percentage rose from an average of less than 75 per cent of the national average in 1957–65 to 80 per cent in 1966 and over 90 per cent in 1967–8.

Number of Employees

The proportion of employees (employed and unemployed) in the different regions has changed partly, but not entirely, inversely with the levels of unemployment (see Table 3·8). As might have been expected from the unemployment figures, the main increase is in the share of the South-East, East and South, which in 1968 had just over 37 per cent of all employees in Great Britain, as compared with rather over 35 per cent in 1957. On the other hand, the share of the other area with considerably less than the national average of unemployment, the Midlands, Yorkshire and Humberside, has fallen slightly, whereas that of the South-West, with about the national average of unemployment, has risen a little.

Among the high unemployment regions, the North-West, where the unemployment percentage has recently fallen to about the national average, has suffered the largest reduction in its share of employees, from 13·7 per cent in 1957 to 12·8 per cent in 1968, while Scotland, where unemployment is less above the national average than it used to be, has also seen its share of employees fall considerably, from 9·9 per cent in 1957 to 9·3 per cent in 1968. On the other hand the North of England, where unemployment has tended to rise relatively to the national average, and Wales, where it has remained about the same, have suffered little fall in their share of employees. These results seem to suggest that, whereas workers tend to move into areas where unemployment is low, they

TABLE 3.8

DISTRIBUTION OF EMPLOYEES, 1957–68

	Number of employees (employed and unemployed) in Great Britain	*Employees in regions as percentages of number in Great Britain*						
		South-East, East and South	*Midlands, Yorks. and Humberside*	*South-West*	*North-West*	*North*	*Scotland*	*Wales*
1957	21,910	35·3	25·2	5·5	13·7	5·9	9·9	4·4
1958	21,899	35·4	25·2	5·5	13·7	5·9	9·9	4·4
1959	22,032	35·6	25·1	5·6	13·5	5·9	9·9	4·4
1960	22,388	35·8	25·2	5·6	13·4	5·8	9·8	4·4
1961	22,705	36·0	25·3	5·6	13·3	5·8	9·6	4·3
1962	23,025	36·2	25·3	5·7	13·2	5·7	9·6	4·3
1963	23,165	36·3	25·3	5·7	13·1	5·7	9·5	4·3
1964	23,263	36·3	25·3	5·8	13·1	5·7	9·5	4·3
1965	23,463	36·8	25·1	5·8	12·9	5·7	9·4	4·3
1966	23,653	36·8	25·2	5·8	12·9	5·7	9·3	4·3
1967	23,376	36·9	25·1	5·8	12·8	5·7	9·4	4·3
1968	23,200	37·1	25·0	5·8	12·8	5·7	9·3	4·3

also tend to reduce unemployment in the areas from which they are best able to move.

The number of employees in Great Britain, after rising from 21·90 million in 1958 to 23·65 million in 1966, fell to 23·20 million in 1968. Part of this fall was cyclical, but part probably represented a downward trend, due mainly to a temporary conjunction of a smaller number of young people reaching working age with a larger number of elderly people reaching retirement age. This downward trend, which will be reinforced by the effects of the rise in the minimum school-leaving age to 16 in 1972, is not likely to be reversed until the mid-1970s.

4

The Management of the British Economy[1]

THE continual argument about the management of the British economy since the war has been confused by widespread mid-understanding, both about the effects of government measures and about the way in which the economy in fact behaves. The publication of Mr J. C. R. Dow's book[2] should serve to remove much, if not of the confusion, at any rate of the excuse for it. It is the fruit of many years of research, mainly at the National Institute of Economic and Social Research, and is by far the best-documented and argued work which has appeared in this field. It will undoubtedly become a leading textbook in applied economics.

Dow's main purpose is to discuss the way in which successive governments have attempted to regulate the general level of demand in the economy. He therefore does not deal, except incidentally, with other possible objectives of government economic policy, such as a more equal distribution of incomes or of wealth. In considering the effects of policy, however, he is obliged to devote much space to the discussion of a wide range of inter-relations within the economic system, which throws a great deal of light on the way in which the economy actually seems to work.

The book is not an easy one to summarise. This is partly because of the way in which it is arranged. It is divided into four parts. In the first, we get a rapid factual survey of the economic and financial history of the United Kingdom, first under Labour and then under Conservative Chancellors. The second part is devoted to a detailed analysis of the various measures taken, and the third part to a

[1] First published in *Lloyds Bank Review*, Apr 1965.

[2] *The Management of the British Economy, 1945–60*, by J. C. R. Dow (National Institute of Economic and Social Research and Cambridge University Press, 1964).

discussion of the general behaviour of the economy. Not until Part IV do we hear Dow's own conclusions, though some indications of these appear here and there on the way. Under this arrangement the same general subject may be discussed two, three, or even four times at different levels and from different aspects, and to obtain a complete idea of Dow's views on any particular question it is necessary to collate passages from different, and often widely separated, sections of the book. An additional difficulty is that much, not only of the information but also of the argument, is presented in the form of small-scale diagrams and charts, and that even where information is presented in tabular form the figures are often highly processed, making them difficult to check without laborious reconstruction from the original data.

In view of these difficulties, no attempt will be made in this review article to follow Dow through the whole of his work. Instead, a limited number of questions will be selected for discussion and followed through the different sections of the book, often by assembling elements separated by many pages of other matter.

THE CYCLICAL PATTERN OF THE ECONOMY

The best place to start the discussion seems to be with the cyclical pattern of changes in demand; for without a picture of this it is impossible to form any clear judgements about the appropriateness of the timing of government measures. The most convenient measure of the pressure of demand at any given time is an index showing how fully the resources of the economy are employed. To construct such an index we need three pieces of information. The first is an index of production; the second is an index of the growth of capacity to produce, or what the Treasury, in their *Economic Report for 1963*, call 'productive potential'; and, thirdly, we need to be able to relate the two indexes on some particular date, from which we can then proceed to measure their relative variations.

Dow's index of the growth of productive potential (which he calls productive capacity) is shown in a small-scale diagram on p. 115. This is transcribed (within the limits of accuracy possible) in the second column of Table 4.1. Dow relates his index to that of gross domestic product (apparently measured from the output side) by making it equal to gross domestic product whenever the number of unemployed is equal to the number of unfilled vacancies; for intervening dates he makes it differ from the output index by twice the difference between the percentage of unemployment and the percentage of vacancies. In Table 4.1, Dow's index is compared both with the index of gross domestic product and with two other indexes of productive potential, one published by myself in 1962[1] and one by W. A. H. Godley and J. R. Shepherd in their article on 'Long-term Growth and Short-term Policy' in the August 1964 issue of the *National Institute Economic Review*. The National Institute index is made equal to that of gross domestic product on dates when unemployment stands at 1½ per cent, and mine when it stood at 1 per cent in the last quarter of 1955, the lowest level recorded since the war. To facilitate comparison, all three indexes and the index of output are shown, in the last four

TABLE 4.1

INDEXES OF PRODUCTIVE POTENTIAL AND GROSS DOMESTIC PRODUCT, 1946–64

	Index of gross domestic product (1958 = 100)	*Indexes of productive potential (own bases)*			*Index of gross domestic product*	*Indexes of productive potential (common bases)*		
		Dow ('full employment' output)	*National Institute (1½% unemployment output)*	*Paish (1% unemployment output)*		*Dow*	*National Institute*	*Paish*
					(Oct–Dec 1955 = 100)			
1946	75·6	70·7			76·3	73·5		
1947	76·3	74·0			77·0	77·0		
1948	79·8	77·3		81·8	80·5	80·4		82·6
1949	82·6	80·6		83·8	83·4	83·8		84·6
1950	85·7	83·4		85·9	86·5	86·7		86·8
1951	87·6	85·8	85·1	88·0	88·4	89·2	89·0	88·9
1952	87·0	88·1	87·5	90·3	87·8	91·6	91·4	91·2
1953	90·5	90·5	89·8	92·5	91·4	94·1	93·8	93·4
1954	94·3	92·9	92·2	94·8	95·1	96·5	96·2	95·7
1955	97·5	95·2	94·7	97·8	98·5	99·0	98·9	98·8
1956	98·4	97·5	97·4	100·8	99·3	101·4	101·6	101·8
1957	100·1	100·0	100·0	103·9	101·0	103·9	104·3	105·0
1958	100·0	102·8	102·8	107·0	100·9	106·8	107·2	108·2
1959	104·5	107·5	105·6	110·4	105·4	111·7	110·2	111·5
1960	110·0	112·2	108·4	112·7	111·0	116·6	113·1	113·8
1961	112·0		111·6	116·0	113·1		116·4	117·2
1962	113·5		115·2	119·6	114·5		120·1	120·8
1963	117·2		119·0	123·4	118·3		124·2	124·6
1964	(123·6)		122·8		(124·8)		128·2	

[1] *Studies in an Inflationary Economy* (Macmillan, 1962) chap. 17, p. 333.

columns of Table 4.1, on a common base of 100 for the last quarter of 1955.

It will be seen that all three indexes of productive potential move very similarly in the years between 1951 and 1958. From 1958 to 1960, however, Dow's index rises much more sharply than either of the other two. This seems to be partly because he fails to allow for the effects of a sharp reduction in the average length of the working week. Where the indexes differ, that of the National Institute, which has been prepared with the aid of much more refined statistical methods than either of the other two, is to be preferred. For the period before 1951, which the National Institute index does not cover, Dow's index may well be nearer the mark than mine. While since 1951 it is reasonable to assume that the critical factor limiting the growth of output has been labour, it is likely that before 1951 supplies of materials, and especially of semi-finished products, were also limiting factors, and that as these shortages were progressively removed output was able to grow at a rate which could not be maintained once the shortages had disappeared.

THE MARGIN OF POTENTIAL AND UNEMPLOYMENT

If we can assume that the economy was quite fully employed in the last quarter of 1955, and accept the National Institute's index of productive potential for the years from 1951 onwards, we can calculate the average percentage of potential utilised, and with it the unused margin of potential, in each year. If we further assume that an average of 1 per cent unemployment in Great Britain (equivalent to about 0·7 per cent in the Midlands and South, where two-thirds of the working population live) is an irreducible peace-time minimum, we can also calculate the unused margin of manpower.

The comparison of the two series in Table 4.2 shows that the unused margin of potential fluctuates much more widely than the unused margin of manpower. Dow's method of estimation requires the fluctuations in the margin of unused potential should be about four times as large as those in unemployment, but he does not explain why the difference should be of just this size. Godley and Shepherd, however, explain at some length why each 1 per cent rise or fall in output above or below productive trend is accompanied by a rise or fall of just over 0·5 per cent in the number employed, and why a rise or fall of 250,000 in the number employed is accompanied by a fall or rise of about 100,000 in the number of unemployed. A combination of the two relationships shows that a rise or fall of 1 per cent in output above or below productive trend is accompanied by a fall or rise in unemployment of just over 0·2 per cent, giving a ratio of about 4½ to 1. To facilitate comparison between the unused margins of potential and manpower, we therefore multiply the unused margin of manpower by 4½. The result is shown in the last column of Table 4.2.

TABLE 4.2

UNUSED MARGINS OF PRODUCTIVE POTENTIAL AND LABOUR, 1951–64

	Productive potential		*Labour*		
	Percentage employed	*Unused margin*	*Percentage employed*	*Unused margin*	*Unused margin* × 4½
1951	99·3	0·7	98·8	0·2	1·0
1952	96·1	3·9	98·0	1·0	4·5
1953	97·4	2·6	98·4	0·6	2·9
1954	98·9	1·1	98·7	0·3	1·5
1955	99·6	0·4	98·9	0·1	0·4
1956	97·7	2·3	98·8	0·2	0·8
1957	96·8	3·2	98·6	0·4	1·9
1958	94·1	5·9	97·9	1·1	5·0
1959	95·6	4·4	97·8	1·2	5·3
1960	98·1	1·9	98·4	0·6	2·9
1961	97·1	2·9	98·5	0·5	2·3
1962	95·4	4·6	98·0	1·0	4·6
1963	95·3	4·7	97·5	1·5	6·7
1964	(97·3)	(2·7)	98·4	0·6	2·9

It will be seen that changes in unemployment tend not only to be much smaller than changes in the margin of potential, but also to lag behind them, both on the upswing and on the downswing of the cycle. The lags are particularly marked in 1955–7, when unemployment rose much more slowly than the margin of potential; in 1958–9, when it continued to rise after the margin of potential had begun to fall; and in 1960–1, when it continued to fall after the margin of potential had begun to rise. Godley and Shepherd attribute this lag largely to delay by employers in adjusting the size of the labour force to changes in the amount of work to be done.

THE MARGIN OF POTENTIAL AND THE RISE IN INCOMES

Before accepting an index of the unused margin of productive potential as a reliable frame of reference against which to judge the timing of government measures, we must test it against the most reliable measure of the pressure of demand: the rate of rise of money incomes. Such a comparison between a static and a dynamic concept is similar to that between the age-structure of a population and its rate of increase or decrease. In Table 4.3 the average margin of productive potential in each year is compared with the annual rates of increase of a number of the components of national money income and of its total.

It is clear from Table 4.3 that changes in the unused margins of productive potential and manpower are accompanied or closely followed by opposite changes in the rates of rise of money incomes.

TABLE 4.3

MARGIN OF PRODUCTIVE POTENTIAL AND RATES OF GROWTH OF OUTPUT AND INCOMES, 1951–64

	Margin of productive potential	*Margin of manpower*	*Percentage increase over previous year*						
			Output		*Money incomes*				
			Productive potential	*Gross domestic product*	*Wage rates: Weekly*	*Wage rates: Hourly*	*Weekly earnings*	*Gross company trading profits*	*Net national income money*
	(%)	(%)							
1951	0·7	0·2	(2·6)	2·3	9·1	9·1	9·3	16·8	10·0
1952	3·9	1·0	2·7	−0·7	8·3	8·3	8·0	−12·2	7·6
1953	2·6	0·6	2·6	4·0	4·3	4·3	6·8	6·1	7·7
1954	1·1	0·3	2·7	4·2	4·1	4·2	7·4	11·5	5·8
1955	0·4	0·1	2·7	3·5	6·7	6·7	9·2	12·3	6·9
1956	2·3	0·2	2·8	0·9	7·4	7·4	7·0	1·6	8·8
1957	3·2	0·4	2·7	1·7	5·0	5·1	4·5	5·3	5·7
1958	5·9	1·1	2·8	−0·1	3·3	3·5	3·3	−3·0	4·3
1959	4·4	1·2	2·8	4·5	2·6	2·7	5·0	10·9	5·1
1960	1·9	0·6	2·6	3·2	2·0	3·4	8·4	12·8	6·7
1961	2·9	0·5	2·9	1·8	4·0	6·2	5·6	−2·8	6·8
1962	4·6	1·0	3·2	1·3	2·8	3·7	2·8	1·5	4·1
1963	4·7	1·5	3·4	3·3	2·8	2·9	4·2	8·0	5·6
1964	(2·7)	0·6	3·2	(5·5)	5·0	5·4	(7·0)		

Dow estimates that each 1 per cent rise or fall in the level of unemployment is associated with a fall or rise of about 3 per cent in the annual rate of increase in wage rates. Since, as we have seen, the ratio of changes in the margin of productive potential to changes in unemployment is about $4\frac{1}{2}$ to 1, this would imply that a change of $1\frac{1}{2}$ per cent in the margin of productive potential would be associated with a change of about 1 per cent in the rate of increase of wage rates. Further, since, on the average, fluctuations in weekly earnings and national money income are considerably larger than those in wage rates, this would seem to imply that each rise of 1 per cent in the proportion of productive potential employed is accompanied by a rise of nearly 1 per cent a year in money incomes.

We still have one step to take before we can use the unused margin of productive potential as a frame of reference for judging government policies. This is to determine at what point the rate of rise of money incomes begins to be too rapid, and therefore what margin of potential represents a level of demand which is neither inadequate nor excessive. The highest rate of rise of money incomes which is consistent with the absence of inflation is that which can be achieved without its exceeding the rate of rise of real income.

Of the three constituents which determine the level of real national income – the output of goods and services, the international terms of trade and the net foreign investment income – output, in the long run, is by far the most important. In most periods, therefore, we can determine the point at which the rate of rise of money incomes becomes excessive by comparing it with the rate of rise of output. But if output is rising at a rate greater than can be permanently maintained (i.e. faster than the rate of rise of productive potential), money incomes, though rising no faster than output, are rising at a rate faster than can be permanently maintained, without generating excess demand. In such conditions, therefore, the balance between the rate of rise of incomes and the rate of rise of output is temporary and unstable; it occurs only during the upswing of the business cycle and breaks down into excess demand as soon as the margin of productive potential approaches exhaustion. To achieve a stable equilibrium, we must therefore ensure not only that incomes are rising only as fast as output, but also that output is rising only as fast as productive potential – that is to say, at present rates of growth, by rather less than 3½ per cent a year.

Reference to Table 4.3 shows that there has been no year since 1951 (and in fact since the war) in which national money income has risen by less than 4 per cent, the lowest being 4.3 per cent from 1957 to 1958, when the margin of potential rose from 3.2 to 5.9 per cent, and 4.1 per cent from 1961 to 1962, when the margin of potential rose from 2·9 to 4·6 per cent. A rough inspection therefore suggests that the margin of potential needed to prevent an excessively rapid rise of money incomes is over 5 per cent, equivalent to an unemployment percentage of over 2 per cent.

UNEMPLOYMENT AND THE RISE OF PRICES

Confirmation of this impression is provided by some very interesting calculations by Dow, based on earlier research by L. A. Dicks-Mireaux. These are shown in diagram form on p. 362, and are transcribed, as accurately as the small-scale chart permits, in Table 4.4. In this, the actual rise in prices (of final expenditure at factor cost) from 1947 to 1959 is compared with what it is estimated it would have been if the level of unemployment, instead of fluctuating widely about an average of 1½ per cent, had been held steady at (*a*) 1¾ per cent and (*b*) 2¼ per cent. It is assumed that, with unemployment steady, output per head would have risen steadily instead of fluctuating cyclically.

It will be seen that, after the end of the rise in import prices in 1951, with 2¼ per cent unemployment (the equivalent to a margin of unused productive potential of about 5½ per cent) prices up to 1959 remain roughly stable. With 1¾ per cent unemployment (corresponding to a margin of potential of about 3½ per cent) the rise in prices averages 1½ per cent a year, while with the actual level fluctuating about 1½ per cent unemployment (equivalent to about 2¼ per cent of potential) the rise in prices averaged about 2¼ per cent a year.

Dow chooses a level of 1¾ per cent unemployment because this corresponds to his concept of zero excess demand for labour, with unemployment equal to unfilled vacancies. This concept appears to have a strong resemblance to my own of a margin of unemployment which would be just high enough to prevent price increases (apart

TABLE 4.4

RECONSTRUCTION OF PRICE TRENDS TO SHOW EFFECT OF LOWER PRESSURE OF DEMAND, 1947–59
(index of factor cost of final expenditure, 1947 = 100)

	Actual course of prices (unemployment average 1½%)	*Estimated course of prices at levels of unemployment of*	
		1¾%	*2¼%*
1947	100	100	100
1948	107	104	103
1949	110	106	104
1950	112	108	105
1951	126	120	115
1952	135	126	119
1953	135	125	117
1954	137	127	116
1955	141	130	115
1956	147	135	118
1957	151	138	119
1958	156	140	120
1959	157	140	117

from those caused by higher import prices) with a purely competitive labour market.[1] The figure of 1¾ per cent is, however, in my view probably too low. I should put it nearer 2 per cent.

While Dow recognises that the evidence of his 'artificial history' for the consistency between a 2¼ per cent level of unemployment and price stability is not conclusive, he attaches sufficient weight to it to commit himself to the view that 'if unemployment were kept at 2 to 2½ per cent, instead of the post-war average of 1½ per cent, this would probably make a major difference to the rate of rise in prices'.

THE LEVEL OF DEMAND AND GROWTH

Before finally accepting the maintenance of a somewhat larger margin of productive potential as an objective of policy, there is one further argument to be considered. This is that, even if a somewhat lower level of demand is necessary to prevent inflation,

[1] *Policy for Incomes?* (Institute of Economic Affairs, 1964), p. 30.

such a policy would slow down the rate of growth, and that a measure of inflation must therefore be accepted. Dow does not agree with this view. He holds that 'if the pressure of demand had been somewhat lower, and the margin of unused capacity somewhat larger, than in most of the post-war years, there could have been steady expansion of expenditure, output and output per head as rapid as that which in fact occurred' (p. 361). He therefore considers that 'the pursuit of faster growth requires action aimed directly at accelerating the growth of capacity. A faster expansion of demand without such action seems likely to lead to an insupportable degree of excess demand' (p. 403).

On this question I myself would go further than Dow, and would support a policy of providing a somewhat larger margin of unused potential as a means not only of checking inflation and reducing the magnitude of cyclical fluctuations, but also of promoting faster growth. Without a margin of unused potential there can be no effective competition; without effective competition it is impossible to ensure the elimination of inefficient managements; and the surest way of slowing down the rate of growth is to conserve inefficiency.

From his long and careful investigation of the way in which the system works, Dow draws the following conclusions for government policy:

> Fiscal and monetary policy should:—(I) aim to produce a steady growth of demand in line with the growth of capacity: this seems desirable partly because 'stop/go' policies probably upset the process of growth; partly because such policies would produce periods of excess demand, which would speed up the rise in prices. (II) aim to keep demand at a point which left a rather greater margin of spare capacity than on average in the past. This seems desirable because a wages policy on its own seems unlikely to be sufficiently effective, at least at first; and greater price stability seems desirable, partly for its own sake, but largely as a means of getting the growth of exports to pay for the imports needed for faster growth (p. 404).

THE BALANCE OF PAYMENTS

It will be observed that, in his prescription for policy, Dow makes no reference to the balance of payments, except to say that greater price stability would facilitate the growth of exports. This relegation of the balance-of-payments problem to the position of a side-effect of the pressure of internal demand is no doubt the reason why, apart from some purely descriptive references in Part I, and a discussion of the accuracy of balance-of-payments forecasts in Chapter V, he devotes only about a dozen pages to the subject, right at the end of the book. Here he again emphasises the distinction, invariably blurred in popular discussion, between cyclical and secular movements. The cyclical effects of changes in the level of internal demand are seen mainly in imports. There may well be cyclical effects also on exports, but these are frequently concealed, as in 1952 and 1958, by the larger effects of developments in the outside world. In the longer run, a cyclical excess of demand is likely to result in a permanent rise in the level of costs, and if this is greater than in other countries the ability to compete in export markets may be permanently impaired. Thus, while the cyclical effects of excess demand are shown mainly in imports, the long-term effects are shown mainly in exports.

Table 4.5 overleaf shows, with the margin of productive potential, annual percentage changes in the volumes of imports and exports of goods and services, and annual values, at constant prices, of the balance of payments on income account and of the physical increase in stocks and work-in-progress. The table also shows the totals of the balance of payments and of stock changes, which, apart from errors and omissions, are together equal to the difference between saving and domestic fixed investment and are in themselves quite a good index of the secular trend in the pressure of internal demand.

As will be seen from Table 4.5, the four years (1951, 1955, 1960 and 1964) in which sharp rises in imports led to substantial adverse balances of payments were also years of high stock accumulation. The rise in stocks occurs, not in the early stages of the upswing of the cycle, but in the second or, as in 1955, even in the third year of the rise. Table 4.5 also indicates a long-term deterioration in exports, since the rise in volume was smaller in 1962–4 than it had been in 1958–60, and smaller again than in 1953–5, although the margin of unused potential became progressively larger. The rate of rise in imports, on the other hand, shows little change from one cycle to the next.

Although, for purposes of analysis, it may well be justified to regard changes in the balance of payments as mere side-effects of changes in the level of internal demand, in discussions of government policy they surely deserve a more central position. In place of the policy objectives set up by Dow, governments hitherto seem

TABLE 4.5.

BALANCE OF PAYMENTS AND INCREASE IN STOCKS, 1951–64

	Margin of productive potential	*Imports of goods and services*	*Exports of goods and services*	*Balance of payments on current account*	*Physical increase in stocks*	*Balance of payments plus stock increase*
	(%)	*(annual percentage increase at 1958 prices)*		*(£ m. at 1958 prices)*[1]		
1951	0·7	+7·0	−1·0	−308	+615	+307
1952	3·9	−6·9	−1·9	+169	+65	+234
1953	2·6	+6·9	+4·2	+154	+135	+289
1954	1·1	+3·8	+5·8	+123	+54	+177
1955	0·4	+8·5	+5·9	−157	+313	+156
1956	2·3	+0·5	+4·3	+205	+243	+448
1957	3·2	+2·7	+2·5	+208	+242	+450
1958	5·9	+1·1	−1·7	+345	+100	+445
1959	4·4	+6·4	+2·8	+153	+174	+327
1960	1·9	+11·1	+5·6	−254	+592	+338
1961	2·9	−0·2	+2·9	−1	+319	+318
1962	4·6	+1·3	+1·6	+113	+101	+214
1963	4·7	+4·0	+4·3	+109	+147	+256
1964 (est.)	2·7	+9·0	+1·5	−350	+470	+120

[1] Average of import and export prices for balance-of-payments figures.

to have reacted mainly to two types of stimulus: an adverse balance of payments, especially when reinforced by pressure on sterling, as a stimulus to restrict demand; and a rise in unemployment as a stimulus to expand it. Since both these developments normally lag well behind changes in the margin of unused potential, it is natural that government action tends always to be taken too late.

THE INSTRUMENTS OF GOVERNMENT POLICY

For their contra-cyclical measures, the various governments since the war have relied on four types of instrument: physical controls, control of public-sector fixed investment, fiscal policy and monetary policy (including financial controls). With the release of resources from the war effort, the war-time physical controls became increasingly difficult to make effective, although control of private-sector housing remained very important up to 1951, and its relaxation in 1952 was the main reason for the housing boom of 1952–4. Import controls were also important in the early post-war years, and Dow attributes about half the drop in imports from 1951 to 1952 to their reimposition. Since 1952 physical controls have not played an important part.

Control of public-sector investment, which before the war was often advocated as the main contra-cyclical instrument, has also proved ineffective. This has been largely because of the long time-lag between the time when policy is changed and the time when its effects are seen in a change in the actual use of resources. Thus an expansion of public-sector investment decided on during a recession is likely to become effective (as in 1964) as an aggravation of an excessive increase in demand a couple of years later, while the effects of a policy of restriction may well be seen (as in 1958) as aggravating a subsequent recession. The occasions when public investment policy has acted contra-cyclically (as in 1955) seem to have been the accidental results of changes in general policy rather than of contra-cyclical design. Until it becomes possible to make allowance for so long a time-lag, and perhaps to inaugurate measures to expand public investment while at the same time taking action to restrict consumption, attempts to use public investment as a contra-cyclical weapon are likely to do more harm than good.

FISCAL POLICY

Since 1951, effective contra-cyclical policy has depended mainly on fiscal and monetary measures. Contra-cyclical fiscal measures have consisted almost entirely of changes in taxation (or in subsidies and other transfer payments which, as Dow points out, can be regarded as negative taxes). Changes in government current expenditure on goods and services are so difficult to make, and have to be planned so far in advance, that they are of little practical use as contra-cyclical measures. Not all tax changes, however, are equally effective. Measures designed to encourage or discourage private-sector fixed investment, even if effective, operate with so long a time-lag that, like government investment policy, they run the risk of aggravating, rather than reducing, cyclical fluctuations. The only tax changes likely to act as contra-cyclical measures are those designed to affect personal consumption within the next few months, and Dow publishes (pp. 198–9) an extremely interesting table showing his estimates of the impact of tax changes on personal consumption for each year from 1945 to 1960. His conclusions are

TABLE 4.6

TAXATION AND MONETARY CHANGES, 1945–64

	Margin of productive potential	*Tax changes*		*Monetary changes*			
		Est. effect on total yield	*Est. impact on consumption*	*increase over previous year in*		*Ratio of net bank deposits to net national income*	*Yield on 2½% Consols*
				clearing-bank advances	*net clearing bank deposits*		
	(%)	(£m.)		(%)			
1945		−385	+242	+2	+13	53·5	2·92
1946		−146	+87	+16	+8	61·3	2·60
1947 Apr		+54	−8	+25	+11	63·5	2·76
1947 Nov		+197	−120				
1948		+49	+42	+19	+5	59·4	3·21
1949		−92	+38	+ 9	+1	56·7	3·30
1950		−1	+37	+11	+1	54·2	3·54
1951	0·7	+387	−84	+14	+2	50·2	3·78
1952	3·9	−67	+176	+1	−1	46·1	4·23
1953	2·6	−412	+128	−6	+3	43·9	4·08
1954	1·1	−10	+3	+4	+4	43·0	3·75
1955 Apr	0·4	−155	+90	+12	−1	40·2	4·17
1955 Oct		+113	−59				
1956	2·3	−2	+10	−6	−3	35·9	4·73
1957	3·2	−131	+70	+3	+2	34·6	4·98
1958	5·9	−108	+52	+3	+3	34·2	4·98
1959	4·4	−359	+215	+31	+5	34·2	4·82
1960	1·9	+71	−4	+24	+4	33·3	5·42
1961	2·9	+193	−123	+7	+3	32·0	6·16
1962	4·6	+10	+8	+2	+3	31·6	6·00
1963	4·7	−269	+228	+14	+5	31·4	5·59
1964	(2·7)	+103	−80	+12	+7	31·3	6·03

summarised in Table 4.6, together with rough estimates on the same lines for 1961–4.

To obtain his estimates of the effect of tax changes on personal consumption, Dow first eliminates all changes in company taxation. He then evaluates the remainder on a scale, ranging from 100 per cent of the change in income tax at reduced rates and allowances to 80 per cent of changes in taxes on personal expenditure, 67 per cent of changes in the standard rates of income tax or surtax, 50 per cent of changes in taxes on dividends and trading incomes, and 10 per cent of changes in taxes on capital. The effect of his evaluation is greatly to modify the impression given by the crude tax changes. Thus the immediately disinflationary effects of the apparently drastic budget of 1951 are seen to be quite moderate, while the expansionary effects of the modest total tax reductions in 1952 are seen to be considerably greater than those of the much larger aggregate tax reductions of 1953.

Over the whole period, the net effects of budgetary changes are shown as having been substantially expansionary. The main expansionary budgets have been concentrated into four short periods: 1945–6, 1952–3, 1959 and 1963. In the intervening periods budgetary net effects have either been slightly restrictive, as in 1947–51 and 1960–2, or slightly expansionary, as in 1954–8. Dow points out that the net tax reductions cannot be justified on the ground that they were needed to offset the impact of rising incomes on a progressive structure of direct taxation, for this was largely or wholly offset by their opposite effects on the very large amount of specific indirect taxation.

Apart from the quite unjustifiable tax reductions of April 1955, which were largely reversed in the October budget of the same year, the major tax reductions since 1947 have all taken place in years in which the level of unemployment was, or had recently been, unusually high – 2·0 per cent in 1952, 2·1 per cent in 1958 and 2·2 per cent in 1959, and 2·5 per cent in 1963. The main restrictive budgets of November 1947, April 1951, October 1955, April 1961 and April 1964 were in years in which the balance of payments on current account was, or had recently been, highly adverse – minus £351 millions in 1947, minus £322 millions in 1951, minus £157 millions in 1955, minus £258 millions in 1960, and probably about minus £370 millions in 1964. Government policy thus seems to be an automatic reflex to unemployment on the one side and balance-of-payments trouble on the other – both of which lag very much as indicators of an inadequate or excessive level of internal demand.

THE EFFECTS OF FISCAL POLICY

The annual percentage changes in various types of national expenditure, set out in Table 4.7 overleaf, confirm the impression that the main contra-cyclical effects of fiscal policy must be looked for in personal consumption, which accounts for about two-thirds of all expenditure. Although in most years the combination of fiscal and monetary measures makes it impossible to attribute effects with certainty, it seems reasonable to conclude that the tax reductions of 1952–3 contributed greatly to the rise in consumption of 1953–5, those of 1959 to the rise of 1959–60, and those of 1963 to the rise of 1963–4. The effects of the relatively smaller tax increases of 1951, 1955 and 1961 were more strongly supplemented by monetary measures, but they presumably contributed to the checks to the rise of consumption in 1951–2, 1956 and 1961–2.

TABLE 4.7

GROWTH IN EXPENDITURE AT 1958 PRICES, 1951–64

	Margin of productive potential (%)	*Percentage change from previous year*						
		Gross domestic product	*Public sector*			*Private sector*		
			Current expenditure on goods and services	*Gross fixed investment*		*Personal consumption*	*Gross fixed investment*	
				Housing	*Other*		*Housing*	*Other*
1951	0·7	+2·3	+7·8	−2·4	+13·0	−1·4	−1·5	−7·1
1952	3·9	−0·7	+9·9	+13·1	+4·5	−0·5	+55·5	−10·3
1953	2·6	+4·0	+2·7	+19·6	+8·1	+4·5	+71·4	+2·9
1954	1·1	+4·2	−0·5	−7·9	+3·2	+4·1	+34·3	+17·2
1955	0·4	+3·5	−3·1	−20·5	+1·9	+4·0	+10·9	+15·2
1956	2·3	+0·9	−0·5	−9·5	+5·2	+0·9	+6·6	+9·8
1957	3·2	+1·7	−1·5	−7·3	+6·9	+2·1	−0·3	+8·2
1958	5·9	−0·1	−2·1	−15·7	+1·3	+2·5	+5·9	+1·8
1959	4·4	+4·5	+2·0	+0·4	+8·7	+4·6	+24·2	+5·3
1960	1·9	+3·2	+2·2	+3·0	+4·6	+4·0	+21·0	+12·4
1961	2·9	+1·8	+4·1	+1·4	+6·6	+2·2	+8·9	+11·2
1962	4·6	+1·3	+2·9	+12·4	+2·4	+1·8	−2·3	−4·6
1963	4·7	+3·3	+2·9	+10·1	+6·0	+4·0	−0·6	−2·2
1964 (est.)	2·7	+5·5	+3·0	+26·0	+15·0	+4·0	+19·0	+11·0

Dow considers that changes in company taxation probably had a substantial effect on industrial and commercial fixed investment, though only after a considerable time-lag. He doubts whether changes in initial and investment allowances had any greater effect than other fiscal changes resulting in similar alterations in the amount of tax paid.

MONETARY POLICIES

Monetary policies are those which directly affect, not spendable incomes, as suitable fiscal policies do, but the availability or cost of borrowed money. They can be divided into two types: financial controls, which attempt to restrict the availability of loan money to particular classes of would-be borrowers; and the restriction of the quantity of money, which raises the cost of borrowing everywhere. Of the financial controls, Dow dismisses as of little practical effect the regulation requiring, until 1959, the permission of the Capital Issues Committee before borrowing or otherwise raising more than £50,000 (from 1956 to 1958 more than £10,000) in any twelve months. Restrictions on hire-purchase finance, in the form both of minimum requirements for deposits and maximum periods for repayment, were more important. Their imposition in 1952–4, 1955–8 and 1960–2 undoubtedly affected the demand for cars and other durable consumer goods. Dow puts their effect on total consumer expenditure at from £100 to £200 millions a year, or from about 0·5 to 1·0 per cent of all consumer expenditure – an effect probably greater than that of tax changes during the same periods. But this result was obtained at the cost of causing fluctuations in the demand for the relatively small quantity of goods involved of 10 or 20 per cent, and of severe dislocation in the industries concerned. It would be greatly preferable to obtain a corresponding result by much less concentrated pressure on a much wider range of products.

The third main type of financial control took the form of 'requests' to the banks to restrict their advances, either to particular classes of borrowers or in total. After 1951 these requests were reinforced by efforts to force the banks to restrict advances by starving them of liquid assets – efforts which, so long as the banks held more government securities than they needed, were largely frustrated by sales of securities, and were therefore supplemented in 1960 by the introduction of 'special deposits'. The Government failed to prevent a rapid rise in advances (from a very low level) in the years before 1952 and again in 1955, but achieved considerable success in 1956–8 (as evidenced by the rapidity of the rise in advances after the withdrawal of restrictions in 1958) and again in 1961–2. Since, even without special directions, the types of advances which suffered most in periods of restriction were personal and financial, the impact effect was probably felt most strongly on the demand for durable consumption goods.

In addition to the financial controls on particular types of loans or sectors of demand, the restrictions on bank advances, the limitation of government short-term borrowing and the institution of special deposits slowed down the rate of rise of bank deposits and so reduced the ratio of bank deposits to national income. As Table 4.6 shows, between 1946 and 1964 net clearing-bank deposits rose by about 60 per cent, while the national money income rose by 220 per cent and the ratio of deposits to income fell by nearly half. At the same time (and, in my view, consequently), the long-term rate of interest more than doubled. From 1947 to 1952 the long-term rate of interest rose at an average rate of about 9 per cent a year, from 1954 to 1957 by 10 per cent a year, and in 1959–61 by over 13 per cent a year. Only in 1952–4, 1957–9 and 1961–2 was the rise interrupted by short periods of stable or declining rates. It can thus be said that, whereas fiscal policy shows short periods of rapid tax reduction interspersed by long periods of little change, interest-rate policy shows long periods of rapid increase interspersed by only short periods of little change. Since 1961, the fall in the bank deposits–national income ratio has virtually ceased and, with the introduction of the fiscal 'regulator' of a 10 per cent increase or decrease in rates of indirect taxation, government policy seems to have relied less on monetary and more on fiscal measures of restraint.

The multiplicity of measures taken and the long time-lags involved make it difficult to trace the connection between government measures and fluctuations in private-sector investment. Dow thinks it likely that monetary measures had nearly as much effect on private-sector industrial and commercial investment as tax changes. My own view is that more important than either were the lagged effects of changes in consumption expenditure, probably operating through the much wider changes in the level of business profits (see Table 4.3), and that, so long as consumption and the profits of consumption goods industries remain high, neither changes in company taxation nor monetary measures are likely to have decisive effects. The one place where changes in interest rates do seem to have had a direct effect is in private-sector house-building (which accounts for perhaps 2 per cent of total expenditure). This effect is probably due less to the actual rise in interest rates than to the restrictions which building societies impose on the volume of their loans in their efforts to avoid, or limit, increases in the rates of interest which they pay and charge.

Dow makes two general criticisms of government contra-cyclical policies in the post-war period. The first is of the general tendency towards over-expansion whenever an increase in the margin of productive potential has reduced the rate of rise of money incomes to a non-inflationary level. He even goes to the extent of suggesting that government contra-cyclical policies, so far from moderating the extent of cyclical fluctuations, have actually intensified them. This charge must, however, be regarded as not proven. The fact that corrective action has, in general, been over-expansionary and insufficiently restrictive, as well as usually taken too late, does not prove that fluctuations would have been less without any action at all.

His other criticism is that too much reliance has been placed on monetary policy for restraining demand, and that long-term interest rates have therefore been forced higher, perhaps much higher, than was either necessary or desirable. While there is much to be said for this view, before accepting it we must look at the other implications of maintaining a lower level of interest rates and of a greater reliance on fiscal policies for restraining demand. These include a slower rise in personal consumption, a higher level of total saving and a more favourable balance of payments on current account; but they also include a higher level of net long-term foreign investment. In other words, our balance of payments troubles might have come to resemble those of the United States. Only if consumption demand had been so restrained as to provide a level of saving sufficient not only for investment at home but also for a high level of foreign investment, while at the same time leaving a margin of potential sufficient to prevent the emergence of excess demand, would a policy of lower interest rates have proved practicable.

5

Government Policy and Business Investment[1]

IN approaching the question of the influence of government policy on business investment there seem to be three main questions to answer. The first is whether the Government is justified in making an attempt to encourage business investment; the second is whether government action has in fact succeeded in raising business investment since the war above the level which it would otherwise have reached; and the third is whether it now has the means of intervening successfully to raise the level of business investment above what it is today.

Our reply to the first question must turn initially on what we think is the relationship between an increase in business investment and an increase in the long-term rate of growth of output. Views on this question are by no means as clear-cut today as they were a few years ago, when it was regarded as axiomatic that a high level of investment was directly correlated with a high rate of economic growth. Recent investigations have, however, shown that the relationship is by no means as simple as this, and that some countries with a high rate of investment have shown a lower rate of growth than other countries where the proportion of national income devoted to investment is appreciably lower.

Today it is generally accepted that the most important factor in the long-term rate of growth is technical progress, including not only new productive techniques but improvements in efficiency at all levels, especially that of management. Since it is possible to combine a high rate of new investment with low rates of technical innovation and of increases in managerial and other efficiency, a high rate of investment is no guarantee of a high rate of growth. It is, however, probably safe to say that a higher rate of investment

[1] Lecture first delivered at the University of York, 8 June 1965.

gives the opportunity, if it can be taken, of a higher rate of innovation. If, therefore, management and workers are able and willing to take advantage of the opportunity, a higher rate of investment will facilitate a higher rate of growth. But in a country where the inhabitants are reluctant to make the, often very uncomfortable, changes in their traditional methods and habits which a high rate of innovation involves, much of the benefit of a high rate of investment will inevitably be lost. It may well be, therefore, that the best contribution which a government can make towards an acceleration of the rate of economic growth is not so much by encouraging physical investment as by persuading its citizens to reduce their resistance to change.

Even in a country where an increase in the rate of business investment would clearly serve to accelerate the rate of long-term growth, there still remains the question of whether the Government is justified in making an economy grow faster than it would have done by the spontaneous efforts of its inhabitants. This is largely a political decision, on which everyone is entitled to have his own views. In my opinion, however, the Government in this country would need to do quite a lot in the way of stimulating growth merely to offset the effects of its other measures, mainly those designed to promote social justice and to redistribute incomes or wealth, which would otherwise have slowed it down. In so far, therefore, as a higher rate of business investment can be regarded as leading to a higher rate of growth, I should regard quite a considerable effort by the Government to encourage it as no more than an attempt to restore the *status quo*.

Whatever the arguments on points of principle, all British Governments since the war have accepted the desirability of an attempt to stimulate economic growth by the encouragement of industrial fixed investment. The measures used have taken two main forms: special depreciation allowances on certain types of recent fixed investment; and lower rates of tax on retained than on distributed profits.

To facilitate the examination of the effects of these policies, I have set out in the accompanying chart (Fig. 5.1) and in Tables 5.1 and 5.2 some economic statistics for the years 1948–64. The smooth upper curve on the chart shows the growth in the index of what the Treasury has called 'productive potential' – the maximum

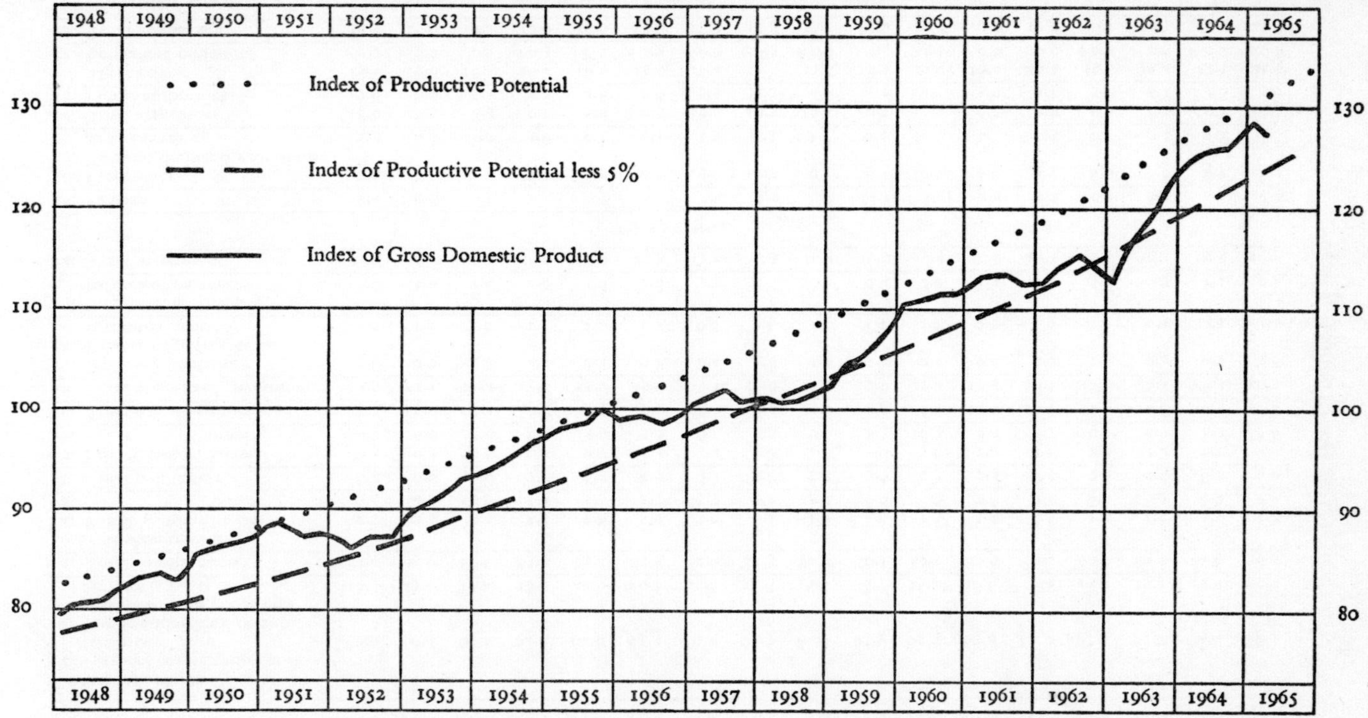

Fig. 5.1 *Output and productive potential, 1948–65 (last quarter of 1955 = 100)*

TABLE 5.1

PERCENTAGES OF GROSS NATIONAL PRODUCT OF UNITED KINGDOM, 1948–64

(a) USES OF RESOURCES

	1948	1949	1950	1951	1952	1953	1954	1955	1956	1957	1958	1959	1960	1961	1962	1963	1964
Current expenditure																	
1. Personal consumption at factor cost	66·9	66·4	66·1	64·6	62·8	62·4	63·0	63·6	61·7	61·5	62·3	62·4	62·0	61·4	61·7	61·6	60·5
2. Public authorities' current expenditure on goods and services	16·5	17·6	17·5	18·8	20·6	20·1	19·6	18·8	18·8	18·7	18·2	18·6	18·4	18·6	19·1	19·0	18·8
3. Total consumption	83·4	84·0	83·6	83·4	83·4	82·5	82·6	82·5	80·5	80·1	80·5	80·9	80·4	80·0	80·8	80·6	79·3
Gross fixed investment[1]																	
4. Public section: houses	2·7	2·5	2·4	2·5	2·8	3·0	2·6	2·1	1·8	1·6	1·3	1·2	1·2	1·2	1·3	1·4	1·8
5. other	3·5	4·3	4·6	5·2	5·5	5·7	5·5	5·6	5·7	6·0	6·0	2·6	6·1	6·2	6·3	6·6	7·2
6. Total public sector	6·2	6·8	6·9	7·7	8·3	8·7	8·2	7·7	7·5	7·7	7·3	7·4	7·3	7·4	7·7	8·0	9·0
7. Private sector: houses	0·4	0·5	0·4	0·5	0·7	1·1	1·4	1·6	1·6	1·6	1·6	1·9	2·1	2·2	2·2	2·1	2·4
8. other	6·7	6·8	7·0	6·5	5·9	5·8	6·5	7·3	7·8	8·3	8·3	8·2	8·7	9·3	8·6	8·2	8·8
9. Total private sector	7·1	7·3	7·4	6·9	6·7	6·9	7·9	8·9	9·4	9·9	9·9	10·1	10·8	11·5	10·8	10·3	11·2
10. Total gross fixed investment	13·3	14·1	14·4	14·6	15·0	15·6	16·1	16·6	16·9	17·6	17·2	17·5	18·1	18·9	18·5	18·3	20·2
11. Stock accumulation[2]	1·6	0·6	−1·8	4·4	0·4	0·8	0·4	1·8	1·4	1·2	0·5	0·8	2·6	1·3	0·3	0·7	1·8
12. Balance of payments on current account[3]	1·5	1·4	3·8	−2·5	1·2	1·0	0·8	−0·9	1·1	1·1	1·7	0·7	−1·2	−0·1	0·4	0·4	−1·4
13. Stock accumulation + balance of payments	3·2	1·9	2·0	2·0	1·6	1·8	1·1	0·9	2·6	2·3	2·2	1·5	1·4	1·2	0·7	1·1	0·4
14. Total investment	16·5	16·0	16·4	16·6	16·6	17·5	17·2	17·5	19·5	19·9	19·4	19·0	19·5	20·1	19·1	19·3	20·6

(b) SAVINGS

	1948	1949	1950	1951	1952	1953	1954	1955	1956	1957	1958	1959	1960	1961	1962	1963	1964
15. Persons	−0·4	0·8	0·5	—	2·8	3·0	2·4	2·9	4·2	4·1	3·3	4·4	5·2	6·8	6·1	5·9	6·2
16. Companies	7·3	7·5	7·6	7·2	8·9	9·0	9·0	10·0	9·3	9·5	10·0	9·8	9·7	8·8	8·6	8·7	8·7
17. Tax and dividend provisions and reserves	1·3	−0·2	1·0	3·6	0·1	0·4	1·5	0·3	1·1	0·4	—	−0·1	2·3	0·7	−0·4	0·7	1·6
18. Total companies	8·6	7·3	8·5	10·8	9·0	9·3	10·5	10·3	10·3	10·0	10·0	9·7	12·0	9·5	8·2	9·4	10·3
19. Public authorities	7·6	8·4	7·4	5·4	4·6	3·6	3·5	4·5	4·0	4·4	4·7	4·0	3·2	3·6	5·1	3·8	5·0
20. Total saving	15·8	16·6	16·5	16·2	16·4	15·9	16·4	17·8	18·5	18·5	18·0	18·2	20·4	19·9	19·4	19·1	21·4
21. Errors and omissions	+0·7	−0·6	−0·1	+0·3	+0·1	+1·5	+0·8	−0·3	+0·9	+1·4	+1·4	+0·8	−0·9	+0·2	−0·3	+0·2	−0·8
22. Total investment	16·5	16·0	16·4	16·6	16·6	16·4	17·2	17·5	19·5	19·9	19·4	19·0	19·5	20·1	19·1	19·3	20·6

[1] Including depreciation. [2] Physical increase in stocks and work-in-progress (excluding stock appreciation). [3] Including foreign aid.

(Errors due to rounding.)

TABLE 5.2

PERCENTAGE CHANGES ON PREVIOUS YEAR, 1948–64

	1948	*1949*	*1950*	*1951*	*1952*	*1953*	*1954*	*1955*	*1956*	*1957*	*1958*	*1959*	*1960*	*1961*	*1962*	*1963*	*1964*
1. *Output:* Productive potential	(+2·5)	(+2·5)	(+2·6)	(+2·6)	+2·6	+2·62	+2·60	+2·75	+2·75	+2·75	+2·89	+2·85	+2·64	+2·74	+3·30	+3·45	+3·22
2. Gross domestic product	+4·5	+3·6	+3·8	+2·2	−0·7	+4·0	+4·2	+3·4	+1·0	+1·7	−0·1	+4·5	+5·3	+1·8	+1·3	+3·3	+5·8
3. *Companies:* Trading profits[1]	+14·2	+5·0	+0·8	+19·6	+9·1	+7·0	+7·0	+9·9	+0·1	+6·2	−2·3	+8·0	+12·5	−3·5	+0·6	+7·8	+12·0
4. Undistributed income[1]	+58·8	+8·8	6·3	+4·8	+33·4	+8·0	+5·4	+18·7	—	+8·6	+10·3	+8·7	+2·7	−3·1	+2·1	+7·3	+7·3
5. *Personal incomes:* Income after tax[1]	+6·3	+5·4	+5·2	+7·0	+9·4	+6·7	+5·1	+8·3	+7·3	+5·3	+4·3	+6·2	+6·5	+7·7	+4·6	+5·8	+6·9
6. Consumer prices	+7·2	+2·3	+2·8	+9·3	+6·0	+1·8	+1·9	+3·4	+4·7	+3·7	+2·5	+0·4	+0·9	+3·0	+3·7	+1·1	+2·8
7. Real personal incomes after tax	−0·8	+3·1	+2·4	−2·1	+3·1	+4·8	+3·1	+4·8	+2·5	+1·6	+1·8	+5·8	+5·6	+4·6	+0·9	+4·7	+4·0
Current expenditure (at 1958 prices)																	
8. Personal consumption	−0·6	+1·9	+2·8	−1·4	−0·6	+4·5	+4·0	+4·0	+0·8	+2·1	+2·6	+4·6	+4·0	+2·3	+2·0	+4·6	+3·8
9. Public authorities' current expenditure on goods and services	−0·7	+5·9	+0·3	+7·8	+9·9	+2·7	−0·4	−3·1	−0·5	−1·4	−2·0	+2·1	+2·2	+3·9	+3·1	+1·8	+1·9
10. Total consumption	−0·6	+2·6	+2·2	+0·5	+1·7	+4·0	+3·1	+2·4	+0·6	+1·3	+1·6	4·1+	+3·7	+2·7	+2·2	+4·0	+3·3
Gross fixed investment (at 1958 prices)																	
11. Public sector: houses		−5·7	−0·9	−2·3	+13·0	+19·6	−7·9	−20·5	−9·5	−7·3	−15·7	+0·4	+3·0	+1·4	+12·4	+10·1	+32·5
12. other		+27·2	+9·4	+12·9	+4·5	+8·0	+3·1	+1·9	+5·2	+6·9	+1·4	+8·7	+4·6	+6·6	+2·4	+7·4	+14·1
13. Total public sector		+12·8	+5·5	+7·6	+7·1	+11·7	−0·6	−5·2	+1·3	+3·5	−2·3	+7·2	+4·3	+5·7	+4·0	+7·7	+17·4
14. Private sector: houses		+21·4	−7·4	−1·6	+55·5	+71·4	+34·2	+10·8	+6·6	−0·3	+5·8	+24·2	+21·0	+8·9	−2·3	−0·6	+22·0
15. other		+4·3	+4·9	−7·2	−10·5	+2·9	+17·2	+15·2	+9·8	+8·3	+1·6	+5·3	+12·4	+11·1	−4·3	+0·4	+13·2
16. Total private sector		+5·3	+4·2	−6·8	−6·5	+9·8	+19·8	+14·4	+9·2	+6·8	+2·3	+8·3	+14·0	+10·7	−3·9	+0·2	+14·9
17. Total fixed investment	+9·7	+8·7	+4·9	+0·2	+0·5	+10·8	+8·5	+4·5	+5·6	+5·4	+0·3	+7·9	+9·9	+8·7	−0·8	+3·3	+16·0

[1] At current prices. Includes depreciation; excludes stock appreciation.

output which the country would be physically capable of producing in any year if demand were unlimited. Its rates of growth are those estimated by W. A. H. Godley and J. R. Shepherd in their article published in the *National Institute Review* for August 1964, with my extrapolations for the years 1948–51 and 1964–5. As is shown in line 1 of Table 5.2, the annual increase rises from about 2½ per cent in 1947–8 to 3·45 per cent in 1962–3 and (with a smaller rise in working population) 3·22 per cent in 1963–4. The lower smooth curve represents 95 per cent of productive potential, leaving the 5 per cent margin which I regard as the least which is necessary to prevent an over-rapid rise in money incomes. On the curves is superimposed a quarterly index of gross domestic product at constant prices, on the assumption that the economy was producing all of which it was physically capable in the last quarter of 1955, when the average level of unemployment in Great Britain was down to 1 per cent. On this assumption, the gap between the index of gross domestic product and the index of productive potential represents the margin of unused resources in the economy, and provides the best indication of where the country stands in relation to the business cycle. Fluctuations in this margin are roughly five times as large as in the percentage of unemployment, with 1 per cent unemployment corresponding to a zero margin of unused resources and 2 per cent unemployment to a 5 per cent margin; fluctuations in unemployment, however, tend to lag behind those in output, usually by several months.

Table 5.1 shows the proportions in which the total resources of the country are estimated to have been divided between their different uses in each year from 1948 to 1964. The first two categories, which between them absorb about 80 per cent of total resources, are personal consumption and public authorities' current expenditure on goods and services. The remainder represents, on the one hand, total investment and on the other (apart from errors and omissions) total savings. Total investment is divided into three main categories: fixed investment, stock accumulation and net foreign investment, which, if we include gold as a foreign investment, is the same thing as the balance of payments on current account.

Fixed investment is divided into the public and private sectors and these again into investment in housing and other investment. Although private-sector fixed investment, other than houses, includes such things as golf clubs, churches and schools, we shall probably not go seriously wrong if we take it as the equivalent of industrial and commercial investment, that is to say, the type of investment which in recent years has absorbed between 8 per cent and 9 per cent of total resources, to whose fluctuations we shall here be paying particular attention.

Since total saving is equal to total investment, the remaining two categories of investment, stock accumulation and the balance of payments, are together equal to the excess of total saving over total fixed investment. While since 1948 the balance of payments has become actually adverse only in years (1951, 1955, 1960 and 1964) when stock accumulation has risen sharply, it is the total of the two which provides the best measure of the external viability of the economy, for a favourable balance of payments secured only by keeping stock accumulation abnormally low (as particularly in 1950) is inevitably precarious.

Saving is divided into three main categories: personal saving (including the increase in life-assurance and pension funds); company saving; and saving by public authorities. There is also in some years a substantial amount of saving in the form of an increase in the reserves set aside out of profits to meet future tax, dividend and interest payments. As these reserves are mainly under the control of companies, the increases in them have been added to company savings.

In Table 5.2 the figures show the percentage changes in a number of items over the previous year. Lines 1 and 2 show the annual percentage changes in the indexes of productive potential and gross domestic product. These figures are the same as those used in the construction of the chart, except that the index of gross domestic product is on an annual instead of a quarterly basis. Lines 3 and 4 show the changes in the trading profits and savings of companies, lines 5 to 7 in retail prices and in money and real personal incomes after tax, and lines 8 to 10 in personal and public consumption. Lines 11 to 17 show annual percentage changes in fixed investment, sub-divided as in Table 5.1.

DEPRECIATION ALLOWANCES

The additional depreciation allowances granted for tax purposes on recent industrial fixed investment have taken two main forms:

initial allowances, which allow an asset to be depreciated by an additional amount in the first year of its life, but with no increase in the total amount allowed over its whole life; and investment allowances, which allow increased depreciation in the first year without any reduction in subsequent depreciation allowances, so that an asset can be depreciated over its whole life by more than its original cost. Investment allowances reduce the tax liability of all businesses receiving them; initial allowances, that of all businesses (presumably the great majority) whose expenditure on fixed capital (in money terms) is on a rising scale. The scales of initial and investment allowances in force at different dates since the war are shown in Table 5.3.

TABLE 5·3

INITIAL AND INVESTMENT ALLOWANCES, 1945–63

(percentages of cost)

	Initial allowances		*Investment allowances*	
	Industrial buildings	*Plant*	*Industrial buildings*	*Plant*
1945	—	20	—	—
1949	—	40	—	—
1951	—	—	—	—
1953	10	20	—	—
1954	—	—	10	20
1955	10	20	—	—
1958	15	30	—	—
1959	5	10	10	20
1963	—	—	15	30

Still larger allowances have been given for investments in ships and mines, and for appropriate investments in development areas.

The result of these allowances has been to give total depreciation allowances greatly in excess of the estimated cost of making good fixed capital actually consumed. According to official estimates, in 1964 depreciation allowances to companies totalled £1,967 million, as against estimated fixed capital consumption in that year of only £948 million (Table 5.4).

TABLE 5.4

COMPANIES' DEPRECIATION AND CONSUMPTION OF FIXED CAPITAL, 1948–64

(£m.)

	1948	*1951*	*1953*	*1957*	*1963*	*1964*
Depreciation allowed for tax						
Initial and investment allowances	95	238	104	269	664	767
Other allowances	208	254	303	569	1052	1200
Total allowed for tax	303	492	407	838	1716	1967
Capital consumption at replacement cost	296	360	429	632	894	948
Total allowances as percentages of capital consumption	102	137	95	133	192	208

The 1964 reduction of £767 million in taxable income must have implied a reduction of over £400 million in actual tax paid.

The effects of these depreciation allowances on the volume of industrial investment have presumably been twofold. In the first place, the relation of the tax concession to the amount of investment in the previous year offers a direct increase in the profitability of an investment after tax and, if effective, would increase the amount of investment well in advance of the actual reduction in tax paid. Secondly, by reducing the amount of tax paid, they increase the amount of profit left in the hands of the companies after tax. In so far as the increase is not distributed in higher dividends, it goes to increase the level of company saving and the internal funds available for investment.

How far the depreciation allowances have in fact acted as incentives to increased fixed investment has been much debated. Their effectiveness is said to have been much reduced by the custom of many businessmen of estimating the yield of a proposed new investment before tax, thus ignoring the effects of the depreciation allowances in increasing the net yield after tax. In addition, it is said that previous attempts to use the allowances as contra-cyclical devices, resulting in the suspension of initial allowances in 1951 and the conversion of investment allowances to initial allowances in 1955, have reduced the willingness of businessmen to rely on their continuation when formulating their long-term capital plans. There is also no evidence of any strong correlation, at least for quoted companies having access to the capital market, between the amount of a company's savings and the amount of its new fixed investment.

Any additional incentive which the special depreciation allowances have given to new investment in the past will presumably be reduced by the introduction of corporation tax, under which the amount of tax saved on the allowances falls from 56¼ per cent to 35 per cent or 40 per cent.

Whatever our views on the effectiveness of special depreciation allowances in encouraging industrial fixed investment, any conclusions we may reach are largely irrelevant for the purpose of considering the ability of the Government effectively to promote a long-term increase in the proportion of the national resources devoted to industrial investment. The rate of growth of industrial fixed investment can exceed that of the economy as a whole only if some other use or uses of resources grow more slowly than the total. The successful stimulation of industrial investment without the corresponding restraint of some other use or uses of resources can lead only to an increase in total demand and in pressure on resources as a whole. In a closed economy, the effect of an increase in demand greater than in the long-term rate of growth of output is a reduction in the margin of unused resources, an acceleration of the rise in incomes, and, as the margin of resources approaches depletion, a rise in prices and visible inflation. The process is likely in its early stages to be delayed by a depletion of stocks, and in its later stages to be accelerated by their replenishment. In an open economy, however, a rise in the proportion of resources devoted to industrial fixed investment can be achieved without a fall in that of consumption or of other forms of fixed investment, not only by running down stocks but also by reducing net foreign investment. Historically, it seems that the worsening of the balance of payments on current account does not occur until stocks begin to rise rapidly in the later stages of the boom. In each cycle, the Government has reacted to this worsening of the balance of payments by a severe restriction of credit, which has tended to reverse its policy of encouraging industrial fixed investment.

The long-term trends of the post-war period can be seen more

TABLE 5.5

PERCENTAGES OF GROSS NATIONAL PRODUCT, 1948–51 TO 1960–4

(*a*) USES OF RESOURCES

	1948–51	*1952–5*	*1956–60*	*1961–4*
Current expenditure				
Personal consumption	66·0	63·0	62·0	61·4
Public authorities' expenditure on goods and services	17·6	19·8	18·5	18·8
Total current expenditure	83·6	82·8	80·5	80·2
Fixed investment				
Public sector: housing	2·5	2·6	1·4	1·4
other	4·4	5·6	6·0	6·5
Total public sector	6·9	8·2	7·5	7·9
Private sector: housing	0·4	1·2	1·7	2·2
other	6·8	6·4	8·3	8·7
Total private sector	7·2	7·6	10·0	10·9
Total fixed investment	14·1	15·8	17·5	18·8
Stock accumulation	1·2	0·9	1·3	1·3
Balance of payments on current account	1·1	0·5	0·7	−0·4
Stock accumulation plus balance of payments	2·3	1·4	2·0	0·9
Total investment	16·4	17·2	19·5	19·7

(*b*) SAVING

	1948–51	*1952–5*	*1956–60*	*1961–4*
Persons	0·2	2·8	4·3	6·0
Companies	7·4	9·2	9·7	8·9
Tax and dividend reserves	1·4	0·6	0·6	1·0
Total companies	8·8	9·8	10·3	9·9
Public authorities	7·2	4·0	4·1	4·1
Total saving	16·3	16·6	18·7	20·0
Errors and omissions	0·1	0·6	0·8	−0·3
Total investment	16·4	17·2	19·5	19·7

clearly if we exclude cyclical changes by expressing the figures in Table 5.1 as averages for each of the four business cycles, 1948–51, 1952–5, 1956–60 and 1961–4, concluding each cycle with its peak year (Table 5.5).

The most striking changes between 1948–51 and 1961–4 are the fall in the proportion of gross national product devoted to personal consumption and the even larger rise in the proportion going to personal saving. Unfortunately, the additional resources so provided for other uses, amounting to nearly 5 per cent of G.N.P., were inadequate to meet all the additional demands made on them, and were supplemented by the withdrawal of 1·5 per cent of G.N.P. from the balance of payments. Less than a third of these additional demands, or 1·9 per cent of G.N.P., was for private-sector fixed investment, other than housing, which we may roughly equate with business fixed investment. Public-sector current expenditure absorbed another 1·6 per cent of G.N.P., partly for social purposes, but largely for defence, while public-sector fixed investment, other than housing, absorbed another 2·1 per cent. Housing took another 0·7 per cent, with a rise of 1·8 per cent of G.N.P. in private-sector housing partly offset by a fall of 1·1 per cent in public-sector housing.

The rise in the proportion of G.N.P. devoted to business investment occurred mainly between the second and third periods, when a fall of 1·0 per cent in the share of personal consumption was supplemented by falls of 1·3 per cent in public-sector current expenditure and of 1·2 per cent in public-sector housing. These reductions in the public sector's demands not only allowed the share of industrial and commercial fixed investment to rise from 6·4 per cent to 8·3 per cent of G.N.P., but also permitted the share of stock accumulation plus balance of payments to rise from 1·4 per cent to 2·0 per cent. Conversely, between the third and fourth periods the small further fall in personal consumption was more than absorbed by rises in public-sector current expenditure, public-sector fixed investment and housing, so that a much smaller rise in industrial and commercial investment was achieved only at the cost of a fall from 2·0 per cent to 0·9 per cent in the share of stock accumulation plus balance of payments, and from plus 0·7 per cent to minus 0·4 per cent in the share of the balance of payments itself.

It will be seen that, except in the 1956–60 cycle, the rise in business fixed investment, given all the other claims on the national resources, was greater than could be achieved without robbing the balance of payments. In so far then as the depreciation allowances did in fact succeed in stimulating business investment, it was a success achieved only at the expense of a deterioration of the international viability of the country. It is, however, impossible to be sure whether the effects of the allowances in stimulating investment did in fact outweigh the effects of the periodic bouts of restriction necessitated by the growth of inflationary pressure and adverse balances of payments. A steadier rate of growth, without rapid rises but also without severe checks, might well have proved faster in the long run.

It is possible that the intention of the policy of special depreciation allowances was not only to stimulate investment but also to provide the resources for its expansion by means of a rise in company saving. As we have seen, the special allowances alone must have reduced the liability of all companies collectively for tax by over £350 million between 1953 and 1963. If we include other tax reductions, we find that altogether company taxes, paid and accrued, were over £600 million less in 1963 than they would have been if rates and allowances had remained unchanged at their 1952 levels. If the whole of this reduction had been saved (that is to say, if gross ordinary dividends had formed the same proportion of profits before tax as in 1953), company saving, in spite of a fall in the share of G.N.P. going to company profits, would have risen from 9·0 per cent to about 10½ per cent of G.N.P. – an increase sufficient to cover the greater part of the rise in company fixed investment. In fact, however, the greater part of the tax saving was used to increase dividends (from a very low level), and the balance was no more than sufficient to offset the effects of the fall in the share in G.N.P. of company profits and to maintain the share of company saving at 9 per cent. It is true that the rise in dividends must have contributed to the rise in personal saving, but it is unlikely that more than a fraction of the reduction in company taxation was saved in this way.

While it is doubtful whether, given the demand for resources by the public sector and for housing, the depreciation allowances have been effective in increasing the share of resources going to industrial and commercial investment in total, they may well have caused some diversion of resources within business investment, towards industrial investment, where the benefit of the allowances is mainly felt, and away from commercial investment. Only if we hold the view that industrial fixed investment is in some sense more 'productive' than commercial fixed investment can we regard such a diversion as a desirable objective of government action.

DIFFERENTIAL TAXATION OF DISTRIBUTED PROFITS

The second type of government policy for encouraging business investment, the differential taxation of distributed profits, has gone through several phases since the war. A moderate tax differential in the immediate post-war years was increased sharply in 1951, and further in 1955 and 1956. Then in 1958 the whole of the differential was abandoned, only to be restored, in an extreme form, in 1965, with the introduction of the corporation tax and the withdrawal of income tax on retained profits. The various changes since 1947 are shown in Table 5.6.

For a discriminatory tax on distributed profits to have the effect of directly expanding business investment, two conditions have to be fulfilled. In the first place, the tax must induce companies to distribute less of their profits in dividends and to plough more of them back to reserve than they would otherwise have done; and secondly, the increase in a company's own savings must cause it to spend more on investment than it would have done if it had had to raise more of the capital required from outside.

It is doubtful whether the second condition is at all fully satisfied. Such evidence as exists seems to suggest that, at least for quoted companies, with access to the open capital market, the correlation between company saving and company investment is slight. The absence of such a correlation is not, however, in itself a decisive argument against a policy of seeking to increase business investment by means of a discriminatory tax on distributed profits. As we have seen, the main factor in limiting business investment since the war has been, not the willingness of businessmen to invest, but the availability of resources to enable them to do so without overstraining the economy. If by tax discrimination against dis-

TABLE 5.6

COMPANY TAXATION, 1947–66

	Tax on distributed profits			*Tax on undistributed profits*		
	Income tax	*Profits or corporation tax*	*Total*	*Income tax*	*Profits or corporation tax*	*Total*
	s d	*s d*	*s d*	*s d*	*s d*	*s d*
1947	9 0	5 0[1]	11 9	9 0	2 0[1]	10 1
1948	9 0	6 0[1]	12 3½	9 0	2 0[1]	10 1
1951	9 6	10 0[1]	14 9	9 6	2 0[1]	10 6½
1952[2]	9 6	4 6	14 0	9 6	0 6	10 0
1953	9 0	4 6	13 6	9 0	0 6	9 6
1955						
Apr	8 6	4 6	13 0	8 6	0 6	9 0
Oct	8 6	5 6	14 0	8 6	0 6	9 0
1956	8 6	6 0	14 6	8 6	0 7·2	9 1·2
1958	8 6	2 0	10 6	8 6	2 0	10 6
1959	7 9	2 0	9 9	7 9	2 0	9 9
1960	7 9	2 6	10 3	7 9	2 6	10 3
1961	7 9	3 0	10 9	7 9	3 0	10 9
1965	8 3	3 0	11 3	8 3	3 0	11 3
1966	8 3	(?)7 6[1]	(?)12 8	—	(?)7 6	(?)7 6

[1] Profits tax deductible for income-tax purposes.

[2] In addition, an excess profits levy was imposed for one year on all profits, whether distributed or not. This varied from nothing up to a maximum of 2*s*, according to the position of each company.

tributed profits companies are induced to accumulate additional reserves which they do not use in their own businesses, the result is to reduce the pressure on the resources of the economy[1] and to enable other uses of resources (including increased investment by other companies) to be increased without giving rise to overstrain. Provided, therefore, that other users of resources can be prevented from absorbing the whole of the extra margin so created, it can be said that additional company saving facilitates additional company investment even if the savings are not used to increase the invest-

[1] The pressure is not, of course, reduced by the whole of the induced increase in company savings, for part of this is offset by the reduction in the savings of those whose dividends are lower than they would have been.

ments of the companies which make them. If, therefore, it could be shown that discriminatory taxation of distributed profits was effective in increasing the level of business saving, it could be claimed that it also permitted an increase in business investment.

Unfortunately, it is difficult to find evidence that discriminatory taxation has had much effect of this sort. It is true that, after the increase in the tax on distributed profits in 1951, company savings (excluding increases in tax reserves) rose sharply from 7·2 per cent of G.N.P. in 1951 to 8·9 per cent in 1952. But almost the whole of this rise is explained by the fact that company saving, like gross domestic product, is shown in Table 5.1 net of stock appreciation, which was very large in 1950 and 1951 and slightly negative in 1952, whereas company profits for purposes of tax are calculated gross of stock appreciation. Thus the disappearance of stock appreciation in 1952 brought with it a sharp fall in the proportion of profits, net of stock appreciation, paid in tax, and a rise in company saving, also net of stock appreciation. Seven years later, when tax discrimination against distributed profits was abandoned in 1958, the fall in company saving was hardly perceptible. It will be interesting to observe if the introduction of corporation tax and the removal of income tax from undistributed profits, which together mean that in future the difference between the tax on distributed and undistributed profits will return almost to its 1956–8 level, will have any marked effect on the aggregate level of company saving in 1966.

Whatever the measures used to encourage business investment, it is clear from the history of the post-war period that we cannot afford to increase the share of business investment in the total resources of the country without at the same time taking steps to reduce the shares of other uses. These are several directions in which reductions might conceivably be made. We might, as in 1953–8, reduce the share of public-sector current expenditure; or, as in 1954–9, of public-sector housing. Or we might reduce the share of public sector 'other' fixed investment, which, apart from a slight check in 1954, has risen steadily since 1948; or of private-sector housing, which has risen almost continuously since 1950. The one thing we cannot do is to reduce further the share of stock accumulation plus balance of payments; this must share with business investment any saving of resources on other uses.

Of these choices, a reduction in the share of public authorities' current expenditure on goods and services looks both the most attractive and the most possible, especially if a reassessment of British international responsibilities makes it possible to reduce the share of defence expenditure, recently running at about 7 per cent of G.N.P. But the most that can be hoped for here is probably a slow and gradual reduction, with current expenditure continuing to rise, in real terms, by 2 per cent or 2½ per cent a year, as against perhaps 3¼ per cent for G.N.P. And any saving here is likely to be more than absorbed by the continuing rise in public-sector fixed investment, where there are urgent demands for higher capital expenditures on houses, roads, schools, universities, hospitals and prisons, as well as on the Post Office, electricity and other nationalised industries, and where the recent cut-backs are unlikely to achieve more than a temporary slowing-down of the rate of increase.

If these expectations are justified, the only source to which we can look for the release of resources for increasing the shares of business investment and of stock accumulation plus balance of payments is personal consumption, which is still absorbing some 60 per cent of all resources. It is possible that, as real personal incomes continue to rise, the proportion of G.N.P. voluntarily set aside as personal savings will also continue to rise and that the share of personal consumption will continue to fall without government intervention; but it looks as if the rise in personal saving has levelled out after its spurt of 1960–1, and it seems unlikely that its cyclical peak of 1965 will equal that of 1961. At the best, it does not look as if any voluntary rise in personal saving would do much more than cover the rise in private-sector investment in new houses, for which the (real) income elasticity of demand seems to be very high. For a release of resources from personal consumption large enough to cover the combined demands of private-sector housing, increased business investment, and stock accumulation plus balance of payments, we probably have to look to government intervention.

Any effective government action to reduce the share of total resources going to personal consumption would have to affect the general mass of the public. An attempt to operate only on the share of the higher income groups would be largely ineffective, partly because their total consumption is now relatively small and partly because they are able to postpone and reduce the effect on their consumption of any reduction in their disposable incomes by reducing their current saving or spending capital. If, therefore, the Government were to attempt to reduce the share of current consumption solely by taxes on the rich, they would have to collect considerably more in tax than the reduction in consumption at which they were aiming. Before doing so they would have to take account of the effect on incentive, perhaps on the migration of people and of capital, and certainly of the increased diversion of valuable resources to tax avoidance and its prevention.

Ideally, any tax designed to divert resources away from personal consumption should be spread as widely as possible, not only over the population but also over the range of resources released. If resources are released only from a narrow range of uses (as, for instance, from the manufacture and distribution of durable consumption goods by hire-purchase restrictions), not only is individual hardship likely to be more severe, but the resources released are likely to be specialised in function and location and may be slow to absorb into new uses. There are three types of taxes which fit this specification: direct taxes on the incomes of a large proportion of the population; indirect taxes on a limited range of goods (such as drink and tobacco) which are in widespread use and of which the price elasticity is low, so that users increase their expenditure on the things taxed and have to reduce it on a wide range of other things; and indirect taxes on a wide range of consumption expenditure. Possibly the first and certainly the second of these types of taxes have already been carried about as far as seems desirable, but more consideration might be given to the third. A retail turnover tax, administered by the Inland Revenue, such as has been recently introduced with success in Ireland, might prove both an effective and a flexible instrument of fiscal policy.

The additional saving resulting from the taxation of personal consumption could be made to appear in the national income accounts under any one of a number of heads. If it were merely added to the budget surplus it would appear as government saving. If it were used to offset a reduction in taxes on capital, such as death duties or stamp duties, it would appear as an increase in personal saving, though there might be some small leak back into consumption. If it were used to reduce the higher ranges of surtax much of it would appear as personal saving, and though the leak back to consumption might be appreciable, there might also be valuable gains in incentive and in the reduction of tax avoidance. Finally, if it were used to reduce business taxation, preferably in a form giving added incentives to investment, part of it would appear in company saving, part in personal saving, and part would leak back to consumption. Of the various possibilities, it would probably be politically easier to allow the extra saving to appear as a larger budget surplus, thus enabling the government to finance more of the capital requirements of the public sector out of its own savings and freeing more private-sector saving to finance private-sector investment.

However the release of resources from personal consumption is achieved, the question arises of how to transfer them to business investment without delay or waste; for if there is inadequate incentive to increase business investment, the resources released from consumption may run to waste or be absorbed in other uses. Some light is thrown on this problem by the following figures of annual changes in personal consumption (Table 5.7), output, company profits and business investment, extracted from Table 5.2.

As can be seen from a comparison of Table 5.7 with Fig. 5.1, cyclical fluctuations in personal consumption and business investment appear to follow a consistent pattern. On the upswing, the initial impetus is given by a rise in consumption, induced by tax reductions (1953, 1959, 1963). This is followed a year later by a rapid rise in business investment (1954, 1960, 1964). By this time the rise in output has depleted the margin of unused productive potential and prices are beginning to rise. There is now a rapid rise in inventory accumulation (1955, 1960, 1964) and an adverse balance of payments on current account. This obliges the Government to take steps to check demand, partly by increased taxes, partly by restrictions on hire purchase and partly by general restrictions on credit and by cutting back plans for public-sector fixed investment. The last two have little immediate effect, but the first two check the rise in consumption to some extent, though not enough fully to restore the necessary margin of potential. The failure to complete the removal of inflationary pressure brings a

TABLE 5.7
PERSONAL CONSUMPTION AND BUSINESS INVESTMENT, 1952–64
(percentage change on previous year)

	Personal consumption	*Gross domestic product*	*Company trading profits*[1]	*'Other' private-sector fixed investment*
1952	−0·6	−0·7	9·1	−10·5
1953	4·5	4·0	7·0	2·9
1954	4·0	4·2	7·0	17·2
1955	4·0	3·4	9·9	15·2
1956	0·8	1·0	0·1	9·8
1957	2·1	1·7	6·2	8·3
1958	2·6	−0·1	2·3	1·6
1959	4·6	4·5	8·0	5·3
1960	4·0	5·3	12·5	12·4
1961	2·3	1·8	−3·5	11·1
1962	2·0	1·3	0·6	−4·3
1963	4·6	3·3	7·8	0·4
1964	3·8	5·8	12·0	13·2

[1] At current prices.

loss of foreign confidence in sterling and heavy withdrawals of foreign balances (1957, 1961, 1964–5), which force the Government to intensify the restriction of credit. The margin of potential is ultimately restored only by a check to business investment, and perhaps also to public-sector fixed investment (1958, 1962, 1966).

With many influences operating simultaneously, it is difficult to be sure of their relative importance. But it seems likely that one of the main causes, if not the main cause, of a change in the rate of increase in business investment is a preceding change in the rate of rise of personal consumption and of total output. If this were the only cause, it would leave us with an awkward problem; for if the only way to make room for more business investment is to restrict consumption, and the only way to induce businessmen to invest more is to expand consumption, any action we take to expand business investment is likely to be self-frustrating. Fortunately, however, it seems unlikely that fluctuations in consumption are the only cause of fluctuations in investment. The checks to consumption, though themselves induced mainly by higher taxes or hire-purchase restrictions, have invariably been accompanied, or preceded, by general credit restrictions and rising interest rates; while tax reductions and the removal of hire-purchase restrictions have been accompanied by easier credit conditions. It is likely, therefore, that part of the fluctuations in investment may be due to the lagged effects of changes in credit policy. If, therefore, stronger restraints on consumption were accompanied by easier, instead of tighter, credit conditions, it is possible that their subsequent check to investment might be partly or wholly offset.

Again, the lagged effect on investment of restrictions on consumption might be offset by direct incentives. Some increase in the special depreciation allowances would be needed merely to counteract the effects of the introduction of corporation tax, and it might also be possible to make the allowances more effective as incentives by persuading more businessmen to do their calculations on the profitability of new investments net of tax instead of gross. Another possibility is that the motivation for increased business investment is not so much rising output as rising profits, which, as can be seen from Table 5.7, usually move closely with output. If this is so, it might be possible to reduce the discouraging effect on business investment of a check to consumption by accompanying higher taxes on consumption with a reduction in taxes on business profits.

The timing of the measures needed for the transfer of resources from consumption to business investment would depend on the point in the business cycle at which the policy was inaugurated. Let us suppose that we start from a position of equilibrium, with output, and its component parts, rising at the same rate as productive potential and the margin of unused resources just large enough to keep money incomes rising at the same rate as output. What we now have to do is to slow down the rise in consumption and accelerate the rise in business investment without affecting the rate of increase of output as a whole. Since taxes on consumption begin to operate at once, while incentives to investment become effective only after a time-lag of a year or so, we shall need to start with measures to encourage investment and to introduce the higher taxes on consumption only when investment begins to rise in the following years.[1]

If, on the other hand, we start in a period of excess demand, with the margin of unused resources below its equilibrium level, our problem will be, not to accelerate investment while checking consumption, but to maintain the rate of rise of investment while throwing on to consumption the whole burden of restoring the margin of unused resources. In this case measures to restrict consumption, such as increased consumption taxes, and to maintain investment, such as cheaper money, would have to be taken simultaneously.

Finally, if the policy were inaugurated at a time when the margin of unused resources was excessive – a condition which has existed since the war only for a few months in 1958 – the problem would be to expand investment without expanding consumption. This would involve either taking steps to expand investment only, and enduring the excess margin until they became effective; or alternatively stimulating both consumption and business investment in the first year and checking back consumption again in the second.

In any case, the smooth transfer of resources from consumption to investment is likely to be an operation of great technical delicacy, only too likely to disturb the balance of the economy in one direction or the other. It would therefore be most unwise to attempt any large and rapid transfer. A series of small and gentle nudges is likely to produce more effect in the long run than a more dramatic policy which has to be reversed later.

POSTSCRIPT (JUNE 1969)

The principal change since 1965 in the incentives provided by the Government for business investment has been the replacement in 1966 of initial and investment tax allowances by investment grants, payable (after some delay) in cash. The main reason advanced for the change was that businessmen were said to calculate the yield on proposed new investments in fixed capital gross of tax, so that tax concessions were likely to provide a less effective

[1] If the measures taken to encourage investment, such as easier money, also have some immediate effect in stimulating consumption, some rise in consumption taxes will be necessary in the first year.

inducement to undertake new investments than cash grants, which could be regarded as a reduction in the cost. Whether or not the new system provides more inducement than the old one is uncertain; what does seem clear is that, at least in its initial stages, the cost to the Treasury of the new concession is appreciably less than that of the old one. Between 1965 and 1967 the total of initial and investment allowances to companies fell from £787 millions to £263 millions, which, with corporation tax at 42½ per cent, represented an increase in liability to tax of £223 millions. Between the same years all initial and investment allowances, including those to unincorporated business, fell by £584 millions, from £890 millions to £306 millions, while the total of investment grants paid in 1967 was only £203 millions. If we deduct, say, 15 per cent for grants to unincorporated businesses, companies' liability for tax in 1967 seems to have been something like £50 millions higher under the new system than it would have been under the old (Table 5.8).

In any case, whatever the incentives, there would have been no resources available in recent years for a higher level of industrial and commercial fixed investment. As is shown in Table 5.9 (a revision and continuation of Table 5.1 on p. 106), between 1962 and 1968 (years between which the rise of output was roughly equal to that of productive potential) more than half of the resources released by the fall in the proportion of output absorbed by personal consumption was taken up by the rise in the share taken by the consumption of public authorities. The balance, 1.1 per cent of G.N.P., was quite inadequate to cover the additional 2·6 per cent of G.N.P. absorbed by public-sector investment. It was therefore possible for private-sector fixed investment to maintain its 1962 share of resources only by robbing the balance of payments. Since the balance of payments in 1962 was already inadequate, the results were disastrous. If government incentives had in fact succeeded in inducing private-sector investment in 1968 to absorb more than its 1962 share of national product, without either reducing the share of personal consumption still further or checking the rise in the share absorbed by public authorities, the effects on the balance of payments would have been even more disastrous.

If we convert the Treasury's projection for 1969 at 1958 market

TABLE 5.8

DEPRECIATION ALLOWANCES AND INVESTMENTS GRANTS, 1962–8

(£m.)

Companies	*1962*	*1963*	*1964*	*1965*	*1966*	*1967*	*1968*
Depreciation allowed for tax:							
Initial and investment allowances	544	653	778	787	410	263	271
Other allowances	907	1099	1262	1378	1505	1511	1495
Total allowances	1451	1752	2040	2165	1915	1774	1766
Capital consumption (other than of houses) at replacement cost	867	912	991	1085	1187	1281	
Total allowances as percentage of capital consumption	167	192	206	200	161	138	
Unincorporated businesses							
Depreciation allowed for tax:							
Initial and investment allowances	89	90	106	103	77	43	41
Other allowances	154	164	196	213	225	251	263
Total allowances	243	254	302	316	302	294	304
Capital consumption (other than of houses) at replacement cost	248	253	271	284	299	318	
Total allowances as percentage of capital consumption	98	100	111	111	101	93	
All businesses							
Depreciation allowed for tax:							
Initial and investment allowances	633	743	884	890	487	306	312
Other allowances	1061	1263	1458	1591	1730	1762	1758
Total allowances	1694	2006	2342	2481	2217	2068	2070
Capital consumption (other than of houses) at replacement cost	1115	1165	1262	1369	1486	1599	
Total allowances as percentage of capital consumption	152	172	186	181	149	129	
Investment Grants						203	

prices (included in the 1969–70 Financial Statement) into its approximate equivalent at the factor cost prices of the second half of 1968, we find that the share of G.N.P. absorbed by private-sector fixed investment is expected to rise from 10·1 per cent to

TABLE 5.9

PERCENTAGES OF GROSS NATIONAL PRODUCT OF UNITED KINGDOM. AT CURRENT FACTOR COST, 1962–70

(*a*) USE OF RESOURCES

	1962	*1963*	*1964*	*1965*	*1966*	*1967*	*1968*	*Projections* *1969*	*Projections* *1970 (1st half)*
Current expenditure									
1. Personal consumption	63·5	63·6	62·6	61·8	61·6	61·7	61·0	60·1	59·3
2. Public authorities' current expenditure on goods and services	18·3	18·1	17·8	18·3	18·8	19·6	19·7	19·3	19·2
3. Total consumption	81·8	81·8	80·4	80·1	80·4	81·3	80·7	79·4	78·5
Gross fixed investment									
4. Public sector: houses	1·3	1·3	1·7	1·7	1·8	2·0	2·1		
5. other	5·9	6·1	6·6	6·7	7·1	7·9	7·7		
6. Total public sector	7·2	7·4	8·3	8·4	8·9	9·9	9·8	8·6	8·7
7. Private sector: houses	2·0	2·0	2·2	2·1	1·9	2·0	1·9		
8. other	8·2	7·7	8·3	8·4	8·1	7·6	8·1		
9. Total private sector	10·2	9·7	10·5	10·5	10·0	9·6	10·1	11·0	11·3
10. Total gross fixed investment	17·4	17·1	18·9	18·9	18·9	19·5	19·9	19·7	20·0
11. Stock accumulation	0·3	0·7	2·1	1·2	0·7	0·4	0·6	1·1	1·3
12. Balance of payments on current account	+0·4	+0·4	−1·4	−0·3	—	−1·2	−1·2	−0·2	+0·2
13. Stock accumulation + balance of payments	0·7	1·1	0·7	1·0	0·7	−0·8	−0·6	0·9	1·5
14. Total investment	18·1	18·2	19·6	19·9	19·6	18·7	19·3	20·6	21·5
(*b*) SAVING									
15. Persons	5·5	5·3	5·3	5·6	5·7	5·0	4·5		
16. Companies	8·0	8·5	8·5	9·3	6·7	6·4	6·1		
17. Tax and dividend reserves	0·5	0·7	1·5	0·5	1·2	1·3	1·8		
18. Public authorities	4·8	3·6	4·5	5·4	6·4	5·7	7·5		
19. Total saving	17·8	18·1	19·8	20·8	20·0	18·4	19·9		
20. Errors and omissions	+0·3	+0·1	−0·2	−0·9	−0·4	+0·3	−0·6		
21. Total investment	18·1	18·2	19·6	19·9	19·6	18·7	19·3		

11·0 per cent. This increase is made consistent with a marked improvement in the balance of payments (which would, however, still leave a small deficit for the year on current account), and with a recovery of stock accumulation to a normal level, only by a sharp further fall in the share of output going to personal consumption and by an appreciable decline in the share taken by public-sector expenditure on both current and capital accounts. If in 1970 the balance of payments were to move, as may be hoped, into surplus without a renewed check to private-sector investment, the share taken by personal consumption would have to continue to decline.

It seems possible that the very severe credit restrictions imposed in the first half of 1969, which have resulted in heavy falls on the stock exchange in prices both of ordinary shares and of fixed-interest securities, may tend to check the rise in private-sector fixed investment. At the same time, it is possible that the approach of the general election may make the Government reluctant to impose still further restraints on personal consumption in the 1970 budget. Any improvement in the balance of payments in 1970 may therefore be less at the expense of consumption and more at the expense of home investment than was envisaged in the Treasury's 1969 projection.

6

How the Economy Works[1]

DISCUSSION of British economic policy in recent years has been marked by three widespread misconceptions. The first is that the long-term growth of the economy would have been faster if it had not been for recurrent balance-of-payments crises. The second is that, even with extreme full employment, it is possible to prevent an excessively rapid rise of money incomes by means of direct restrictions on increases in wage rates, imposed either by law or by obtaining the co-operation of the trade unions and employers' organisations. And the third is that the best way of accelerating the growth of output is to run the economy with extremely full employment of productive resources. The purpose of this paper is to replace these misconceptions with more valid explanations of the working of the economy.

PRODUCTIVE POTENTIAL

Even in a completely closed system, with no international transactions, the amount which an economy can produce in a given year, with its existing resources, institutions, attitudes and tastes, cannot exceed certain limits, however great the demand. The factors which impose a physical limit on output can, no doubt, be different at different times and in different places. Output can, for instance, be checked by shortages of fixed capital, of raw materials or semi-finished goods, or of transport facilities, so that the physical maximum is reached while there is still a large reserve of unemployed labour. But in Britain since the war the main limiting factor has undoubtedly been the supply of labour, and especially of skilled labour, including those with managerial and technical as well as manual skills. This physical limit on output is called the productive potential of the country.

[1] First published in *Lloyds Bank Review*, Apr 1968.

Attempts to exceed the productive potential are, in fact, likely to produce less output, rather than more. The number of projects started may increase, but their completion is delayed by shortages of particular resources, so that other resources are forced into periods of idleness, the production period is lengthened and the increased starts are accompanied by reduced completions. In such conditions it may well be found, as it was in 1947–8, that measures taken to restrict demand bring a faster, instead of a slower, rise of output.

It has fortunately been found that, in post-war Britain, the ceiling imposed on output by productive potential has risen gradually year by year. The most important cause of this increase is the greater efficiency in the use of labour, as shown by the rise in output per man-hour. The main reason for this improvement in efficiency seems to be technical innovation, including not only scientific developments, but also increased skills at all levels, especially at the level of management. More fixed investment seems to contribute to the rise in output per man-hour mainly because it facilitates the introduction of technical improvements. It is, however, possible to introduce a great deal of improvement by means of better management with little or no new capital investment; while it is also possible to spend a great deal on new buildings, plant and equipment without achieving much increase in output per man-hour. It is probably true of all countries, and certainly of Britain, that output could, for a considerable time, be increased more rapidly by making more efficient use of existing equipment than by expanding equipment without raising the efficiency with which it is used.

Given the rate of increase in output per man-hour, the rate of increase of total output is governed partly by the average number of hours worked and partly by changes in the size of the labour force. Output per man-hour is presumably not wholly independent of the number of hours worked, but at existing levels a reduction in the average number of hours worked per week is unlikely to be wholly compensated by an increase in output per hour, so that a reduction in hours worked is likely to be accompanied by some slowing down of the rate of increase of productive potential. On the other hand, the rate of rise of productive potential can be accelerated by a faster rise in the labour force, such as might occur as the result of an increase in net immigration, while a check to the rise of the labour force will tend to slow it down.

Fig. 6.1 shows the estimate rise in the index of productive potential of the United Kingdom from 1952 to 1967, with the last quarter of 1955 as equivalent to 100. From 1952 to 1964

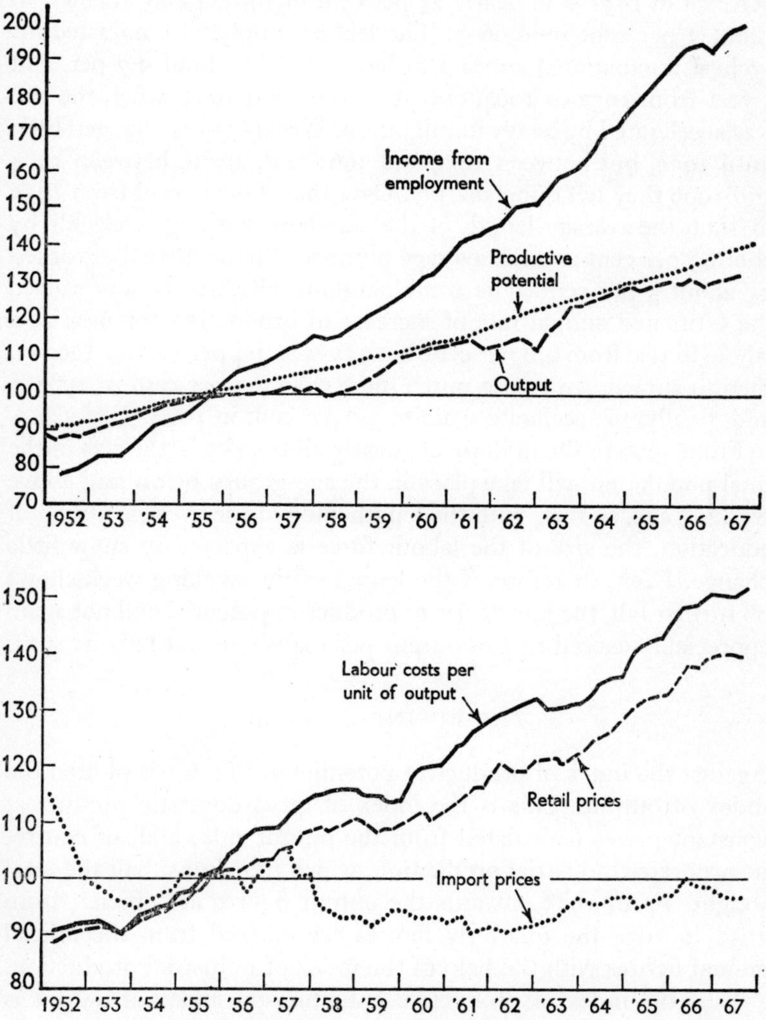

Fig. 6.1 Output, incomes, prices and costs, 1952–67 (last quarter of 1955 = 100)

the rates of growth follow the estimates made by Messrs W. A. H. Godley and J. R. Shepherd,[1] the extrapolation from 1964 to 1967 being derived from estimates by the author.

The annual rate of growth of output per man-hour (adjusted for cyclical fluctuations) is estimated to have increased from about $1\frac{3}{4}$ per cent in 1951–2 to nearly $2\frac{3}{4}$ per cent in 1963–4 and, further, to about 3 per cent in 1966–7. The labour supply (also adjusted for cyclical fluctuations) appears to have risen by about 0·7 per cent a year from 1952 to 1964, except in 1962 and 1963, when the rise was accelerated by heavy immigration. Weekly hours changed little until 1959, but between 1959 and 1961 and, again, between 1964 and 1966 they fell quite sharply. Over the whole period from 1959 to 1966 the average length of the standard working week fell by about 9 per cent and the average number of hours actually worked by about 5 per cent. The combination of all three factors caused the estimated annual rate of increase in productive potential as a whole to rise from 2·6 per cent in 1953–4 to 3·4 per cent in 1962–3, then to slow down to not much more than 2·5 per cent in 1964–6 and, finally, to accelerate again to 3·0 per cent in 1966–7.

From 1966 to the mid-1970s, nearly all the rise in the size of the total population will take place in the age-groups below and above working age, so that, with the lengthening of the average period of education, the size of the labour force is expected to show little change. Even, therefore, if the length of the working week shows no further fall, the rate of rise of productive potential will not again appreciably exceed that of output per man-hour until about 1975.

THE BUSINESS CYCLE

Against the index of productive potential in Fig. 6.1 is plotted the index of output. This is the index of gross domestic product at constant prices (calculated from the output side) and, of course, incorporates industrial production, which has almost half the total weight. From 1955 onwards the output figures are official; from 1952 to 1954 the quarterly figures are derived from the official annual figures with the help of the index of industrial production.

Like the index of productive potential, the index of output is

[1] In their paper on 'Long-term Growth and Short-term Policy', *National Institute Economic Review*, Aug 1964.

based on the last quarter of 1955 as 100. Since the economy is assumed to have been fully employed at that date (or, more strictly, since full employment is defined as a condition similar to that which existed in the last quarter of 1955), the gap between the two curves shows the margin of unused productive potential, changes in which indicate the course of the business cycle. It will be seen that there have been three complete cycles since 1952, with clearly defined troughs in 1952, 1958, 1962[1] and 1967. The peaks are less sharply defined, since the rapid rise of output in the upturn is followed by a period of 'bumping along the ceiling' (1954–5, 1960–1, 1964–6), with a very small unused margin, and with output rising at about the same rate as productive potential. More than one peak may be recorded during this period.

MONEY INCOMES

There is strong evidence that the rate of increase of money incomes is inversely correlated with the size of the margin of unused potential. Fig. 6.1 includes an index of income from employment in the United Kingdom. This rises much more rapidly in periods when the margin of unused potential is small, such as 1954–5, 1960–1 and 1964–6, than in periods when it is larger, such as 1952–3, 1958, 1962–3 and 1966–7.

LABOUR COSTS AND RETAIL PRICES

If we divide the index of income from employment by the index of output, we get an index of labour costs per unit of output. Since the index of employment incomes rose by 100 per cent between the last quarter of 1955 and the third quarter of 1967, while the index of output rose by only 32 per cent, the index of labour costs per unit of output increased by over 50 per cent. Fig. 6.1 shows that this index of labour costs moves very closely with the index of retail prices; the slower average rise in retail prices since 1955 seems to have been due mainly to the absence of a rise in import prices.

The rise in labour costs per unit of output has been checked from time to time. These checks have occurred not only in years when the margin of unused potential has been at a peak and the

[1] The fall in output in the first quarter of 1963 can be attributed to the weather and should be disregarded.

TABLE 6.1

USE OF POTENTIAL AND RISE IN INCOME FROM EMPLOYMENT

Twelve months ending	*High use of potential*		*Twelve months ending*	*Low use of potential*	
	Average percentage of potential in use	*% rise in income from employment*		*Average percentage of potential in use*	*% rise in income from employment*
4th qr, 1954	98·9	7·0	2nd qr, 1958	95·3	4·0
4th qr, 1955	99·5	9·0	3rd qr, 1958	94·4	2·6
2nd qr, 1956	99·1	10·0	1st qr, 1959	93·6	2·7
3rd qr, 1960	98·2	8·7	2nd qr, 1962	96·0	4·8
2nd qr, 1961	98·0	8·9	4th qr, 1962	95·3	5·0
			2nd qr, 1963	94·9	4·8
4th qr, 1964	97·9	7·9	2nd qr, 1967	95·2	2·4
4th qr, 1965	97·8	7·5	3rd qr, 1967	94·6	2·7
2nd qr, 1966	97·7	7·8			

rise in earnings small, but also in years of rapidly rising output, in spite of a rise in earnings which accelerates as the margin shrinks. As soon, however, as output approaches potential, its rise has necessarily to slow down, while the increase in incomes continues, so that labour costs and prices rise. These rises normally continue not only while the margin of potential remains small, but also while it is widening after the boom has been checked. For during this period the rise in output is checked as much as, or more than, that in earnings, so that earnings continue to rise faster than output and the rise in prices is not checked. Only when the necessary margin of potential has been re-created, the rise in earnings slowed down to equality with that of potential, and the expansion of output resumed, does the increase in labour costs and prices cease.

These movements are shown more clearly in Fig. 6.2, where cyclical fluctuations in the proportion of potential in use are compared with the percentage changes over the previous twelve months in income from employment, output, labour costs and prices.

INCOME FROM EMPLOYMENT

The most important conclusion to be drawn from Fig. 6.2 is that, at least since 1954, the annual rate of rise in employment income is closely related to the proportion of potential in use.

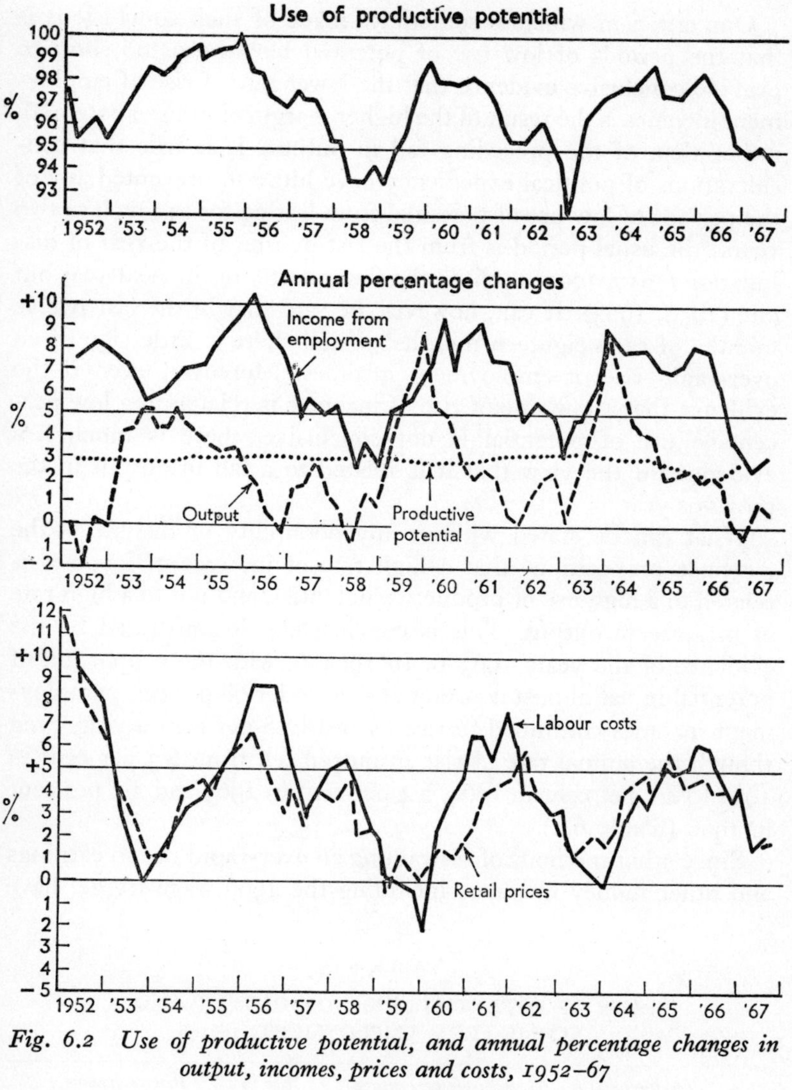

Fig. 6.2 *Use of productive potential, and annual percentage changes in output, incomes, prices and costs, 1952–67*

It would seem that, with a use of potential of 98 per cent, we may expect a rise in employment incomes of something like 8 per cent a year, while, when the use of potential is down to about 94 per cent, the rate of rise of employment incomes is in the neighbourhood of 3 per cent.

One criticism which is sometimes made of such conclusions is that the periods of low use of potential have been too short to provide conclusive evidence that the lower rate of rise of employment incomes is the result of the higher margin of unused potential, rather than of the preceding fall in output. It is true that considerations of political expediency have hitherto prevented any of the periods of low use of potential from lasting for as much as two years: the usual period is from the last quarter of the year of disinflation (1957, 1961, 1966) to the first quarter of the next year but one (1959, 1963). It can, however, be said that in the last twelve months of each eighteen months' period there is little sign of an over-rapid rise of employment incomes. Moreover, even if the evidence that a low rate of rise of incomes is related to a low percentage use of potential is not conclusive, there is much less evidence for the view that it is related to a fall in output in the previous year.

What can be stated without any possibility of dispute is the converse proposition: that a high rate of increase of incomes is related to a high use of productive potential, and not to a high rate of increase in output. This is conclusively demonstrated by the evidence of the years 1963–6. In 1964–6, with the proportion of potential in use almost constant at just under 98 per cent, employment incomes continued to rise by nearly 8 per cent a year, even though the annual rate of rise in output fell from 6·3 per cent in 1963 to 4·1 per cent in 1964, 2·4 per cent in 1965 and 2·2 per cent in 1966 (Table 6.2).

Since other methods of restraining an over-rapid rise in earnings and other money incomes, including the 1966 wage-freeze, have

TABLE 6.2

USE OF POTENTIAL, RISES IN OUTPUT AND INCOME FROM EMPLOYMENT, 1963–6

Twelve months ending	*Average percentage of potential in use*	*Rise in output* (%)	*Rise in income from employment* (%
4th quarter, 1963	95·8	6·3	6·4
4th quarter, 1964	97·9	4·1	7·9
4th quarter, 1965	97·8	2·4	7·5
2nd quarter, 1966	97·7	2·2	7·8

either failed or at best achieved only very temporary success, would it not be desirable for the policy of maintaining a rather larger margin of unused potential to be given a sufficiently long trial to provide conclusive evidence about its permanent effectiveness?

Another phenomenon which is clearly brought out in Fig. 6.2 is the regular alternation of periods when labour costs and prices are rising little, or are even falling, with periods in which they are rising rapidly. To understand what lies behind these fluctuations it is necessary to divide the cycle, not into two phases, but into four.

The rise in prices first slows down when the proportion of potential in use is at or near its minimum and output is rising at about the same rate as potential. This phase (1958, 1962, 1967) could, in principle, become permanent, with output and incomes both rising at the same rate as potential and with prices stable. This, however, is not true of the next phase of the cycle, when the second half of the period of steady prices is inherently unstable. In this phase (1953, 1959–60, 1963–4) an increase of demand, usually generated by tax reductions, brings with it a rapid rise of output, so that, though the rate of rise of incomes is also accelerated, the rise is matched or more than matched by the increase of output, and labour costs and prices remain steady or may even fall. Unfortunately, as soon as the margin of unused potential has been absorbed and output approaches its ceiling, the rate of rise of output falls to equality with the rate of rise of potential, while the rise of incomes continues with undiminished speed (1954–5, 1960–1, 1964–6). In this third phase of the cycle, therefore, prices rise rapidly. This phase, like the first, could in principle continue indefinitely (apart from its effects on the balance of payments), provided that the country were willing to tolerate a continuous inflation. Historically, however, the continued inflation has sooner or later brought a general loss of confidence, at home and abroad, in the government's determination or ability to maintain the value of the currency, and heavy precautionary and speculative sales of sterling have forced the authorities to take sufficiently strong disinflationary action to bring this phase of the cycle to an end. It is possible for such a loss of confidence in the currency to occur, as in 1957, even though the balance of payments is in surplus, when it is seen that the use of potential is being maintained at too high a level to allow the inflation to be checked.

The fourth phase of the cycle, like the second, is inherently temporary. In this phase (1956–8, 1961–2, 1966–7) measures taken to restrict expenditure have the effect of slowing down the rise of output as rapidly as they slow down the rise of incomes, so that the rise of prices continues or may even accelerate for a time. But as the margin of unused potential widens, the rate of rise of incomes falls towards equality with that of productive potential. When it reaches this level, output can again be allowed to rise as fast as productive potential, and the rise of prices ceases. We are now back in phase 1, except that incomes and prices are permanently higher. Although, as we have seen, this phase is potentially permanent, any renewed rise of output which is faster than the rise of potential will initiate a new cycle.

The fourth phase of the 1962–6 cycle was distorted by the introduction of the temporarily effective 'wage-freeze' in the second half of 1966. This had the effect of slowing down the rise of employment incomes much sooner than in either 1957–8 or 1961–2. It would seem, however, that much, if not all, of the rise inhibited in the second half of 1966 has merely been postponed and that the rise between July 1966 and December 1967 has been little, if any, less than in the corresponding periods of previous cycles. If so, the rise in incomes during 1967 will have been faster than in either 1958 or 1962.

BALANCE OF PAYMENTS

One side-effect of a rapid rise of output and of the consequent fall in the margin of unused productive potential is that the balance of payments on current account becomes markedly adverse. It is this development, which usually occurs in the second year of the upturn, rather than the inflation itself, which alarms the Government and induces it to introduce some tentative measures to restrict demand.

As these measures are shortly followed by a marked slowing down of the rate of rise of output, it is natural that the check to output should be popularly attributed to the effects of the adverse balance, and that there should be a widespread belief in the first of the fallacies listed at the beginning of this article: that, but for the balance-of-payments difficulties, the rapid rise of output could have continued indefinitely. There is, therefore, a demand for such measures as devaluation, a floating pound, import restrictions or export subsidies which, it is claimed, would solve the balance-of-payments problem and allow output to continue to rise rapidly for ever.

In fact the effects of rapidly rising output on the balance of payments do not appear until the margin of unused potential has already fallen to a low level, so that output could not, in any case, have continued its rapid rise for more than a short time longer. The only effect of removing the restraints imposed by the balance of payments would be to allow the margin of unused potential to be completely exhausted and to accelerate the rise of money incomes even further, while not preventing the slowing down of output, within a very few months, certainly to the rate of rise of productive potential and, very possibly, with the development of bottlenecks, to below it.

The effects on the balance of payments of an over-rapid rise of output and the running down of the margin of unused potential seem to be felt in three ways. In the short run, the most noticeable effect is that the rapid rise of output leads, with a time-lag of about a year, to a sharp increase in stock accumulation and in imports. As can be seen from Table 6.3, the rapid import rises and adverse balances of payments of 1955, 1960 and 1964 were all accompanied by very considerable additions to stocks. Table 6.3 also makes it clear why the adverse balance of payments of 1955 did not occur until the third, instead of the second, year after the upturn of output, and also why the Government was not obliged by balance-of-payments difficulties to take steps to restrict demand until the margin of unused potential had fallen almost to zero. Stock accumulation in the private sector did, in fact, rise rapidly at the usual time, in 1954, but this rise was more than offset by a heavy fall in the stocks, mainly government trading stocks, held by the public sector. A further decline in public-sector stocks partially offset a still larger rise in private-sector stocks in 1955, and undoubtedly prevented the adverse balance of payments which appeared in that year from being as large as it would otherwise have been.

A favourable balance of payments is highly precarious if it is

TABLE 6.3

USE OF POTENTIAL, BALANCE OF PAYMENTS AND STOCK ACCUMULATION, 1952–66

	Average potential in use	Balance of payments on current account								Stock accumulation				Balance of payments and stocks	
		Commodity trade			Net invisibles			Balance on c/a		Public authority	Other	Total			
		Exports and re-exports	Im-ports	Visible balance	Govt.	Other	Total		% of G.N.P.				% of G.N.P.		% of G.N.P
	(%)	(£m.)	(£m.)	(£m.)	(£m.)	(£m.)	(£m.)	(£m.)		(£m.)	(£m.)	(£m.)		(£m.)	
1952	96·1	2,769	3,048	−279	−61	+503	+442	+163	+1·2	128	−78	50	0·4	+213	+1·5
1953	97·3	2,683	2,927	−244	−66	+455	+389	+145	+1·0	27	98	125	0·8	+270	+1·8
1954	98·9	2,785	2,989	−204	−131	+452	+321	+117	+0·7	−188	244	56	0·4	+173	+1·1
1955	99·5	3,073	3,386	−313	−138	+296	+158	−155	−0·9	−93	393	300	1·8	+145	+0·9
1956	97·8	3,377	3,324	+53	−175	+330	+155	+208	+1·1	−8	267	259	1·4	+467	+2·5
1957	96·8	3,509	3,538	−29	−144	+406	+262	+233	+1·2	18	220	238	1·2	+471	+2·4
Average 1952–7	**97·7**	**3,033**	**3,202**	**−169**	**−119**	**+407**	**+288**	**+119**	***+0·7***	**−19**	**191**	**171**	***1·0***	**+290**	***+1·7***
1958	94·0	3,407	3,378	+29	−219	+537	+318	+347	+1·7	28	83	111	0·5	+458	+2·2
1959	95·6	3,522	3,640	−118	−227	+494	+267	+149	+0·7	1	173	174	0·8	+323	+1·5
1960	98·2	3,733	4,141	−408	−282	+432	+150	−258	−1·1	−42	644	602	2·6	+344	+1·5
1961	97·2	3,892	4,045	−153	−332	+490	+158	+5	0	4	330	334	1·4	+339	+1·4
Average 1958–61	**96·3**	**3,639**	**3,801**	**−162**	**−265**	**+488**	**+223**	**+61**	***+0·3***	**−2**	**307**	**305**	***1·4***	**+366**	***+1·6***
1962	95·3	3,994	4,098	−104	−359	+590	+231	+127	+0·5	11	72	83	0·3	+210	+0·8
1963	95·8	4,287	4,370	−83	−381	+580	+199	+116	+0·4	−30	258	228	0·8	+344	+1·3
1964	97·9	4,471	5,016	−545	−432	+575	+143	−402	−1·4	21	628	649	2·2	+247	+0·8
1965	97·8	4,784	5,065	−281	−446	+617	+171	−110	−0·4	24	392	416	1·3	+306	+1·0
1966	97·0	5,110	5,262	−152	−460	+553	+93	−59	−0·2	60	149	209	0·6	+150	+0·5
Average 1962–6	**96·8**	**4,529**	**4,762**	**−233**	**−416**	**+583**	**+167**	**−66**	***−0·2***	**17**	**300**	**317**	***1·1***	**+251**	***+0·9***

achieved in a year when the rise in stocks is unusually small, and is likely to be maintained only if stock accumulation in the same year is at or above its normal level of rather over 1 per cent of gross national product. If we put the current account surplus needed to cover exports of long-term capital and to strengthen the reserves of gold and foreign exchange at a minimum of £300 millions, or about 1 per cent of G.N.P., the lowest level of current account surplus plus stock accumulation (which is identical, apart from errors and omissions, with the surplus of saving over domestic fixed investment) which can be regarded as satisfactory is rather over 2 per cent of G.N.P. – a level not achieved since 1958. For the 1962–6 cycle the average was less than 1 per cent of G.N.P., and in 1967 seems to have been very small indeed, or even negative.

A second short-term effect of a rapid rise of output – this time a result of the shrinking margin of unused potential rather than of the rise of output itself – is the appearance of shortages, exemplified by lengthening order-books and delays in delivery. These shortages tend to draw in additional imports from abroad and to divert products from export to the home market. It is difficult to trace these effects, for they are often obscured by the effects of changes in world markets; but they are likely to continue, even after the initial rapid rise in stock accumulation has been checked, so long as the margin of unused potential remains inadequate.

Both these short-term effects of an over-rapid rise of output can be expected to disappear as soon as output is checked sufficiently to restore the margin of unused potential. This is, unfortunately, not true of the third effect of over-expansion, which is a permanent and largely irreversible rise of costs and prices. This will, of course, affect the competitive position of British producers both in home and in export markets only if British costs and prices have risen more than those of our main competitors. There is strong evidence to support the view that this is what they have done.

If we abstract from cyclical fluctuations by calculating the yearly averages for whole cycles, we find that, in spite of an improvement in the average terms of trade of 12 per cent between the first and second cycles and of 4 per cent between the second and third, the average balance of payments on current account deteriorated progressively from a surplus of £119 millions in 1952–7 to one of £61 millions in 1958–61 and to a deficit of £66 millions in 1962–6.

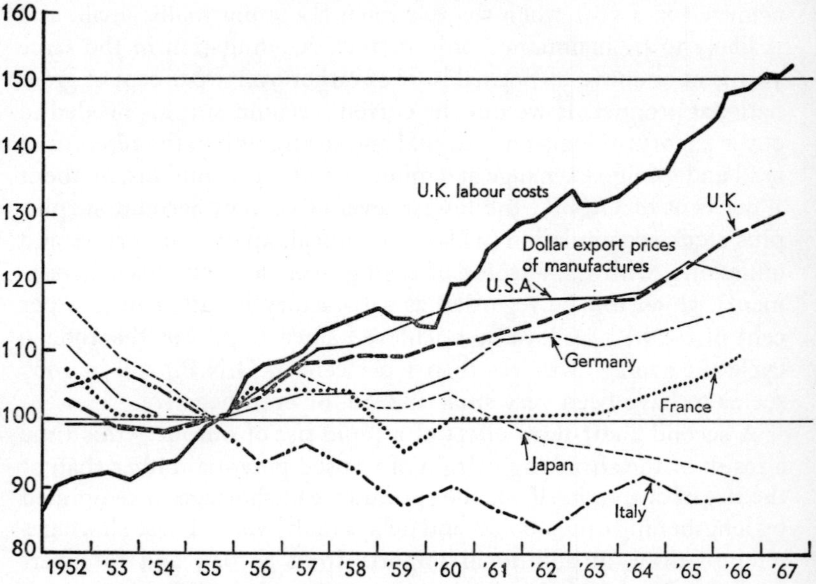

Fig. 6.3 U.K. labour costs and dollar export prices of manufactures, 1952–67 (1955 = 100)

The worsening between the first and second cycles was due almost entirely to a greater rise in public-sector payments abroad on invisible account than in private-sector invisible earnings, but between the second and third cycles the worsening of the trade balance was greater than that on invisible account.

That the underlying cause of the worsening of the visible balance, especially since 1959, is the excessive rise of British labour costs is strongly suggested by Fig. 6.3. Between 1959 and 1966 the index of British labour costs per unit of output rose by 28 per cent. Export prices of British manufactures increased by 17 per cent, or by much less than labour costs. But during the same period the prices of manufactured exports from France rose by 15 per cent, from Germany by 12 per cent, from the United States by 6 per cent, and from Italy by 1 per cent, while export prices of Japanese manufactures fell by 10 per cent. This suggests that while, with the rise of British costs, the rise in export prices of British manufactures has been too little for them to be profitable, it has been too much for them to be competitive.

UNEMPLOYMENT

Unemployment and the Margin of Unused Productive Potential

Since the principal factor which sets a physical limit to the level of output in any given year is the supply of labour, it is inevitable that any widening of the margin of unused productive potential should be accompanied by a rise in unemployment. The increase in the percentage of unemployed labour is, however, much smaller than the increase in the percentage of unused potential. Godley and Shepherd, in the paper mentioned above, estimate that fluctuations in unemployment are not much more than one-fifth as large as those in the margin of potential, partly because the rise in the margin is nearly twice as large as the fall in employment, and partly because the fall in employment is some two and half times as large as the rise in unemployment.

The difference between the changes in employment and in unemployment seems to be due to the fact that, in periods of severe labour shortage, a number of 'fringe workers', who were not registered as unemployed, are sucked into employment, and that these, when the shortage of labour is relieved, drop out of the figures again. It is clear, nevertheless, that the ratio of nearly five to one cannot be continued indefinitely as unemployment and the margin of potential rise: taken to the extreme this would mean that output would fall to nothing before unemployment reached 25 per cent.

In curves *A* and *B* of Fig. 6.4 the percentage of unemployment in Great Britain is plotted against the margin of unused potential for the years 1952 to 1967. One per cent of unemployment, the level in the last quarter of 1955, is equated with a zero margin of potential, and the scale used for unemployment is five times that for the margin. The two curves generally move closely together, though there seems to be some tendency for the curve of unemployment to rise higher at the peaks. This may be because, by the time unemployment is reaching the neighbourhood of 2 per cent, the margin of fringe workers is becoming exhausted, so that the gap between the fall in the number employed and the rise in the number unemployed is beginning to shrink.

Another relationship revealed by Fig. 6.4 is that changes in

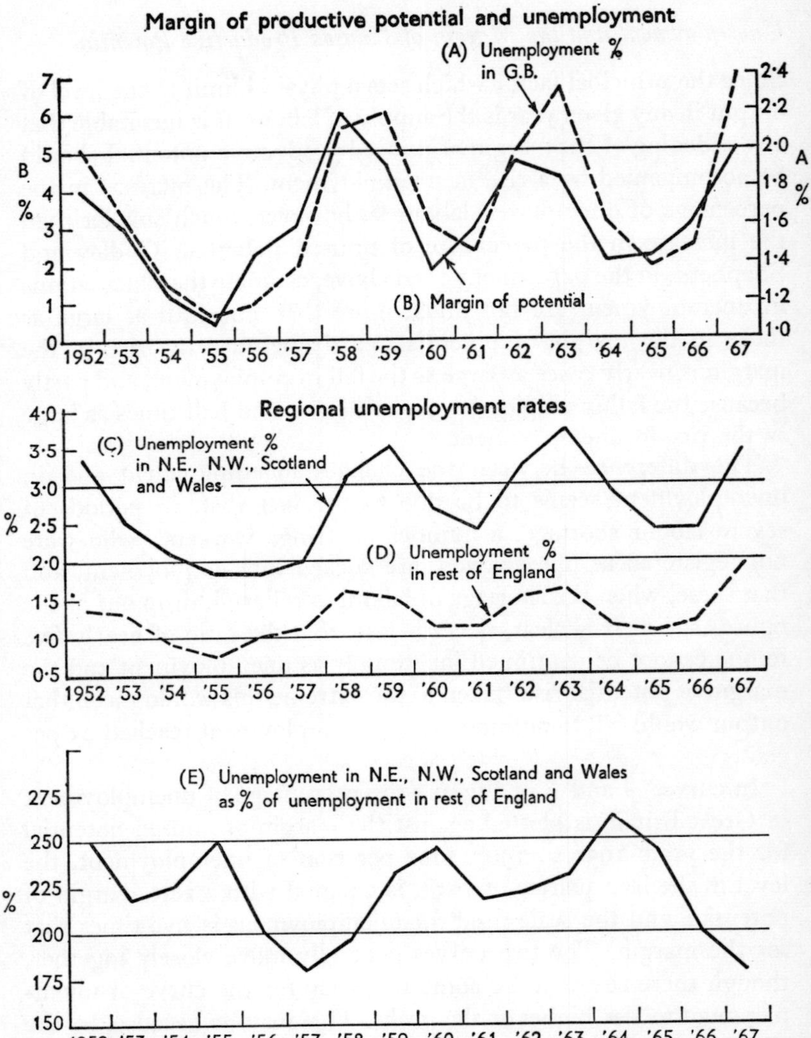

Fig. 6.4 Margin of productive potential and unemployment, and regional unemployment rates, 1952–67 (1963 figures are adjusted for the exceptional weather)

unemployment tend to lag behind those in the margin of unused potential. Thus in 1959 and 1963 unemployment continued to rise after the margin of potential had begun to fall, while in 1961 and 1965 it continued to fall after the margin had begun to rise. The lag seems to average about six months, but it is very variable. In spite of the promptness with which unemployment figures are published, this highly variable lag makes unemployment a poor indicator for purposes of policy.

Regional Differences in Unemployment

It is the cost in terms of unemployment of maintaining a margin of unused potential sufficient to prevent an excessively rapid rise of incomes which has probably been the main reason why successive Governments have failed to maintain such a margin for more than brief periods. The resistance to the maintenance of an adequate margin is intensified by the fact that unemployment is distributed unequally through the country, being much higher in the North of England and in Scotland and Wales than in the Midlands and in South, East and South-East England. As will be seen from the *C* and *D* curves in Fig. 6.4, the average unemployment percentage in the high unemployment area has varied cyclically from 1·8 (in 1955 to 1956) to 3·7 (in 1963), while in the low unemployment area it has varied only from 0·7 (in 1955) to 1·9 (in 1967).

There is also a difference in the timing of the cyclical movements in the two areas, for unemployment in the low unemployment area begins both to rise and to fall sooner than it does in the high unemployment area. Thus, in the checks to output of 1956 and 1966, unemployment in the North, Scotland and Wales remained unchanged after it had begun to rise in the rest of England, while in the recovery of 1959 it continued to rise in the North after it had begun to fall in the South. The reason for this difference in timing seems to be that both upswings and downswings of the cycle have been initiated by changes in consumption expenditure, induced by alterations in taxation or in hire-purchase rules, which affect industries located mainly in the Midlands and South. It is only after a time-lag of about a year that the changes in consumption are reflected in changes in fixed investment and in the demand for the capital goods produced largely in the North and Wales.

This difference in the timing of cyclical movements in unemployment in the two parts of the country seems to be the main cause of the fluctuations in the difference between the unemployment percentages, shown in curve *E* of Fig. 6.4. Thus the average unemployment percentage in the high unemployment area was about two and a half times as high as in the rest of England at the activity peaks of 1955, 1960 and 1964, not much more than twice as high in the checks of 1956 and 1961, and less than twice as high in the recessions of 1957, 1958, 1966 and 1967.

In spite of continual and increasing efforts by Governments to decrease the disparity between the high and low unemployment areas, there does not seem to be any continuing trend towards greater equality. The low ratio recorded in 1967 (which was about the same as in 1957) seems to have been due, not so much to an exceptionally low percentage for this stage of the cycle in the high unemployment area, as to an unusually high percentage in the rest of the country, and especially in the Midlands, caused, perhaps, by the exceptional severity of the restrictions imposed on hire-purchase.

Effective and Non-effective Unemployment

If unemployment could be spread more equally between the different regions, it would be possible to reduce the amount of *total* unemployment which would be consistent with the absence of an over-rapid rise in incomes from employment. For it seems unlikely that the pressure of excess demand for labour generated in the low unemployment areas of the South and Midlands, where two-thirds of the employed population work, is appreciably moderated by the labour surpluses of the high unemployment areas of the North, Scotland and Wales. The reduction in unemployment which could safely be achieved in this way should not, however, be exaggerated.

There is one factor, in particular, that makes it impossible to achieve complete equality between regions in unemployment as at present recorded. This is the existence of a considerable number of people, now classified as unemployed, who suffer from various personal disabilities which make them 'likely to spend long periods on the register even when the local demand for labour is high'. These people, who cannot be regarded as competing effectively for the vacancies available, are put in the Ministry of Labour's survey of October 1964[1] at over 180,000, or about 0·8 per cent of the employed population, a figure which now may well be higher. These 'non-effective' unemployed are distributed very unequally between the regions, with 98,000, or 1·3 per cent of employees, in the North and North-West of England, Scotland and Wales, and only 83,000, or 0·5 per cent, in the rest of England. If we deduct the non-effectives, as in Table 6.4 below, we reduce the amount of

TABLE 6.4

UNEMPLOYMENT: EFFECTIVE AND NON-EFFECTIVE, OCTOBER, 1967

	Non-effective		*Effective*		*Total*	
	('000)	(%)	('000)	(%)	('000)	(%)
High unemployment area						
North-West	30	1·0	45	1·5	75	2·5
North	21	1·6	34	2·5	55	4·1
Scotland	35	1·6	49	2·2	84	3·8
Wales	12	1·2	28	2·8	40	4·0
Total	98	1·3	156	2·1	254	3·4
Low unemployment area						
London and South-east	27	0·5	66	1·1	93	1·6
East and South	14	0·5	35	1·3	49	1·8
South-West	10	0·8	23	1·6	33	2·4
Midlands	17	0·5	67	1·7	85	2·2
Yorks. and Humberside	14	0·6	33	1·6	47	2·2
Total	83	0·5	224	1·4	307	1·9
Great Britain	181	0·8	380	1·6	561	2·4

unemployment in the high unemployment area in October 1967 (a month in which the seasonal adjustment was small) from 254,000, or 3·4 per cent, to 156,000, or 2·1 per cent, and in the low unemployment area from 307,000, or 1·9 per cent, to 224,000, or 1·4 per cent. The percentage in the high unemployment area then becomes 50 per cent higher than in the low unemployment area.

It would clarify the position if the greater part of the non-effectives could be removed from the unemployment figures and transferred to some other register of the welfare state.

[1] See Ministry of Labour *Gazette*, Apr 1966.

Equilibrium Unemployment

We start our attempt to estimate the maximum amount by which unemployment could safely be reduced by greater equality between regions by ascertaining the gap in each region between the number effectively unemployed and the number of vacancies in October 1965, when unemployment was low, and in October 1967, when it was high. We then determine how much of the change in each gap was due to rising unemployment and how much to falling vacancies. From this we can calculate how large would be the changes in vacancies and unemployment to bring the two to equality in either of these months, and from this the amount of unemployment which would exist if effective unemployment were equal to vacancies in each region. The results of this calculation are set out in Table 6.5.

It will be seen that this calculation gives an equilibrium level of effective unemployment of 1·0 per cent in the high unemployment area, as compared with one of 1·3 per cent in the low unemployment area. But this difference is much more than offset when we

TABLE 6.5

EQUILIBRIUM UNEMPLOYMENT

	Non-effective		*Equilibrium effective (equals vacancies)*		*Total equilibrium unemployment*	
	('000)	(%)	('000)	(%)	('000)	(%)
High unemployment area						
North-West	30	1·0	32	1·1	62	2·1
North	21	1·6	12	0·9	33	2·5
Scotland	35	1·6	21	1·0	56	2·6
Wales	12	1·2	12	1·2	23	2·4
Total	98	1·3	77	1·0	175	2·3
Low unemployment area						
London and South-East	27	0·5	70	1·2	97	1·7
East and South	14	0·5	38	1·4	53	1·9
South-West	10	0·8	17	1·3	27	2·1
Midlands	17	0·5	48	1·3	66	1·8
Yorks. and Humberside	14	0·6	25	1·2	39	1·8
Total	83	0·5	199	1·3	282	1·8
Great Britain	181	0·8	276	1·2	457	2·0

add back the non-effectives: we then get equilibrium total unemployment of 2·3 per cent in the high unemployment area, as against 1·8 per cent in the low unemployment area and 2·0 per cent in Great Britain as a whole.

Equalisation of Unemployment

We can now compare these estimates of equilibrium unemployment with the unemployment which actually existed in October 1965 and October 1967. This is done in Table 6.6.

TABLE 6.6

UNEMPLOYMENT SURPLUSES AND DEFICITS

('000)

	Equilibrium unemployment	*October 1965*		*October 1967*	
		Total unemployment	*Surplus or deficit*	*Total unemployment*	*Surplus or deficit*
High unemployment area					
North-West	62	45	−17	75	+13
North	33	32	−1	55	+22
Scotland	56	60	+4	84	+28
Wales	23	27	+3	40	+16
Total	175	164	−11	254	+79
Low unemployment area					
London and South-East	97	50	−47	93	−4
East and South	53	26	−27	49	−4
South-West	27	22	−5	33	+6
Midlands	66	33	−33	85	+19
Yorks. and Humberside	39	23	−16	47	+8
Total	282	154	−128	307	+25
Great Britain	457	318	−139	561	+104

Table 6.6 indicates that in October 1965 the supply and demand for labour were approximately in balance in the North of England, Scotland and Wales, while in the rest of England there was a shortage of 145,000. In October 1967, on the other hand, demand and supply were about in balance in the South-East, East and South of England, with a surplus of supply over demand of 112,000

in the rest of the country. On this basis, the exact matching-up of supply and demand for labour in each region separately would have reduced unemployment in Great Britain from 561,000, or 2·4 per cent, to 457,000, or 2·0 per cent. This is the most that could be achieved even by perfect success. The most that could be reasonably hoped for in practice would be much less than this – perhaps a saving of unemployment of 50,000, or 0·2 per cent.

INCOMES POLICIES

In their attempts to render compatible the irreconcilable objectives of maintaining extreme full employment and of preventing inflation, or at least its effects on the balance of payments, successive Governments have from time to time followed policies based on the second of the three fallacies enumerated at the beginning of this article: that, even with extreme full employment, it is possible to prevent an excessively rapid rise of money incomes by means of direct restrictions on increases in wage rates. The assumption behind such a policy seems to be that earned incomes rise too rapidly, not as the result of competition between employers for scarce labour, but because trade unions are using their monopoly power to force wages up. It has, of course, been the popular habit for centuries to attribute the price effects of inflation to the use of monopoly power by some section or other of the community; and it does not seem that this particular attribution has much more justification than its predecessors.

It is possible that, if imposed at a time when the supply of labour is nearly in balance with demand, or when used in conjunction with severe measures of disinflation, an 'incomes policy' may have some effect on the rate of rise of incomes from employment. The experience of 1966–7, however, seems to indicate that such effects are unlikely to be more than temporary. The rise in weekly earnings, after being checked completely in the second half of 1966 by the 'wage-freeze', has been resumed so vigorously in 1967, in spite of the continued co-operation with the Government by the Trades Union Congress, that, during the eighteen months to the end of 1967, it seems likely to have been at least as large as in the corresponding periods of previous cycles, when there was no effective wage-freeze (see Table 6.7).

TABLE 6.7

UNEMPLOYMENT AND WEEKLY EARNINGS

	1957–58		1961–62		1966–67	
	Unemployment	*Weekly earnings*	*Unemployment*	*Weekly earnings*	*Unemployment*	*Weekly earnings*
	(%)		(%)		(%)	
Apr	1·6	100·0	1·5	100·0	1·3	100·0
Oct	1·3	103·5	1·6	101·6	1·8	100·5
Apr	2·0	104·5	2·0	103·3	2·4	102·0
Oct	2·4	106·1	2·2	104·1	2·4	105·5

If the effects of an 'incomes policy', even when imposed under the most favourable conditions, are likely to be only temporary, when imposed in continuing conditions of extreme full employment it is unlikely to enjoy even this limited success. Apart altogether from the political difficulties of instituting such a policy, its enforcement would encounter insuperable obstacles. With the demand for labour in most parts of the country greatly in excess of the supply at the permitted price, many employers would find themselves with equipment they could not man and profitable orders they could not fulfil. In such conditions, it is doubtful if they could be prevented, even by penal legislation, from using methods which would increase their labour costs in order to attract and retain the labour they urgently needed. Even if standard wage rates were effectively controlled, there are innumerable methods of giving higher remuneration, in cash and in kind: guaranteed overtime; up-grading; revised piece-rates; merit payments; bonus or incentive schemes; profit-sharing; pension schemes or other fringe benefits; even improved canteen or other amenities. All are means of bidding up the price of labour, so that the gap between the standare rate and the actual remuneration paid widens continuously.

Even if we assume that, by means of drastic penalties, it is possible to prevent employers from offering too much for their labour, a wages policy would be likely to break down from the labour side. Even if the trade unions could be induced to give their official support to the policy, their members would rapidly become out of sympathy with them. Unofficial strikes and the formation of breakaway unions would become increasingly frequent. And finally, the government would have to choose between abandoning the policy and introducing measures of compulsion which would be intolerable in a free society.

If an incomes policy can, at best, secure only a very temporary check to the excessively rapid rise of incomes from employment so long as there is an excess demand for labour; and if a policy of securing greater equality of unemployment between regions is unlikely to reduce the level of unemployment compatible with the absence of an excess demand for labour by more than about 50,000, or 0·2 per cent, it would seem that the country must face the fact that, to check inflation permanently and to prevent the emergence of yet another balance-of-payments crisis, it must accept a permanent unemployment of some 500,000, or rather over 2 per cent. This would be reduced to rather over 300,000, or about 1·4 per cent, if we could exclude those who, while now included in the register, are not in fact able effectively to compete for the vacancies available. It could be hoped that few of the 300,000 would be unemployed for very long. Since their number would be no greater than that of vacancies, they would constitute a continually changing population in transition from one job to another, though not always to one in the same industry or in the same place. Attention could then be concentrated on alleviating hardship and on reducing the average period out of work by increasing mobility, especially by making it easier for a newcomer to a district to find a house and by suitable provisions for re-training.

GROWTH AND INVESTMENT

In recent years much criticism has been directed at the rate of growth of output in the United Kingdom, as compared with that of many countries on the continent of Europe. Yet both by historical standards and in comparison with such advanced industrial countries as the United States and Canada, the growth in output per head in Britain since the war has been not only quite rapid, but increasingly rapid. The real question, which is rarely asked, is not why the rise in British output has been so slow, but why the rise in the output of some other European countries has been so unprecedentedly fast.

The main answer seems to be that, even after their recovery

from the immediate effects of the war, many Continental countries still had a number of technologically backward sectors in their economies, offering great scope for rapid technological improvement. The most important of these was farming, with a large number of peasant farmers with a low real output per head. While these technological gaps were being closed, there was scope for a very rapid increase in output. Now that many of them have been narrowed, the rate of growth of these countries' productive potentials seems to have slowed down, with the result that in most of them outputs have caught up with potentials, necessitating measures to restrain demand. As a result, the rise in output has been sharply checked and, though it now seems about to be resumed, it is unlikely that it will be as rapid as in the past. It is likely, however, that it will continue to be appreciably faster than either in Britain or in the United States, for most Continental countries still have quite large low-productivity farming sectors, technical improvements in which will both raise output per head in farming and release labour for higher-productivity industrial production.

It is a paradox, but none the less true, that the agitation for faster growth in Britain has probably served, in the long run, to slow it down. For, confusing growth of output with growth of productive potential, it has added to the pressures for permitting too fast a rate of rise of output. The consequent periodical depletions of the margin of unused potential have resulted, not only in over-rapid rises of incomes and in balance-of-payments difficulties, but also in reductions in the pressure of competition and in the need for firms to be efficient in order to survive. A condition of excess demand, in which all a dissatisfied customer can do is to go to the bottom of another supplier's long order-book, provides an ideal climate for keeping inefficient firms alive and thus for slowing down the improvement in the average efficiency of the system as a whole. For a high rate of growth of output per man-hour we need an economic climate in which all producers are under continual pressure to keep down their costs.

One argument which is frequently advanced in support of the third of the three fallacies listed in the introduction to this article – that a high rate of growth is best achieved by running the economy with little or no margin of unused potential – is that only in these conditions is there an incentive for the rapid growth of industrial and commercial investment, held to be essential for a faster growth of output. It has already been pointed out that a high rate of investment will lead to a rapid growth of output only if it is accompanied by a high rate of improvement in both technical and managerial efficiency, and that much of its benefit will be lost if it takes place in conditions which permit inefficient managements to survive. In

TABLE 6.8

GROWTH OF INDUSTRIAL AND COMMERCIAL INVESTMENT, 1952–66

	Margin of potential (%)	*Output*	*Company trading profits*	*Private-sector fixed investment (other than in houses)*		
				Vehicles, etc.	*Buildings, plant and machinery*	*Total*
		(annual percentage increases at 1958 prices)				
1952	3·9	−0·7	−17·4	−9·4	−10·2	−10·0
1953	2·7	4·0	6·1	17·4	−1·4	2·9
1954	1·1	4·2	10·2	11·9	19·0	17·2
1955	0·5	3·4	7·3	7·3	18·5	15·7
1956	2·2	0·9	−3·5	4·0	12·0	10·2
1957	3·2	1·7	1·2	5·3	8·1	7·5
1958	6·0	−0·1	−5·2	7·3	0·3	1·8
1959	4·4	4·5	10·3	13·4	2·5	5·0
1960	1·8	5·4	11·3	12·5	13·7	13·4
1961	2·9	1·8	−5·1	−4·7	16·0	11·0
1962	4·7	1·2	−4·3	−11·4	−1·5	−3·6
1963	4·2	3·3	12·3	8·0	−2·4	−0·4
1964	2·1	6·1	9·3	24·4	13·5	15·8
1965	2·2	2·6	0·6	−3·1	7·1	4·8
1966	3·1	1·6	−3·1	4·1	−2·6	−1·2

addition to this, there are strong reasons for doubting the claim that a very low margin of unused potential is necessary for a high rate of private-sector investment.

If is true that high rates of growth of industrial and commercial fixed investment have usually occurred in, or immediately after, years when the margin of potential was low. But there is another explanation of this phenomenon, which fits the facts always as well, and sometimes better. This is that a rise of industrial and commercial investment follows, not a low margin of potential, but a rise in output and in business profits. That there is usually a time-lag between the rise of output and that of investments in buildings, plant and machinery (though not in vehicles) is explicable by the interval between the date of the decision and the time when actual expenditure begins to become substantial.

In a four-year cycle, such as that of 1958–61, both explanations appear to fit the facts, for the year after that in which the upswing begins is also the year in which the margin of potential is at its lowest. But in a longer cycle, such as those of 1952–7 and 1962–6, the two do not necessarily coincide. Thus we find that in 1952–7 the fastest growth of investment occurs, not in 1955, at the peak of the cycle, but in 1954, the year after output begins to rise in 1953, while the fastest rise of investment in vehicles occurs actually in 1953. Again, in 1962–6 we find that fixed investment rises much less rapidly in 1965 than in 1964, although the margin of unused potential is almost the same in both years.

If the relationship between rises in output and profits and increases in investment is the true one, the fact has important implications for policy. It means that we can expect an increase in output and profits to be followed by an increase in investment, whether the margin of potential is 2 per cent or 5 per cent, and that we could expect a steady increase in output of 3 per cent a year with a 5 per cent margin of unused potential to be accompanied by a rise of investment at least as great as with an increase of output, also averaging 3 per cent a year, but fluctuating between 6 per cent and nothing. Further, in conditions where plans were not being periodically disorganised by 'stop–go' and where firms were under continuous competitive pressure to keep down their costs, it is likely that a given rate of increase of investment would be accompanied by a faster growth of output.

If we wish to accelerate the rate of growth of industrial and commercial investment, the most important requirement would seem to be, not further incentives to invest, but the freeing of more resources from other uses, so that private-sector investment can expand faster without over-straining the economy. In recent years, the continued fall in the proportion of the national income taken by personal consumption (see Table 6.9) has been more than absorbed by the increased share taken by public expenditure, so that it has been possible to maintain the share going to private-sector fixed investment only by robbing the balance of payments.

TABLE 6.9

USES OF GROSS NATIONAL INCOME, 1952–66
(percentages, at factor cost)

	Consumers' expenditure	*Public authorities' current expenditure on goods and services*	*Fixed capital formation*		*Stock accumulation*	*Balance of payments on current account*
			Public sector	*Private sector*		
1952	64·8	19·8	7·7	6·2	0·4	1·1
1953	64·4	19·2	8·1	6·5	0·8	1·0
1954	65·2	18·7	7·6	7·4	0·4	0·7
1955	65·6	18·0	7·3	8·2	1·8	−0·9
1956	64·0	17·8	6·9	8·7	1·4	1·1
1957	63·8	17·6	7·1	9·1	1·2	1·2
Average 1952–7	**64·6**	**18·5**	**7·5**	**7·7**	**1·0**	**0·7**
1958	64·4	17·3	6·8	9·2	0·5	1·7
1959	64·5	17·6	7·0	9·4	0·8	0·7
1960	64·0	17·6	6·8	10·2	2·6	−1·1
1961	63·0	17·8	7·0	10·8	1·4	—
Average 1958–61	**64·0**	**17·6**	**6·9**	**9·9**	**1·3**	**0·3**
1962	63·5	18·2	7·2	10·2	0·3	0·5
1963	63·5	18·2	7·4	9·6	0·8	0·4
1964	62·4	18·0	8·3	10·5	2·2	−1·4
1965	61·8	18·3	8·4	10·5	1·3	−0·4
1966	61·7	18·8	8·9	10·0	0·7	−0·2
Average 1962–6	**62·6**	**18·3**	**8·0**	**10·2**	**1·1**	**−0·2**

DEVALUATION AND AFTER

In the third quarter of 1967, the latest for which official estimates of gross domestic product are available, the margin of unused productive potential is estimated to have been about $5\frac{1}{2}$ per cent (see Fig. 6.2). This was almost up to the level at which income from employment could be expected to rise at about the same rate as productive potential (once the deferred reaction from the 1966 wage-freeze had been absorbed) and at which the rise of prices could be expected to become quite small or cease. If such a condition of internal balance had been reached in 1965, or even in 1966, instead of in 1967, it is probable that devaluation would never have become necessary. For not only would the rise in British costs and prices have been arrested at a lower level, but the check would have coincided with a still rising level of activity on the continent of Europe. Even as late as 1967, the stopping of internal inflation might have been sufficient to inaugurate a steady improvement in the balance of payments if it had not happened to coincide not only with a business recession in most Continental countries but also with the closing of the Suez Canal.

Even if devaluation had not taken place, action would probably have had to be taken within the next few months to prevent output from rising faster than potential and so initiating a new period of excess demand. The slower rise of output than of potential during the first nine months of 1967 occurred in spite of a rapid rise in public-sector expenditure on goods and services and a considerable increase in personal consumption, and was due mainly to a much reduced rate of stock accumulation and the worsening balance of payments. To leave room for even a gradual improvement in the balance of payments and a more normal rate of stock accumulation, without an over-rapid rise of output, steps would have had to be taken in 1968 either to slow down the rapid rise of public expenditure, or to impose additional checks on consumption, or both.

The devaluation of sterling on 18 November from a basic rate of \$2·80 to the pound to \$2·40, or by 14·3 per cent, and from a market rate of about \$2·78¼ to about \$2·41, or by 13·5 per cent, reverses the internal and external positions. Instead of an economy in internal balance, but with a level of costs and prices too high for external balance, we have one where costs and prices are again competitive with those of other countries, but where the tendency towards internal over-expansion has been greatly intensified. This disturbance has occurred because the improvement in the balance of payments, and the change in the terms of trade needed to bring it about, instead of taking place gradually over a period of five years or more, are now likely to be concentrated into two or, at most, three. As the changes in the terms of trade and the balance of payments are once for all, the more rapidly they take place the greater the strain they put on the economy.

It was estimated (p. 141) that, to provide an adequate balance of payments on current account in a year when stocks are rising at a normal rate, we need to devote to the balance of payments and stock increase combined rather more than 2 per cent of gross national product at factor cost. To provide for the repayment of the large amounts borrowed in recent years on short term from abroad, the Government has put its objective higher than this, and is aiming at a favourable balance of £500 millions a year on current account. This, together with an average increase of about £360 millions a year in stocks, brings the combined total for the two to £860 millions, equal to about 2·6 per cent of G.N.P. at factor cost. In the third quarter of 1967 there were a current account deficit of £116 millions and a rise of £2 millions in stocks, giving a deficit of £114 millions in the total. Part of this deficit was seasonal, but even after adjustment it remains at about £75 millions for the quarter, or at a rate of £300 millions a year. If we add this deficit to the surplus of £860 millions we require, we find that we need a total improvement of £1,160 millions, or £290 millions a quarter, plus a small annual increase to keep the increase in stocks in line with rising output. It is clear that it would not be possible to achieve such an increase by the third quarter of 1968, but the effects of achieving it by the third quarter of 1969 are shown in Table 6.10(*a*) on p. 160. Table 6.10(*a*) also shows the effects of the worsening of the terms of trade, which is expected to involve a loss of real national income of about £300 millions, the whole of which will be borne in 1968. If we add this to half the required rise in balance of payments plus stocks, we find that we have absorbed £220 millions out of the growth of output. If output is permitted to rise only at the same rate as productive potential in order to prevent the reappearance of inflationary pressure, there would be left only about £70 millions of the 1967–8 rise of output to cover all other increases in expenditure.

During recent years the expenditure of public authorities on goods and services, on both current and capital accounts, has risen in real terms at an average rate of over 5 per cent a year, or well over the 4 per cent rate of increase allowed for in the over-optimistic National Plan. In the first nine months of 1967 it was running at over 7 per cent above the level of the corresponding period of 1966. In the absence of the cuts in expenditure announced since devaluation, it could have been expected to rise by at least 6 per cent between the third quarter of 1967 and the third quarter of 1968. This would have much more than absorbed the balance of resources available, and would have involved a fall of about £90 millions for the private sector as a whole. Even if private-sector fixed investment showed no rise, there would have been a fall of nearly 1½ per cent in personal consumption, implying, with the rise in population, a fall of about 2 per cent in consumption per head. Such a fall in consumption, in a year in which incomes from employment can be expected to rise by at least 4 per cent, could be secured only by an increase in taxation so large that it is doubtful if it would be politically acceptable.

The position in 1968–9 would not have been much better. Public expenditure would probably have risen less rapidly, while there would probably not have been any further deterioration in the terms of trade, but on the other hand allowance must be made for some rise in private-sector fixed investment. On balance, there seems no scope for any rise in personal consumption, so that consumption per head would fall again. Only in 1969–70, after the task of building up the balance of payments is assumed to have been completed, could consumption be expected to show any appreciable rise, though this would still leave the average standard of living well below its present level.

The cuts in government expenditure announced since devaluation will probably not do very much to reduce the pressure on resources by the third quarter of 1968, although, as Table 6.10(*b*) shows, they can be expected to have more effect in subsequent years. In the information so far available, it is difficult to distinguish reductions in expenditure on goods and services from changes in transfer payments, the effect of which, if any, will be mainly on consumption. But if we estimate that the increase in public-sector expenditure on goods and services will be reduced from 6 per cent to 5 per cent in 1967–8, and from 4 per cent to 2 per cent in subsequent years, we shall probably not be underestimating the effect of the cuts. Even after allowing for these, it seems that the standard of living would still have to fall substantially in 1968 and would show little rise in 1969, though it would improve sharply in 1970.

In these conditions, there would undoubtedly be very strong pressure on the Government, both in 1968 and in 1969, to allow

TABLE 6.10

PROJECTED USES OF NATIONAL PRODUCT

(changes between third quarters, at 1967 market prices)

(*a*) 3 PER CENT GROWTH OF OUTPUT; IMPROVEMENT IN BALANCE OF PAYMENTS OVER TWO YEARS; NO CUTS IN GOVERNMENT EXPENDITURE

	1967 to 1968		*1968 to 1969*		*1969 to 1970*	
	(%)	(£m.)	(%)	(£m.)	(%)	(£m.)
Consumers' expenditure	−1·4	−88	—	−3	+2·3	+145
Private-sector investment	—	—	+5·0	+43	+5·0	+45
Public-sector expenditure	+6·0	+161	+4·0	+114	+4·0	+118
Stocks plus balance of payments		+145		+148		+3
Gross national income	+2·2	+218		+302		+311
Terms of trade		75		—		—
Gross national product	+3·0	+293	+3·0	+302	+3·0	+311

(*b*) RATE OF INCREASE OF PUBLIC EXPENDITURE REDUCED

	1967 to 1968		*1968 to 1969*		*1969 to 1970*	
	(%)	(£m.)	(%)	(£m.)	(%)	(£m.)
Consumers' expenditure	−1·0	−61	+0·9	+55	+3·3	+206
Private-sector investment	—	—	+5·0	+43	+5·0	+45
Public-sector expenditure	+5·0	+134	+2·0	+56	+2·0	+57
Stocks plus balance of payments		+145		+148		+3
Gross national income	+2·2	+218		+302		+311
Terms of trade		75		—		—
Gross national product	+3·0	+293	+3·0	+302	+3·0	+311

(*c*) BALANCE OF PAYMENTS IMPROVEMENT SPREAD OVER THREE YEARS

	1967 to 1968		*1968 to 1969*		*1969 to 1970*	
	(%)	(£m.)	(%)	(£m.)	(%)	(£m.)
Consumers' expenditure	−0·2	−12	+1·6	+104	+1·7	+107
Private-sector investment	—	—	+5·0	+43	+5·0	+45
Public-sector expenditure	+5·0	+134	+2·0	+56	+2·0	+57
Stocks plus balance of payments		+96		+99		+102
Gross national income	+2·2	+218		+302		+311
Terms of trade		75		—		—
Gross national product	+3·0	+293	+3·0	+302	+3·0	+311

(*d*) 4 PER CENT GROWTH OF OUTPUT IN 1967–8

	1967 to 1968		*1968 to 1969*		*1969 to 1970*	
	(%)	(£m.)	(%)	(£m.)	(%)	(£m.)
Consumers' expenditure	+1·4	+86	+1·6	+107	+1·7	+110
Private-sector investment	—	—	+5·0	+43	+5·0	+45
Public-sector expenditure	+5·0	+134	+2·0	+56	+2·0	+57
Stocks plus balance of payments		+96		+99		+102
Gross national income	+3·2	+316		+305		+314
Terms of trade		75		—		—
Gross national product	+4·0	+391	+3·0	+305	+3·0	+314

output to expand by considerably more than productive potential. But, while a rise of 4 per cent in output might be tolerated for a single year, a 4 per cent rise for two years consecutively would bring the percentage of potential in use up to 96½, and would greatly accentuate the pressure of demand for labour, as well as running the risk of again destroying the reluctantly reviving confidence in sterling. A rise of 4 per cent for three years, bringing the percentage up to 97½, would fully re-create the conditions of excess demand from which the country suffered so disastrously between 1964 and 1966, and would certainly be followed by another sterling crisis.

The difficulties of 1968 and 1969 would be greatly mitigated if the rise in the balance of payments plus stocks could be spread over three years instead of two. Since there may well be a considerable replenishment of stocks in 1968, this would mean that the improvement in the balance of payments would take place mainly in 1969 and 1970. Such a development should be greeted with relief rather than alarm, for a gradual improvement based on stable costs and prices is preferable to a rapid improvement achieved by means of an over-rapid rise of output and likely to be subsequently reversed by renewed inflation and rising costs.

The effects of such a prolongation of the period of building up the balance of payments are indicated in Table 6.10(*c*). It would permit an appreciable improvement in the standard of living in 1969 at the cost of a slower improvement in 1970. It would, however, still leave an appreciable fall in the standard of living in 1968, when the country will be feeling the whole of the impact of the worsening of the terms of trade. To offset this the Government would probably be justified in allowing output to rise by 4 per cent for one year only. A rise of 4 per cent in output in 1967–8 (see Table 6.10(*d*)) would permit a modest rise in the standard of living and would still leave the percentage of potential in use at no more than 95½, or about the same as in the first nine months of 1962. This would probably enable Britain to keep her rise of costs and prices down to the level of most other industrial countries, and to preserve the competitive advantage gained by devaluation. But to turn an output rise of 4 per cent in 1967–8 into one of 3 per cent in 1968–9 and subsequent years would be no easy matter. Quite apart from the usual difficulties of the lateness, inadequacy and unreliability of statistical information, and the uncertainties about the amount and timing of the effects of fiscal and monetary measures, there is always a tendency, so long as there is an appreciable margin of unused productive potential, for a rise in output to accelerate. The authorities would therefore have to stand ready to take rapid action to check back consumption, either because of its own excessive rise or to leave room for a faster rise in private-sector investment. Nevertheless, there does seem to be a course, though a narrowly confined one, for the country to achieve the balance-of-payments surplus which it needs without imposing, in any year, a reduction in the standard of living of the great mass of the population.

7

Inflation and the Balance of Payments in the United Kingdom, 1952–67[1]

THERE is no doubt that, even after the ending of the inflations associated with the after-effects of the war of 1939–45 and with the Korean War, there has continued to be a substantial amount of inflation in the United Kingdom; there is also no doubt that, at least since 1958, there has been a considerable deterioration in the balance of payments on current account. This lecture attempts to examine the causes of the inflation and the connection between it and the balance of payments.

BALANCE OF PAYMENTS

A summary of the balance of payments on current account is shown in Table 7.1. Its markedly cyclical pattern will be discussed in a subsequent section. Here it is sufficient to note its worsening trend, as shown by comparing the averages for the three complete cycles which occurred between 1952 and 1966.

Between the first cycle, from 1952 to 1957, and the second, from 1958 to 1961, the worsening of the average balance, from plus £119 million to plus £61 millions, was caused entirely by a large rise in net government expenditure abroad than in net private-sector receipts from abroad. Between the second and third cycles, on the other hand, more than half the accelerated worsening in the balance of payments, from an average of plus £61 millions to one of minus £60 millions, was caused by the deterioration of the average balance of commodity trade from minus £162 millions to minus £232 millions. It must, however, be remembered that between the

[1] The third annual Scottish Economic Society Lecture delivered in the University of Dundee on 17 April 1968; first published in the *Scottish Journal of Political Economy*, xv (1968) 213–26.

TABLE 7.1

U.K. BALANCE OF PAYMENTS ON CURRENT ACCOUNT, 1952–67
(£m.)

	Commodity trade			*Net invisibles*			*Balance*
	Exports and re-exports	*Imports*	*Visible balance*	*Govt.*	*Other*	*Total*	
1952	2,769	3,048	−279	−61	+503	+442	+163
1953	2,683	2,927	−244	−66	+455	+389	+145
1954	2,785	2,989	−204	−131	+452	+321	+117
1955	3,073	3,386	−313	−138	+296	+158	−155
1956	3,377	3,324	+53	−175	+330	+155	+208
1957	3,509	3,538	−29	−144	+406	+262	+233
Average 1952–7	**3,033**	**3,202**	**−169**	**−119**	**+407**	**+288**	**+119**
1958	3,407	3,378	+29	−219	+537	+318	+347
1959	3,522	3,640	−118	−227	+494	+267	+149
1960	3,733	4,141	−408	−282	+432	+150	−258
1961	3,892	4,045	−153	−332	+490	+158	+5
Average 1958–61	**3,639**	**3,801**	**−162**	**−265**	**+488**	**+223**	**+61**
1962	3,994	4,098	−104	−359	+590	+231	+127
1963	4,287	4,370	− 83	−381	+580	+199	+116
1964	4,471	5,016	−545	−432	+575	+143	−402
1965	4,784	5,065	−281	−446	+617	+171	−110
1966	5,116	5,263	−147	−461	+577	+116	−31
Average 1962–6	**4,530**	**4,762**	**−232**	**−416**	**+588**	**+172**	**−60**
1967	5,023	5,673	−650	−449	+585	+136	−514

first and second cycles the heavy fall in prices of imported commodities in 1957–8 brought with it an average improvement of over 15 per cent in the terms of trade, while between the second and third cycles the average improvement was only 3½ per cent. Without the great improvement in the terms of trade, the balance of visible trade would almost certainly have shown a marked deterioration from the first to the second cycle, as well as from the second to the third.

Of the £650 millions adverse balance of commodity trade in 1967, something like £120 millions seems to have been due to the temporary holding-up of export shipments by the dock strike.

OUTPUT AND INCOMES

Inflation can perhaps be best defined as a faster increase in money incomes than in the supply of goods and services on which to spend them. It can conveniently be measured by an index of labour costs per unit of output, obtained by dividing an index of income from employment by an index of output. Such an index is shown in Table 7.2. It will be seen that between 1952 and 1967 output rose by about 50 per cent, or at an average rate of 2·9 per cent a

TABLE 7·2

OUTPUT AND INCOMES, 1952–67

	(1952 = 100)			*Percentage increase over previous year*		
	Output	*Income from employment*	*Labour cost per unit of output*	*Output*	*Income from employment*	*Labour cost per unit of output*
1953	104·0	105·7	101·8	4·0	5·8	1·7
1954	108·4	112·9	104·2	4·2	6·7	2·2
1955	112·0	123·4	110·2	3·4	9·3	5·5
1956	113·0	134·6	119·1	0·9	9·1	8·1
1957	114·9	142·4	123·8	1·7	5·8	4·1
Average 1952–7				**2·9**	**7·4**	**4·4**
1958	114·8	148·0	128·9	−0·1	3·9	4·0
1959	119·9	154·7	129·0	4·4	4·5	0·1
1960	126·4	166·4	131·6	5·4	7·5	2·9
1961	128·7	179·9	139·8	1·8	8·1	6·1
Average 1957–61				**2·9**	**6·1**	**3·1**
1962	130·2	189·4	145·4	1·2	5·4	4·2
1963	134·6	199·0	147·9	3·4	5·1	1·7
1964	142·8	215·0	150·6	6·1	8·1	1·9
1965	146·6	231·9	158·1	2·6	7·7	5·0
1966	148·9	246·7	165·7	1·6	6·4	4·7
Average 1961–6				**3·0**	**6·6**	**3·5**
1967	150·6	255·4	169·5	1·1	3·5	2·4
Average 1952–67				**2·9**	**6·5**	**3·6**

year, while income from employment rose by over 150 per cent, or 6·5 per cent a year, and labour cost per unit of output by nearly 70 per cent, or 3·6 per cent a year. Retail prices rose rather less than labour costs, by 57 per cent or an average of just over 3 per cent a year, presumably because there was, on balance, no rise in import prices.

The rates of increase in all three series show wide cyclical fluctuations, which will be discussed in a subsequent section.

LABOUR COSTS AND EXPORT PRICES

While British labour costs per unit of output rose by nearly 70 per cent between 1952 and 1967, prices of exports of British manufactures rose by only 26 per cent, as shown in Table 7.3. Between 1952 and 1961, with a rise of 40 per cent in labour costs, the rise in export prices was only 9 per cent, while between 1961 and 1967 a rise of 21 per cent in labour costs was accompanied by a rise of 15½ per cent in export prices. The disparity in 1952–61 between the rise in labour costs and the rise in export prices was no doubt partly accounted for by the fall in prices of imported materials, but it is difficult to escape the conclusion that it also involved a narrowing of profit margins, so that exporting became less attractive; while the faster rise in export prices after 1961 seems to have made British exports less competitive with those of other leading industrial countries.

CYCLICAL FLUCTUATIONS IN OUTPUT AND INCOMES

(1) *Simplified Model*

As Table 7.2 shows, there are marked cyclical fluctuations in the rates of increase of both output and incomes. In the first year of the cycle output rises little, if at all, and although incomes are rising relatively slowly, there is a moderate rise in labour costs. In the second and third years the rise in output accelerates greatly, and although incomes also rise faster the rise in labour costs is small. During the remainder of the cycle, however, the rate of rise of output declines while the rate of rise of incomes remains high. During this period, therefore, labour costs rise rapidly. We thus get alternating periods of rapidly and slowly rising labour costs.

TABLE 7.3

LABOUR COSTS AND EXPORT PRICES, 1952–67

(1952 = 100)

	U.K. labour costs per unit of output	*Dollar prices of exported manufactures*			
		U.K.	*U.S.A.*	*Germany*	*France*
1953	101·8	96	100	94	94
1954	104·2	95	99	90	93
1955	110·2	97	101	90	93
1956	119·1	100	105	93	98
1957	123·8	105	111	94	98
1958	128·9	106	112	94	96
1959	129·0	106	115	94	90
1960	131·6	108	118	95	93
1961	139·8	109	119	100	93
1962	145·4	111	119	101	93
1963	147·9	113	119	100	94
1964	150·6	115	119	101	97
1965	158·1	119	123	102	99
1966	165·7	124	122	105	102
1967	169·5	126	121		

The explanation of these fluctuations is facilitated by reference to a very simple model of the post-war business cycle, shown in Fig. 7.1. This starts from the assumption that, given existing resources, institutions, habits, attitudes and tastes, there is a physical limit to the amount that can be produced in any given year, however great the demand. The limiting factors can, no doubt, vary from time to time and from place to place; but in the United Kingdom since the war the main limiting factor has undoubtedly been labour, and especially skilled labour. This physical limit to output is usually called the country's 'productive potential'.

Productive potential fortunately rises from year to year, at a rate determined mainly by the rise in output per man-hour, but modified by changes in the number of hours worked and the size of the labour force. The rate of rise of output per man-hour seems to depend largely on the rate of technical improvement, including not only the introduction of new inventions but also the improvement of efficiency at all levels, especially at the level of management. The rate of investment in new fixed capital seems to be important, less for increases in the quantity of capital than for the higher rate of innovation which a higher rate of investment makes possible.

While output cannot, by definition, exceed the productive potential, it usually falls short of it. This shortfall, measured as a percentage, is called the margin of unused potential. There is evidence, some of which will be given later, that the rate of increase in money

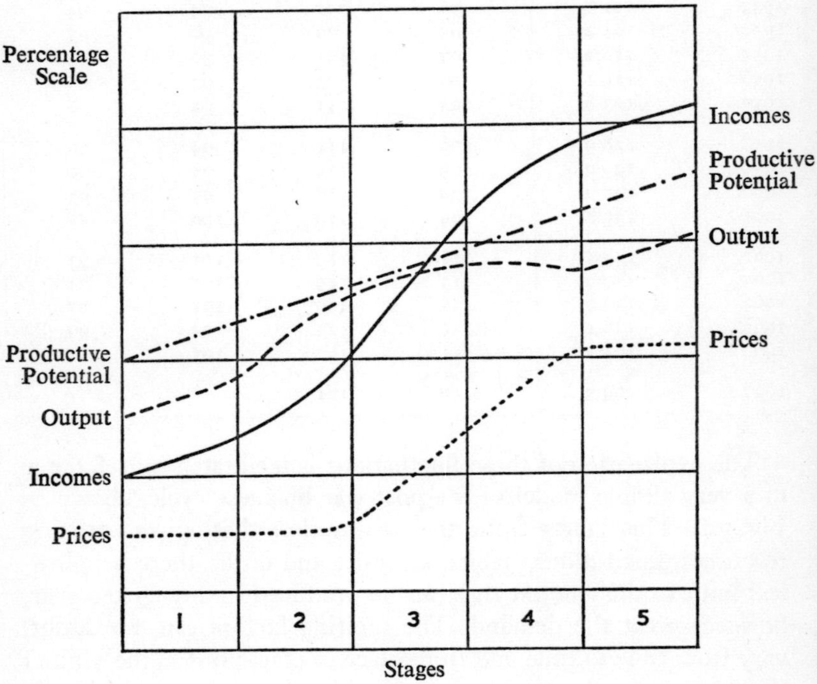

Fig. 7.1 The post-war business cycle

incomes varies inversely with the size of this margin, rising faster as the margin shrinks and more slowly as the margin expands. There must therefore be some margin at which incomes are growing at the same rate as productive potential. If, with this margin, output also grows at the same rate as productive potential, so that the margin is kept constant, the system is in balance, with factor cost prices stable (apart from the effects of changes in import prices). This is the position in stage 1 of Fig. 7.1.

This stage could, in principle, be permanent. Let us, however, assume that something occurs to accelerate the rise in incomes, either spontaneously or (as in post-war cycles) as the results of an increase in government expenditure or a reduction in taxation. To begin with, the existence of a margin of unused resources enables output to rise also, so that costs per unit of output rise little, if at all, and prices remain stable. We are now in stage 2, which is by far the pleasantest part of the cycle, with money incomes rising briskly, but with prices stable, so that real income and the standard of living show substantial improvement. It is at this stage of the cycle that Governments usually choose to hold their general elections.

Unfortunately stage 2 is necessarily temporary, and can last only so long as there remains a margin of unused potential. As soon as this margin approaches exhaustion, the rise of output must slow down to equality with that of productive potential, while the rapid rise in incomes is maintained or may even accelerate. This brings us to stage 3, in which money incomes are rising much faster than output, and costs and prices are rising rapidly, at a rate equal to the difference between the rate of rise of incomes and the rate of rise of output.

Stage 3, like stage 1, could in principle be permanent, provided that the country was prepared to tolerate continuous inflation. Governments have, however, frequently been obliged sooner or later to take steps to bring it to an end, as the result of a worsening balance of international payments. The effects of the cycle on the balance of payments seem to be of three kinds. The faster rise of output in stage 2 entails an increased demand for imported materials, and this in turn leads to increased imports. There is, however, a considerable time-lag before the additional imports arrive, so that imports do not rise much more than normally until towards the end of stage 2, or even the beginning of stage 3. The demand for imports is reinforced by a marked increase in the rate of stock accumulation, which usually occurs also about the beginning of stage 3. The worsening of the balance of payments as the result of the rise in imports usually causes the Government to introduce its first tentative measures to check the rise in incomes. These measures frequently accompany the slowing down in the rise of output caused by the exhaustion of the margin of unused potential. The check to output is therefore popularly attributed to the balance-of-payments difficulties, although in fact the rapid rise could not have continued for long even in their absence.

In stage 3, another effect on the balance of payments appears. This is the effect of running the economy with so little margin of potential that delays in delivery lengthen to the point where export orders are lost and urgent home needs are satisfied by increased imports. This effect persists, even after the rate of stock accumulation has returned to normal, so long as the margin of potential remains small.

The end of stage 3 has in practice not come until the continued inflation brings a loss of confidence in the stability of the currency, heavy withdrawals of sterling and loss of gold reserves. These ultimately force the Government to take effective measures to reduce the pressure of internal demand and to slow down the rise of incomes. This brings us to stage 4 of the cycle.

At first, the Government's disinflationary measures may well seem to do more harm than good, for though they have some effect in slowing down the rise of incomes, they also check the rise of output, so that the gap between the rate of rise of incomes and the rate of rise of output remains large and prices continue to rise. Stage 4, however, is, like stage 2, essentially temporary. When, in due course, the margin of unused potential has widened sufficiently to slow down the rise of incomes to equality with that of potential, output can be allowed to resume its rise, and the rise in prices ceases.

If output now rises at the same rate as potential, stage 5 is the same as stage 1, with the important difference that costs and prices are permanently higher. If the rise in costs and prices is greater than that of competitors in export markets, the competitiveness and profitability of exports will be impaired. The work of replacing the reserves lost during the previous cycle, or of repaying the foreign debts incurred, is therefore made more difficult. It is this third, and permanent, effect of allowing an over-rapid rise of output which has been the main cause of the deterioration of the British balance of trade, as shown in Table 7.1.

(2) *Experience since 1952*

We can now turn from our simplified model of the business cycle to the actual experience of the United Kingdom in recent years. In

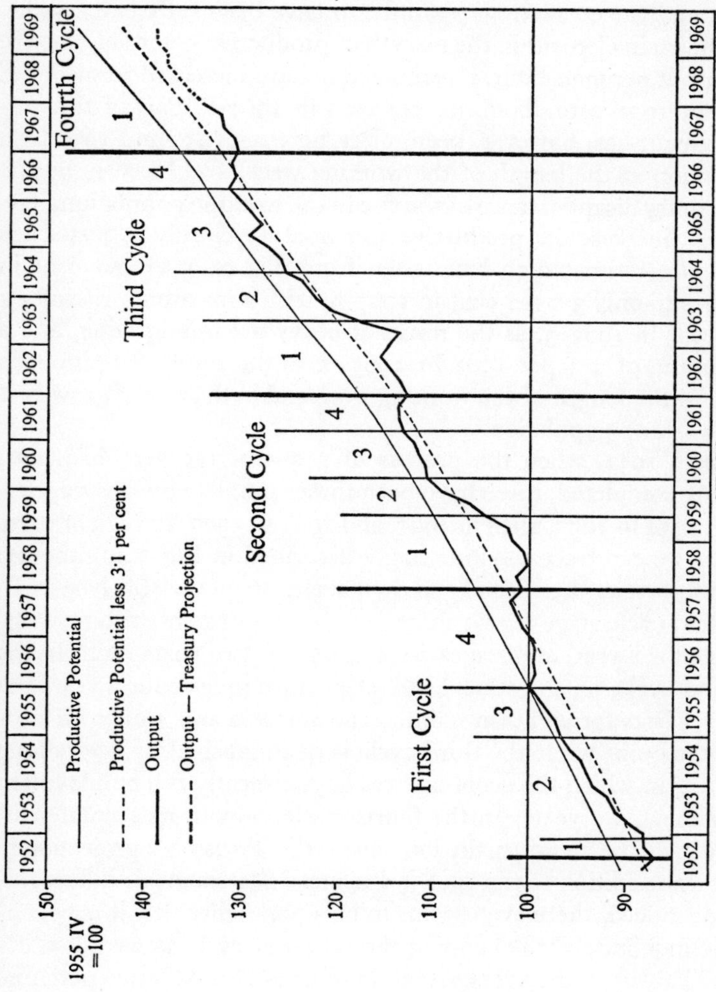

Fig. 7.2 *U.K. business cycles, 1952–68*

Fig. 7.2 an index of gross domestic product (measured from the output side) is related to an index of productive potential.[1] Both series are based on 100 for the last quarter of 1955, when the seasonally adjusted level of unemployment in Great Britain was 1·0 per cent, and the economy is assumed to have been fully employed.

The main element in the growth of productive potential, the rise in output per man-hour, is estimated to have increased from 1¾ per cent in 1951–2 to about 3·0 per cent in 1967–8. Part of this improvement has, however, been offset, between 1959 and 1966 by a reduction in the length of the working week, and recently by the temporary disappearance of the rise in the working population. The annual increase in productive potential (cyclically adjusted) is therefore estimated to have risen from just over 2½ per cent in 1951–2 to only 3·0 per cent in 1967–8, with a maximum rise of 3·4 per cent in 1962–3, as the result of heavy net immigration, and a minimum of 2·3 per cent in 1965–6, as the result of reductions both in the length of the working week and in the rate of growth of the working population.

Since 1952, when the process of post-war recovery had been mainly completed, there have been three complete business cycles, from 1952 to 1957, 1958 to 1961, and 1962 to 1966. In each of these cycles we can trace the four stages described in Fig. 7.1, although both the cycles themselves and their stages are of variable length. In the first cycle stage 1 is so short as to be almost non-existent, stage 3 lasts for a year, and stages 2 and 4 last for two years each. In the second cycle, on the other hand, stage 3 again lasts for a year, but stage 1 lasts for eighteen months and stages 2 and 4 only for nine months each; while the third cycle is distinguished by a very long stage 3, in which the economy was kept at nearly full employment for almost two years. In the fourth cycle, now in its second year, stage 1 will be an unusually long one if the Treasury's projection (a welcome addition to the 1968–9 Financial Statement) is in fact fulfilled; indeed, there even seems to be a possibility that it may continue indefinitely, thus ending the post-war cycle as we know it.

In Table 7.4, the average margin of unused productive potential in each stage of each cycle is related to the average annual rate of

[1] 1952–64: estimates from W. A. H. Godley and J. R. Shepherd, 'Long-term Growth and Short-term Policy', *National Institute Economic Review*, Aug 1964. 1965–8: author's estimates.

TABLE 7.4

CYCLICAL FLUCTUATIONS IN POTENTIAL, OUTPUT, INCOME AND LABOUR COSTS

	Average margin of potential	*Annual percentage increase in*		
		Output	*Income from employment*	*Cost per unit of output*
First cycle				
Stage 2. 1952(IV) to 1954(IV)	2·2	4·8	6·3	1·4
,, 3. 1954(IV) to 1955(IV)	0·6	3·3	9·0	5·4
,, 4. 1955(IV) to 1957(IV)	2·4	0·3	6·7	6·4
Second cycle				
Stage 1. 1957(IV) to 1959(II)	5·9	2·7	3·9	1·2
,, 2. 1959(II) to 1960(I)	3·1	7·4	6·9	−0·5
,, 3. 1960(I) to 1961(I)	1·9	2·2	8·5	6·1
,, 4. 1961(I) to 1961(IV)	2·8	−0·4	6·3	6·7
Third cycle				
Stage 1. 1961(IV) to 1963(II)	5·1	3·0	5·2	2·1
,, 2. 1963(II) to 1964(II)	3·0	6·5	8·3	1·8
,, 3. 1964(II) to 1966(I)	2·1	2·8	7·5	4·5
,, 4. 1966(I) to 1966(IV)	3·0	−1·3	2·0	3·3
Fourth cycle				
Stage 1. 1966(IV) to 1968(I)	4·8	3·4	6·4	3·0

increase in output, income from employment and labour cost per unit of output. In the first cycle, stage 1 is too short to be measurable, but in both the second and third cycles incomes during this stage rise relatively slowly, so that, although the rise in output is only moderate, the rise in labour costs is small. In stage 2 of all three cycles there is a rapid rise of incomes, but as output also rises rapidly the rise in labour costs remains small, or may even fall. In stage 3 of all three cycles the rise of output slows down as it approaches potential, while the rapid rise of incomes is maintained, or even accelerates. Labour costs therefore begin to rise rapidly. This rise in labour costs accelerates in stage 4 of the first two cycles, when the rise in incomes slows down but output rises little or falls. It will, however, be observed that in stage 4 of the third cycle the rise in incomes is very small, and in spite of a fall in output the rise in labour costs is smaller than in stage 3. This is the result of the wage-freeze, successfully imposed in the second half of 1966. The rise prevented in stage 4 of the third cycle seems, however, merely to have been postponed to stage 1 of the fourth cycle, in which incomes and labour costs have risen faster than in either of the previous two-cycles.

INCOMES AND THE MARGIN OF POTENTIAL

The foregoing analysis of the course of the post-war business cycle is sometimes criticised on the ground that the slowing down of the rise in incomes in stage 1 of the cycle may be due, not to the higher margin of potential (and the higher level of unemployment) but to the lagged effects of the preceding rises in the margin and in unemployment, and that there is no conclusive evidence that a continuation of the higher margin of potential would be accompanied by a continuation of the slow rate of income rise. We can obtain some lengthening of the periods for comparison if, instead of comparing stages 1 and 3 (the period of maximum and minimum margins of potential), we compare periods when the margin is above average with those when it is below. The average margin of unused potential during the years 1952–67 was 3·1 per cent, and this is indicated in Fig. 7.2. If we compare the periods between the points at which the 3·1 per cent margin curve cuts the output curve, we shall be comparing periods during which output has risen at the same rate as productive potential, thus avoiding the effects on productivity of exceptionally slow or fast rises of output. It is possible to find quarterly figures which approximate to nearly all the points of intersection; the only exception is in the second

TABLE 7.5

MARGIN OF PRODUCTIVE POTENTIAL AND INCREASES IN INCOMES AND LABOUR COSTS

	Average margin of unused potential	*Average annual percentage increases in*			
		Productive potential	*Output*	*Income from employment*	*Labour cost per unit of output*
1953(II) to 1957(III)	1·6	2·7	2·7	7·3	4·5
1957(III) to 1959(III/IV)	5·2	2·7	2·7	4·3	1·5
1959(III/IV) to 1961(III)	2·0	2·8	2·9	8·3	5·2
1961(III) to 1963(IV)	4·5	3·4	3·3	5·4	2·0
1963(IV) to 1966(III)	2·2	2·8	2·7	7·2	4·4

half of 1959, when we have to average the third and fourth quarters. The results of this investigation are shown in Table 7.5.

It will be seen that, in the three periods when the margin of potential was below average, incomes and labour costs rose much faster than in the two periods when the margin was above average. For the three periods with the margin below average, when the margin averaged 1·9 per cent, the annual rise in income from employment was 7·5 per cent and the annual rise in labour cost per unit of output 4·6 per cent. For the two completed periods with margins above average, the average margin was 4·8 per cent, the average rise in incomes 4·9 per cent and the average rise in labour costs 1·8 per cent.

CYCLICAL FLUCTUATIONS AND THE BALANCE OF PAYMENTS

It remains to examine the effects of cyclical fluctuations on the balance of payments. In Table 7.6 the annual surpluses or deficits of the balance of payments on current account are related both to the average margin of unused productive potential for the year and to the increase in stocks.

It will be seen that, up to 1966, the balance of payments on current account worsens as the margin of unused potential shrinks and improves as the margin widens. The only exception to this rule was in 1963, when a small decline in the balance of payments coincided with an unchanged average margin of potential. But in 1963 the average margin of potential was substantially increased by the effect on output of the severe weather in the first quarter: during the remainder of the year the margin shrank rapidly.

It is also noticeable that changes in the balance of payments generally coincide with opposite changes in the rate of stock accumulation, so that fluctuations in the combined total of the two are much smaller than those in either separately. The large adverse balances of 1955, 1960 and 1964 were all accompanied by exceptionally large increases in stocks, while the subsequent improvements in the balance of payments were accompanied by reduced rates of stock accumulation. The rapid rise in stocks, and the accompanying worsening of the trade balance, usually begin about nine months after the beginning of the upturn, early in the third

TABLE 7.6

MARGIN OF POTENTIAL, BALANCE OF PAYMENTS AND STOCK ACCUMULATION, 1952–67

	Average margin of unused potential	*Balance of payments*		*Stock accumulation*				*Balance of payment plus stocks*	
		Balance on c/a		*Public authority*	*Other*	*Total*			
Year	(%)	(£m.)	(% of G.N.P.)	(£m.)	(£m.)	(£m.)	(% of G.N.P.)	(£m.)	(% of G.N.P.)
1952	3·9	+163	+1·2	128	−78	50	0·4	+213	+1·5
1953	2·7	+145	+1·0	27	98	125	0·8	+270	+1·8
1954	1·1	+117	+0·7	−188	244	56	0·4	+173	+1·1
1955	0·5	−155	−0·9	−93	393	300	1·8	+145	+0·9
1956	2·2	+208	+1·1	−8	267	259	1·4	+467	+2·5
1957	3·2	+233	+1·2	18	220	238	1·2	+471	+2·4
Average 1952–7	**2·3**	**+119**	**+0·7**	**−19**	**191**	**171**	**1·0**	**+290**	**+1·7**
1958	6·0	+347	+1·7	28	83	111	0·5	+458	+2·2
1959	4·4	+149	+0·7	1	173	174	0·8	+323	+1·5
1960	1·8	−258	−1·1	42	644	602	2·6	+344	+1·5
1961	2·9	+5	0	4	330	334	1·4	+339	+1·4
Average 1958–61	**3·8**	**+61**	**+0·3**	**−2**	**307**	**305**	**1·3**	**+366**	**+1·6**
1962	4·7	+127	+0·5	11	72	83	0·3	+210	+0·8
1963	4·7	+116	+0·4	−30	258	228	0·8	+344	+1·3
1964	2·1	−402	−1·4	21	628	649	2·2	+247	+0·8
1965	2·2	−110	−0·4	24	392	416	1·3	+306	+1·0
1966	3·0	−31	−0·1	60	156	210	0·6	+179	+0·6
Average 1962–6	**3·3**	**−60**	**−0·2**	**17**	**300**	**317**	**1·1**	**+257**	**+0·9**
1967	4·8	−514	−1·5	112	−44	68	0·2	−441	−1·3

year of the cycle. Exceptionally, the accelerated rise in stocks and the development of the adverse balance of payments did not occur in the first cycle until 1955, the fourth year of the cycle. The reason for this exceptional delay is made clear in Table 7.6. In 1953 the Government were still holding very large stocks of commodities, originally accumulated against war-time emergencies, and they began to release these in 1954. The result was that, although private-sector stocks began to rise rapidly at the usual time, in 1954, this rise was more than offset by the fall in government stocks, so that total stock accumulation declined. The further decline in government stocks in 1955 served partly to offset the faster rise in private stocks, and probably prevented the adverse balance of payments of that year from being as large as it would otherwise have been. It is these large releases of government stocks which probably provide the explanation of the exceptional duration of the upturn in the first cycle, and perhaps also of why the economy was able to maintain a higher average use of potential than in either of the following cycles.

The year 1967 presents a major departure from the normal relationship between the margin of unused potential and the balance of payments, with a substantial widening of the margin coinciding with a marked worsening of the balance. This deterioration, which occurred entirely in the last quarter of the year, was due partly to the dock strike, which is estimated to have held up some £120 millions of exports, which appear in neither the trade nor the stock figures. Even after allowing for this, however, the total of balance of payments plus stocks fell by over £300 millions as compared with a rise of over £200 millions in 1962, the corresponding year of the previous cycle. Part of the 1967 fall can be explained by the deferment of imports from 1966, when the 10 per cent surcharge was not removed until the end of November; but a more important reason seems to have been that disinflation in the United Kingdom happened to coincide with even sharper business recessions in other European countries – a combination of events which made devaluation unavoidable.

In the absence of restrictions, the surplus on current account needed to finance exports of long-term capital can be put at rather more than £300 millions a year, or about 1 per cent of gross national product. Since the average annual increase in stocks is rather over 1 per cent of G.N.P., to provide for an adequate balance on current account in a year of average stock accumulation would absorb rather over 2 per cent of G.N.P., or over £700 millions a year. In order to provide for the repayment of the foreign short-term debts, including those to the International Monetary Fund, incurred during the past few years, the Government is aiming higher than this, at a current account surplus of £500 millions a year. With an average rate of stock accumulation, this would require nearly £900 millions a year, or over 2½ per cent of G.N.P., for balance of payments and stock accumulation combined, a proportion reached only once since 1952, in 1956. To achieve and maintain this proportion will in any case be difficult; if the margin of unused potential is allowed to fall below its present level it is likely to prove impossible.

8

Rise and Fall of Incomes Policy[1]

I. INTRODUCTION

MANY differences of opinion on matters of economic policy are caused by disagreements about the relative importance of ultimate ends. Thus those for whom increased equality of incomes is more important than a faster reduction of poverty achieved through more rapid growth of national product will naturally disagree with those who would give first priority to growth. And those who believe that extreme full employment is desirable, not only for its own sake but also because they think that rapid growth is possible only with some degree of inflation, will differ from those who believe that inflation is not only grossly unjust in its effects but also leads to the inefficient use of resources and the survival of inefficient managements, and thus in the long run tends to slow down growth.

The difference of opinion analysed in this Hobart Paper is, however, not of this sort. In this discussion both sides agree in giving first priority to the prevention of inflation, that is to say, to preventing rises in money incomes from outstripping the sustainable growth of output. We can therefore say that both sides agree on the necessity of an 'incomes policy'; where they disagree is about the way in which it can be carried out. One side believes that its common objective can best be achieved by inducing or compelling trade unions and employers' organisations to limit rises in wages and profits to rates which are compatible with the growth of output and with long-term price stability. The other holds the view that such a limitation, even if achieved, would be ineffective so long as there was an excess demand for labour and unnecessary if there were not. It believes that the only way to prevent wages and other incomes from rising too fast is to prevent the emergence of an

[1] First published as Hobart Paper 47 by the Institute of Economic Affairs, 1969.

excess demand for goods and services and an excess demand for labour. This requirement implies a level of unemployment as high as would be consistent with the absence of inflation with a fully competitive labour market. In this paper the attempt is made to examine the assumptions which lie behind the two views and to see how far they can be reconciled.

II. INFLATION

Causes of inflation

One, though not the only, cause of the disagreement is a conflict of opinion about the ways in which an inflation can start. Both sides agree that an inflation *can* be generated by an excessive rise in the demand for goods and services, whether by public authorities or by the private sector. This is the so-called 'demand inflation'. Where they disagree is on whether inflation can also be initiated by an excessive rise in wage rates forced on reluctant employers by the use of monopoly power by the trade unions. This is the so-called 'cost inflation'.

The way in which cost inflation is supposed to operate seems simple. Employers are forced by trade union pressure to grant increases in wage rates in excess of the rise in output per head. To maintain profit margins, employers are forced to increase prices. Their higher wages enable consumers to buy as much as before, in spite of the higher prices, while the increase in prices induces further demands by the unions – and so *ad infinitum*. If this view is accepted it follows that, if trade unions can be persuaded not to press claims for excessive wage increases, a cost inflation can be prevented from starting, and can be arrested even after it has begun.

This apparently simple description of a cost inflation, however, conceals some implicit assumptions which are by no means obviously true. First, if an inflation is to be *initiated* by rising costs, it must start from a condition where there is no excess demand – that is to say, a condition in which output is rising by no more than its sustainable rate of growth and incomes are rising no faster than output. In such conditions, no employer under pressure to grant an increase in wages larger than the expected increase in output per head can expect in advance to be able to pass on his higher costs in the form of higher prices without losing sales. He will therefore do his best to resist the demand, even at the risk of a strike, and if he is forced to accept it will consider that some marginal activity, either existing or projected, has been made unprofitable. He will therefore reduce his output and his demand for labour, or more probably in a growing economy with a rising working population, will not increase them as much as he would otherwise have done. He will also tend to restrict his plans for new investment below what they would otherwise have been, thus causing demand for investment goods to be less than expected and intensifying the effects on the profits of investment goods industries of their own wage increases. The higher wages, even if general, are thus achieved only at the cost of lower business profits and rising unemployment. Only if employers confidently expect that they will be able to pass on their higher costs in higher prices without losing sales will they maintain their output and demand for labour at the levels at which they would have stood but for the excessive increases in wages. Excessive wage demands will therefore be granted without rising unemployment *only if inflation is already expected.* 'Cost inflation' thus becomes the way in which inflations are perpetuated rather than initiated.

Inflation and the money supply

Second, even when an inflation is in progress, a further assumption is necessary to enable a cost inflation to continue indefinitely. Each rise in money incomes will require the holding of more money to finance consumption, while each rise in prices of physical assets, and of titles to their ownership, will require additional money to be held for financing investment. If the total quantity of money is not rising, or rising only as fast as real output, money will have to be withdrawn from idle balances in order to increase the average velocity of circulation, and this will be accompanied by a rise in interest rates.[1] As the excessively rapid rise of incomes proceeds,

[1] For a discussion of the relationship between changes in national money income, the quantity of money and the rate of interest, see Paish, *Studies in an Inflationary Economy* (Macmillan, 1962) chap. 1, p. 3, and *Long-term and Short-term Interest Rates in the United Kingdom* (Chapter 1 of the present volume).

the velocity of circulation must continue to increase, and rates of interest will continue to rise until they reach a level which checks the rise in investment and reduces the demand for labour. It is true that if the economy starts from a condition of high liquidity and low interest rates, such as existed in 1946, the process may continue for a long time before it is checked; but to make any inflation truly self-perpetuating requires a suitably expansionary monetary policy.

The checking of an inflation through a shortage of money, often slow, can of course be speeded up by government fiscal policy. If part of the money flow can be diverted, so that it ceases to create increased incomes on its next circuit, the rise in incomes can be directly prevented from perpetuating itself. Such a policy is effective even though it is implemented by a rise in indirect taxes, of which the impact effect is to raise prices further. Unlike higher prices received by producers, the proceeds of which are paid out in increased wages or dividends or used to finance increased investment, a rise in prices due to higher indirect taxes is not self-perpetuating, *provided the Government does not use the proceeds to increase its income-creating expenditure*. The effects of a larger budget surplus will be particularly marked if the increase is used to repay short-term government debt to the banks, thus reducing their liquid assets ratio and accelerating the rise in interest rates.

Trade unions as monopolists of labour

The case for a policy of attempting to induce the unions to refrain from pressing for wage increases in excess of the rise in output per head does not, however, depend only on a belief in the existence of cost inflation. Even if we believe that, in the absence of demand inflation, the unions cannot enforce excessive increases in wages without causing a rise in unemployment, there is still a strong case for trying to persuade them to limit wage increases to amounts which can be paid without either raising unemployment or raising prices. It pays a monopolist to raise his prices even at the cost of some reduction in the volume of his sales, and if the unions are in practice effective monopolists of the supply of labour, the same will be true of them.

When only a *minority* of occupations is effectively unionised, their unions can raise wages above the level at which they would stand in a fully competitive labour market at the cost of some reduction in the number employed in those occupations. They can do this without raising the general level of unemployment provided that people who are prevented from working in the unionised occupations are able to obtain employment in non-unionised occupations, thus driving wages there down below what they would have been in a fully competitive system. If, however, *all* occupations are strongly unionised, the general level of real wages can be kept above its competitive level only by forcing some potential workers out of employment altogether. It is possible, with suitable assumptions, to construct hypothetical cases where the combination of strong and ruthless unions with a Government determined to prevent inflation at any cost will result in an unemployment level of 5 per cent, or even 10 per cent.[1] On such assumptions those still employed would obtain so much larger a share of the national product, at the cost partly of people rendered unemployed and partly of profits, that the rise in the size of their share would more than offset the fall in the size of the product, so that, at least in the short run, they would be better off. Whether they would be better off also in the long run depends on what assumptions we make about the effects on the rate of growth of output.

It is probable, of course, that long before unemployment had reached the levels which, on these assumptions, would be needed to reconcile the unions' policies with the absence of inflation, the Government would find the rise politically intolerable. If they could not induce the unions to change their policies, the Government would be forced to seek a cure for the unemployment by increasing its expenditure or reducing taxes, thus expanding demand and profits, and at the same time raising prices and depriving union members already in employment of part of the rise in real wages which their rise in money wages would otherwise have brought them. This loss of real income would no doubt bring increased union pressure for wage increases and new measures to expand demand, and so on. In this sense it is perhaps possible to speak of a self-perpetuating 'cost-push' inflation.

[1] C. D. Finch, 'Some Problems of Wages Policy' (unpublished London University Ph.D. thesis, University of London Library).

III. APPROPRIATE AND INAPPROPRIATE 'INCOMES POLICIES'

Control of wages

If it could be shown that in practice there existed conditions in which the trade unions were able and willing, even in the absence of demand inflation, to force wage rates up well above the level which would have existed in a competitive labour market, there would be every argument for the Government to try to escape from the choice between inflation and a high level of unemployment by attempting to induce or compel the unions to abandon this use of their monopoly power. If the arguments in favour of a 'wages policy' were based on the need to escape from such a dilemma, the discussion would turn merely on whether the unions, in that economy at that time, were in practice able and willing to hold the rest of the community up to ransom in this way. Once the facts were ascertained, there could be no further argument about the desirability of a 'wages policy', though there could, of course, be differences of opinion about methods of implementation. These would no doubt depend largely on how much the activities of the trade unions were thought to be adding to the cost, in terms of unemployment, of preventing inflation. If it could be shown that this cost was anything like the theoretically possible 5 per cent or more, public opinion would probably support a revision of trade union law,[1] while if the additional unemployment were shown to be relatively small, the support for a revision of the law would be correspondingly less, and the methods used to implement a wages policy would probably continue mainly to be limited to attempts at persuasion.

It would, however, seem that some advocates of a 'wages policy' go further than this and wish, not only to prevent the level of unemployment (consistent with the absence of inflation) from

[1] An approach towards such a policy has recently been made by the publication of the White Paper *In Place of Strife* (Cmnd. 3888, Jan 1969), and by the proposal to introduce a bill into Parliament to implement some of its recommendations. While the approach has so far been tentative, it has aroused strong opposition from many trade unions and its effective implementation is doubtful. It may, however, provide a precedent for stronger measures later.

being forced above what it would have been in a competitive labour market, but also to hold down the levels of wages and of unemployment below their competitive equilibrium levels. The desirability of such a policy is doubtful, its practicability more than doubtful. If it could be implemented, its effects would be identical with those of an employers' monopoly designed to keep wage rates down below their competitive level, and therefore the exact opposite of the effects of a trade union monopoly designed to keep wages above their competitive level. People already employed would lose part of the wage increases they would otherwise have received, there would be less unemployment, and profits would increase.

(i) *Desirability* On the credit side of such a policy can be set a fall in unemployment which, if the policy could be really effectively enforced, might be to an extremely low level. In addition, a fringe of workers, who would otherwise not have taken paid employment at all, may be recruited, often on a part-time basis, to help meet the excessive demand for labour. Thus output, in the short run, would be higher than it would have been with a competitive labour market. At the same time there would be rises in retained profits, very possibly in tax yields and in the Government's budget surplus, and possibly also in personal saving, if the increase in the savings of those receiving higher dividends more than offset the fall in the savings of those receiving lower wages and salaries. Thus it is likely that total saving would rise, and with it total investment, so that there might be a tendency not only for current output to be higher but also for it to grow faster.

On the debit side can be set, not only the lower real incomes and standards of living of the bulk of the population, but also some loss of dynamism in the economy. In conditions in which wage rates are held artificially low and profits artifically high, it is easy for even inefficient managements to stay in business. The pressure for improved efficiency would thus be relaxed, and it is possible that, in spite of the higher rates of saving and investment, in the long run the rate of growth might be slower than in an economy where efficiency was enforced by competition.

(ii) *Feasibility* Of more practical importance than the desirability of such a policy is its feasibility. The difficulties of its inauguration are largely political, while those of its subsequent maintenance are mainly economic. The most obvious difficulty is to persuade the unions to agree to collaborate in keeping wages below the levels at which they would have stood in a competitive labour market. The only argument likely to have any effect in persuading them to accept such a policy is that this is the only way in which unemployment can be kept at an extremely low level without inflation. From the unions' point of view, the chief argument against it is that it would not only keep down wages but also increase profits; and it is likely that, in trying to meet this objection, the Government will offer measures, especially in the form of profit and price controls, which reduce the advantages and increase the disadvantages of the policy itself.

Control of prices or profits

There is no need to consider in detail proposals for the direct limitation of profits. To try to peg profit margins would mean that every firm would be working on a cost-plus basis and would lose all incentive to keep down costs. To attempt to fix all prices at levels which, given the agreed rates of wages, would give normal profits to the reasonably efficient firm would, perhaps, be slightly less impracticable; but if the attempt were successful it would frustrate the whole purpose of the operation. Unemployment can be kept abnormally low only by keeping the demand for labour abnormally high; and the demand for labour can be kept abnormally high only by keeping the employment of labour abnormally profitable. If profits are held down to the same level as would obtain with a competitive labour market, the demand for labour will be correspondingly restrained and unemployment will not fall.

It is more probable that the unions would be offered an agreement whereby, though profits would be allowed to rise, the extra profits would be removed by increased taxation. Such a policy, while technically enforceable, would add substantially to the debit side of a wages policy. A high rate of profits tax has no effect on the inefficient firm which is only just managing to stay in business, while it increases the difficulty of efficient firms in obtaining the finance they need for expansion, both from internal sources and, very probably, in the market. It also reduces the incentive to keep down costs, especially in the form of expenditures such as advertising, which may still be yielding some residual benefit to the firm after the tax, it may be hoped, is reduced or removed. No system could be better designed to slow down growth than one which keeps the inefficient alive, prevents the efficient from expanding, and reduces for everyone the incentive to keep down costs.

Alternatively, the Government might offer, as an inducement to the unions, higher taxation, not of all profits but of distributed profits only. Such a measure, while avoiding some of the disadvantages of heavy taxation of all profits, introduces some new ones of its own. A system of heavier taxes on distributed than on retained profits causes few problems for the well-established but slowly growing company, which is able to finance its capital requirements entirely out of its own resources, but makes it more expensive, and probable more difficult, for a fast-growing company, which needs more capital than it can save, to raise new capital in the market. It also tends to induce companies which are growing little if at all to retain profits for which they have no real use. It thus tends to cause capital to be used for less productive rather than more productive purposes.[1]

Difficulties of enforcement

Even if the political difficulties of obtaining the agreement of the trade unions could be overcome, it is unlikely that a wages policy would be successful for long in holding wages and unemployment below their competitive equilibrium levels. As time went on, the administration of the policy would encounter increasing difficulties. These would arise basically because an attempt was being made to hold wages below the level which would equate the demand for labour with the supply. Although such a policy might be effective for a limited period of emergency, an attempt to maintain it permanently would face the employers, the trade unions

[1] Both these fears have been realised in recent years by the introduction, with effect from 1966, of corporation tax, which causes distributed profits to be taxed much more heavily than retained profits, and by subsequent increases in its rate, which have raised the taxation of all profits.

and probably also the Government with difficulties so acute that they would lead ultimately to its breakdown.

With the demand for labour in excess of the supply at the price, many employers will find themselves with plant and equipment they cannot man, and profitable orders they cannot fulfil, for lack of labour. In these conditions it is extremely difficult, even by penal legislation, to prevent employers from attempting to attract the labour they need by methods which raise their labour costs. Even if standard wage rates can be effectively controlled, the other methods of offering higher remuneration, in cash or kind, are innumerable: guaranteed overtime; upgrading; piece-rates; merit payments; bonus or incentive schemes; profit-sharing; pension schemes and other fringe benefits; even improved canteen and other amenities. All these methods (however desirable some of them may be in themselves) add to labour costs, and to the real, even if not the money incomes, of employees; and all are means of bidding up the price of labour, the excess of which over standard wages rates is likely to become increasingly apparent the longer the wages policy is maintained.

The only effective way yet found to stop such a 'wage drift' is to have a firm agreement between employers for allocating scarce labour, so that they may no longer bid for labour in the market but must draw it from a central pool, sharing the labour shortages on some agreed basis. A scheme of this sort has been successfully operated for many years by the South African mining industry, with the object and result of keeping African wages below the level at which they would have stood if the mines had competed freely with each other for African labour. But it is difficult to believe that a scheme of this sort could be successfully established in this country.

Just as the employers' associations would find it increasingly difficult to ensure that their members kept the spirit, as well as the letter, of the agreement, so the trade unions would find it increasingly difficult to prevent their members from take unofficial action to secure wage increases larger than provided for. As time went on, the unions would find their branches and members increasingly out of sympathy with headquarters; the influence of shop stewards would grow at the expense of the union officials; unofficial strikes and other means of bringing pressure on employers would become increasingly common; breakaway unions would be formed with increasing frequency; and finally, unless the agreement had already broken down as the result of breaches by employers, the unions would be faced with the choice of abandoning the agreement or losing all control over their members.

The Government's difficulties, apart from those caused by unofficial strikes and by the threat of inflation as the agreement gradually collapsed, would arise largely from the need they would feel to set a good example to employers in the private sector, by keeping the agreement strictly in negotiations with their own employees and by trying to insist that local authorities and the managements of nationalised industries did the same. Consequently, as the agreement broke down in the private sector, employees' earnings in the public sector would tend to fall increasingly behind. The result would be not only unofficial strikes and other labour troubles, frequently in occupations where they would cause the maximum of inconvenience to the public, but also an increasing inability to recruit and retain labour for the public service in the numbers and of the quality required. This would be the more disastrous in that most of the really essential public services are now under the control of public authorities.

IV. THE EXTENT OF UNEMPLOYMENT

Even if we accept that, while there is every justification for trying to dissuade trade unions from using their monopoly power to force wage increases larger than would have been consistent with the absence of inflation in a competitive labour market, an attempt to keep wage increases below the equilibrium competitive level is of doubtful desirability and unlikely to succeed for long, we still need the answers to three further questions before we can formulate a practical policy:

1. What, in the existing situation, is the minimum level of unemployment consistent with the absence of inflation? (pp. 190–210).
2. What would that level be with a competitive labour market? (pp. 210–14).
3. How effective can we expect a policy of income restraint to be in closing the gap between the two? (pp. 215–23).

If the existing minimum level of unemployment were found to be substantially higher than the competitive level, it would imply that the unions were exercising considerable monopoly power, and that there would be a strong case for a wages policy; if, on the other hand, the difference were found to be small, the case for a wages policy would be correspondingly less strong. In no case, however, would an attempt be justified to keep wage increases and unemployment below the levels which would have existed in a non-inflationary competitive market.

How much unemployment to prevent inflation?

There is considerable evidence about levels of unemployment which in the past have accompanied various rates of inflation. To measure them we first of all have to decide on a suitable measure of inflation. To define inflation merely in terms of the rate of rise in prices, while broadly valid for large and prolonged changes, is not adequate for the relatively small and short-period movements with which we shall be mainly concerned. Market prices are likely at times to be affected, not only by changes in indirect taxation, but also by changes in import prices which, if accompanied by similar changes in export prices, do not affect the real national income. A better definition of inflation is that it is a condition in which money incomes are rising faster than the flow of goods and services on which to spend them – that is to say, faster than real national income. But this definition is also not adequate, for an accelerated rise of money incomes may be accompanied for a time by an equally rapid rise of output and real income, achieved by a higher level of employment.[1] But while the rise of incomes can continue indefinitely, and indeed is likely to accelerate as unemployment falls, the rapid rise of output can be maintained only until full employment is reached, and must then slow down to equality with the long-term trend of growth. The inflation, already implicit in the rapid rise of incomes, now comes into the open. The definition of inflation must therefore be a condition in which incomes are rising faster, not than the current rise in real national income, but

[1] For fuller descriptions of this process, see Paish, 'How the Economy Works' and 'Inflation and the Balance of Payments in the United Kingdom, 1952–67' (Chapters 6 and 7 of the present volume).

than the *maintainable* rise. Apart from the effects of changes in the terms of trade and in net income from foreign investments, this is the same thing as the maintainable rise of output, or, as it is sometimes called, the rise of productive potential.

In current discussion of the rate of rise of incomes, attention is often concentrated on rises in nationally negotiated wage rates.

TABLE 8.1

WAGE RATES, EARNINGS AND WAGE DRIFT: ALL MANUAL WORKERS, 1956–68

		Unemployment (per cent in G.B.)	*Average hourly wages rates*	*Average hourly earnings (excluding effects of overtime)*	*'Wage drift'*
			(Percentage change compared with corresponding month of previous year)		
1956	Apr	1·2	+8·3	+9·3	+1·0
	Oct	1·2	+7·6	+8·2	+0·6
1957	Apr	1·6	+2·5	+3·8	+1·3
	Oct	1·3	+5·6	+6·6	+1·0
1958	Apr	2·0	+4·8	+5·9	+1·1
	Oct	2·4	+3·7	+3·4	−0·3
1959	Apr	2·4	+3·5	+3·5	+0·0
	Oct	1·9	+1·4	+2·9	+1·5
1960	Apr	1·8	+4·4	+6·4	+2·0
	Oct	1·5	+5·5	+7·3	+1·8
1961	Apr	1·5	+6·2	+6·5	+0·3
	Oct	1·6	+6·4	+6·9	+0·5
1962	Apr	1·9	+4·1	+5·2	+1·1
	Oct	2·2	+4·2	+4·4	+0·2
1963	Apr	2·6	+3·6	+4·0	+0·4
	Oct	2·1	+2·3	+3·6	+1·3
1964	Apr	1·8	+4·9	+6·5	+1·6
	Oct	1·5	+5·7	+8·1	+2·4
1965	Apr	1·5	+5·3	+8·0	+2·7
	Oct	1·4	+7·3	+9·5	+2·2
1966	Apr	1·3	+8·0	+9·7	+1·7
	Oct	1·9	+5·6	+6·5	+0·9
1967	Apr	2·4	+2·7	+3·0	+0·3
	Oct	2·4	+5·3	+5·0	−0·3
1968	Apr	2·5	+8·6	+7·7	−0·9
	Oct	2·4	+6·0	+6·9	+0·9

Source: The source of cols 2 to 4 is Table B15 of the March 1969 issue of *Statistics on Incomes, Prices, Employment and Production.* The negative wage drift in April 1968 was due mainly to special factors.

The index of weekly wage rates has the advantage of prompt publication, but as an indication of income change it suffers from two disadvantages. One is that at certain periods wage increases have taken the form not only of rises in weekly rates but also of a reduction in the number of hours worked to earn them. Since 1958 the length of the standard working week has fallen by over 9 per cent, of which about half has been reflected in a fall in the number of hours worked, the remainder representing a rise in hours worked at overtime rates.

We can partly overcome the difficulty of changes in the length of the working week by using hourly, rather than weekly, wage rates, but the other objection to the use of the index of wage rates is more serious. There are times when changes in weekly, or even hourly, wage rates bear little relationship to changes in pay received. To some extent this is due to changes in the amount of overtime worked; but, even apart from this, there are times when hourly earnings rise much faster than hourly wage rates. This difference is known as 'wage drift', official estimates of which are shown in Table 8.1.

The figures of Table 8.1 have been used for the construction of Fig. 8.1, with the mid-points of the annual increases in wage rates and earnings conciding in time with the unemployment percentages.

Two main conclusions can be drawn from the table and diagram. The first is that there is a clear tendency for both wage rates and earnings to rise faster when unemployment is low, as in 1955–6, 1960–1 and 1964–6, than when it is relatively high, as in 1958–9, 1962–3 and 1967. The anomalous effects for 1966–8 resulting from the 'wage-freeze' imposed in the second half of 1966 will be discussed in a later section (pp. 215–23). And the second is that the faster rise in earnings than in wage rates is significant only in years of low unemployment; in years of high unemployment 'wage drift' is small or may even be negative. The rate of rise of earnings therefore fluctuates more widely than that of wage rates. Since it is wage rates, rather than earnings, which are determined by bargaining between trade unions and employers' organisations, it is for those who believe that excessive increases in earned incomes are caused by trade union pressure (cost-push inflation), rather than by an excessive demand for labour (demand-pull inflation), to explain both how it is that trade union pressure becomes effective only

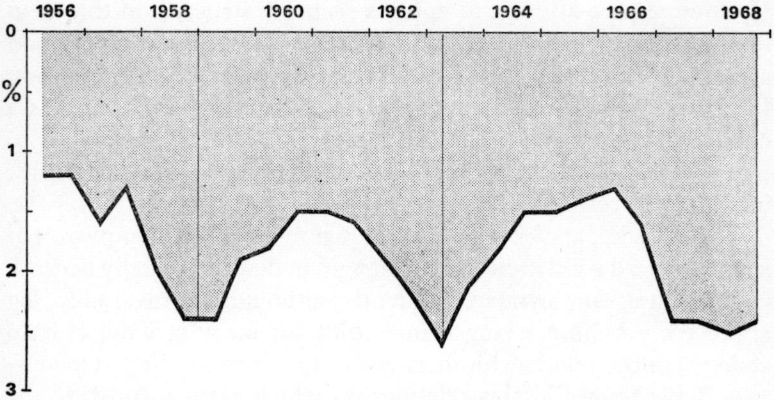

Fig. 8.1(a) *Unemployment in Great Britain, 1956–68 (source: Table 8.1)*

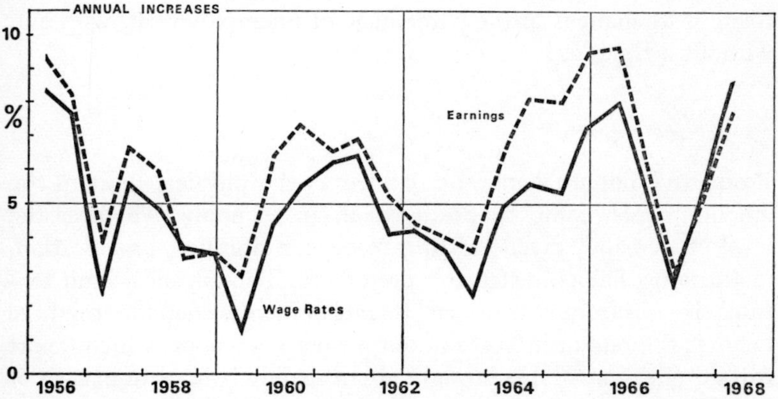

Fig. 8.1(b) Hourly wage rates and hourly earnings, 1956–68 (source: Table 8.1)

when unemployment is low and also why it is only at such times that 'wage drift' occurs.

From an inspection of Fig. 8.1 it would appear that, at one extreme, an unemployment level of about 1·3 per cent is accompanied by a rise in hourly earnings of 9 per cent or more, while at the other an unemployment level of about 2·4 per cent is accompanied by an earnings rise of only 3 to 4 per cent. Thus a decrease of about 1·1 per cent in unemployment is accompanied by a rise of about 5·5 per cent in earnings, an inverse ratio of about 5 to 1.

If, however, we attempt to apply a scale constructed on this ratio to all the data, we find that while in most years there is fairly good agreement, there are also a number of discrepancies (in addition to that in 1967–8, noted above), particularly in the early stages of a change of trend. Indeed, there are years (1957, 1960 and 1966) when earnings move in the same direction as unemployment, instead of inversely.

These discrepancies seem to arise mainly because unemployment is not always a good indicator of changes in demand, chiefly because changes in unemployment frequently, although not invariably, lag appreciably behind changes in output or, more strictly, behind changes in the relationship between output and productive potential. It is changes in this relationship which seem to provide the best indicator of changes in the pressure of demand against which to measure changes in the level of earned incomes. We shall also relate it to changes in the percentage of unemployment, with and without a time-lag.

Productive potential

Productive potential may be defined as the physical limit to the amount which could be produced in an economy, whatever the level of demand, given existing resources, abilities, organisation, institutions, habits, tastes and prejudices. This physical limit fortunately rises from year to year. Its rate of increase depends on three factors: the rate of increase of output per man-hour, which (apart from cyclical factors) is brought about mainly by a combination of improvements in the techniques of production and management with an increasing quantity of capital; the increase, if any, in the number at work; and the change, if any, in the average number of hours worked a year. All three factors fluctuate cyclically, with changes in the level of demand. Output per man-hour is probably also affected by changes in the number of hours worked per week, rising as the length of the working week falls, though not by enough, at the present number of hours, to prevent a net loss of output. For the purpose of the present calculation, it is assumed that a fall of 1 per cent in the number of hours worked raises output per man-hour by 0·4 per cent and reduces output (below what it would otherwise have been) by 0·6 per cent.

As well as fluctuating cyclically the number of hours worked a week has tended to fall, mainly since 1959, although only about half as fast as the standard hours fixed by agreement between employers and unions, the difference being made up by an increase in the number of hours worked at overtime rates. This fall in hours has tended to slow down the rise of productive potential. On the other hand the upward trend in the number at work has until recently helped to accelerate the rise in productive potential. Since 1966, however, the accident of the age distribution of the population has temporarily checked this rise, which is not likely to be resumed until towards the mid-1970s.

To eliminate the effects of cyclical changes in all three factors, we calculate their changes between periods at similar stages of business cycles, in which the pressure of demand is judged to be similar. Three such periods are the second quarters of 1952, 1959 and 1963. All three were periods of fairly high unemployment, just at the beginning of the upturns of output which inaugurated the new cycles. We cannot, however, make similar use of the second quarter of 1968, although unemployment was at almost exactly the same level as in the second quarter of 1963, because in it output was checked by a sharply disinflationary budget, whereas in 1963 it was encouraged by an expansionary one. Fortunately, however, we can make a valid comparison between the last quarter of 1962 and the last quarter of 1967. The increases in output per man-hour during these periods are shown in Table 8.2.

Particular of hours worked are unfortunately available only for industrial employees; we have to assume that the hours worked by the rest of the population have changed similarly. In addition,

TABLE 8.2

INCREASES IN OUTPUT PER MAN-HOUR, 1952–67

Year and Quarter	*Percentage unemployed*	*Employment*	*Hours worked*	*Man-worked hours*	*Output*	*Output per man-hour*
			(average 1958 = 100)			
1952(II)	2·21	97·1	98·9	96·0	86·2	89·8
1959(II)	2·17	100·4	100·7	101·1	103·8	102·7
1963(II)	2·36	104·0	97·7	101·6	116·5	114·8
1962(IV)	2·35	103·7	97·1	100·7	113·7	112·9
1967(IV)	2·47	104·5	95·3	99·5	132·4	133·1

Table 8.2 probably slightly underestimates the fall in hours worked and the rise in output per man-hour, since in addition to the fall in average weekly hours there has probably been some increase in the average length of the annual holiday.

To obtain estimates of the underlying growth of productivity, we must now adjust output per man-hour for the effects of changes

TABLE 8.3

PRODUCTIVITY AND PRODUCTIVE POTENTIAL

(percentage changes)

(*a*) PRODUCTIVITY

Period	*Output per man-hour*	*40 per cent of change in hours worked*	*Underlying productivity*	
			Period	*Average per annum*
1952(II) to 1959(II)	+14·4	+0·7	+15·2	+2·1
1959(II) to 1963(II)	+11·8	−1·2	+10·5	+2·5
1962(IV) to 1967(IV)	+17·9	−0·8	+16·9	+3·2

(*b*) PRODUCTIVE POTENTIAL

Period	*Underlying productivity*	*60 per cent of change in hours worked*	*Employment*	*Productive potential*	
				Period	*Average per annum*
1952(II) to 1959(II)	+15·2	+1·1	+3·4	+20·4	+2·7
1959(II) to 1963(II)	+10·5	−1·8	+3·6	+12·5	+3·0
1962(IV) to 1967(IV)	+16·9	−1.1	+0·8	+16·6	+3·1

in the number of hours worked (Table 8.3(*a*)). From the underlying growth of productivity we obtain the rise in productive potential by allowing both for the remaining effects of the changes in hours worked and for the changes in the number at work (Table 8.3(*b*)).

It will be seen that, whereas in the two earlier periods the rise in the number at work enabled the increase of productive potential substantially to exceed the increase of productivity, in 1962–7 the slowing down of the rise in employment, together with the further fall in hours worked, kept the rise of productive potential below that of productivity. It is this, together with the fall of output below productive potential in 1966–7, which until recently has prevented the much accelerated rise in underlying productivity from being reflected in a corresponding acceleration of the rise in output.

It remains to allocate the aggregate rises calculated for each period to particular years within the periods. Since the increases for each of the first two periods approximate extremely closely to those estimated for the same periods by Messrs W. A. H. Godley and J. R. Shepherd in their paper on 'Long-term Growth and Short-term Policy',[1] we can follow their estimates of annual increases. The closeness of the estimates made here for these two periods to those made by Godley and Shepherd with the use of much more sophisticated statistical methods encourages the hope that our estimates for 1962–7 will provide a valid extrapolation of their series.

Godley and Shepherd estimate that throughout the whole period from 1952 to 1963 the acceleration of the growth of underlying productivity was just under 0·08 per cent a year, raising the rate of increase from 1·85 per cent in 1952–3 to 2·63 per cent in 1962–3. If the same rate of acceleration had continued up to the end of 1967, the rise in productivity from the last quarter of 1962 to the last quarter of 1967 would have been about 15 per cent and the average annual increase for the period under 2·9 per cent, as against the increases of 16·9 per cent and 3·2 per cent shown in Table 8.3. It would seem, therefore, that the acceleration in 1962–7 has been considerably faster than in 1952–63. If we assume a constant rate of acceleration from the second quarter of 1963 onwards, this must have been about 0·25 per cent a year, bringing the annual rise in productivity up from Godley and Shepherd's estimate of 2·63 per cent in 1962–3 to about 3·7 per cent in 1966–7 (Table 8.4).

To convert the estimated annual increases in productivity into increases in productive potential we have to allow for the effects of changes in hours worked and in the size of the population at work. The number at work rose by 2·8 per cent between the last quarter of 1962 and the last quarter of 1965, and then fell cyclically by 2 per cent, leaving a net increase of 0·8 per cent. Since the rise in the population of working age had levelled off by early 1966, we

[1] *National Institute Economic Review*, Aug 1964.

TABLE 8.4

ANNUAL INCREASES IN PRODUCTIVITY AND PRODUCTIVE POTENTIAL, 1962–7
(percentage changes between 4th quarters)

Years	*Productivity*	*25 per cent of change in standard hours*	*Employment*	*Productive potential*
1962–3	+2·70	—	+0·4	+3·10
1963–4	+2·95	−0·2	+0·2	+2·95
1964–5	+3·20	−0·6	+0·2	+2·80
1965–6	+3·45	−0·3	—	+3·15
1966–7	+3·70	—	—	+3·70
Total, 1962–7	+16·9	−1·1	+0·8	+16·6
Annual average	+3·2	−0·2	+0·1	+3·1

allocate the whole of the non-cyclical rise of 0·8 per cent to the first three years of the period. Hours worked rose by 1·4 per cent from 1962 to 1963, and then fell by 3·3 per cent from 1963 to 1967, a net fall of 1·9 per cent. Since much of this movement is clearly cyclical, we cannot use the annual changes in hours worked to calculate yearly changes in productive potential. As, however, standard hours (which do not fluctuate cyclically) fell by 4½ per cent during the period, as against a net fall of 1·9 per cent in hours worked, we can deduct 25 per cent of the fall in standard hours instead of 60 per cent of the fall in hours worked. This concentrates the fall in hours on the three middle years of the period. As the result of these adjustments, the steady rise we have assumed for productivity is concealed for productive potential until 1966–7.

In combination with the estimates of Godley and Shepherd for 1952–63, we now have estimates for a continuous series of annual percentage increases of productive potential from 1952 to 1967. We now have only to choose a common base date in order to relate this series to that of output. A convenient date is the last quarter of 1955, when the seasonally adjusted percentage of total unemployment in Great Britain fell to 1 per cent, and the economy can be regarded as having been fully employed – or rather, full employment is defined as a condition similar to that which existed in the last quarter of 1955. By interpolation between the annual figures, we can estimate a quarterly index of productive potential.

TABLE 8.5

PRODUCTIVE POTENTIAL, OUTPUT, AND INCOME FROM EMPLOYMENT, 1952–68

Year and quarter	*Productive potential*		*Output (4th quarter 1955 = 100)*	*Use of potential (%)*	*Income from Employment*	
	4th quarter 1955 = 100	*Increase over previous year*			*4th quarter 1955 = 100*	*increase over previous year (%)*
1952						
I	90·5		88·1	97·3		
II	91·1	+2·7	87·1	95·6	77·1	+6·9
III	91·7		88·1	96·1		
IV	92·3		88·2	95·6	79·7	+7·3
1953						
I	92·9		89·8	96·7		
II	93·5	+2·6	90·8	97·1	82·3	+6·7
III	94·1		91·8	97·6		
IV	94·7		93·2	98·4	83·5	+4·8
1954						
I	95·3		93·7	98·3		
II	95·9	+2·6	94·7	98·6	87·1	+5·8
III	96·5		95·7	99·2		
IV	97·2		96·8	99·6	89·9	+7·7
1955						
I	97·9		97·1	99·2	93·6	
II	98·6	+2·8	98·0	99·4	95·6	+8·6
III	99·3		98·8	99·5	98·0	
IV	100·0		100·0	100·0	100·0	+10·1
1956						
I	100·6		99·2	98·6	102·2	+9·2
II	101·3	+2·7	99·4	98·1	105·1	+9·9
III	102·0		99·2	97·3	106·8	+9·0
IV	102·7		99·7	97·1	108·0	+8·0
1957						
I	103·4		100·8	97·5	109·4	+7·0
II	104·0	+2·7	101·2	97·2	110·3	+4·9
III	104·8		101·7	97·0	112·8	+5·6
IV	105·5		100·7	95·5	113·8	+5·3
1958						
I	106·2		101·3	95·4	115·6	+5·6
II	107·0	+2·9	100·1	93·5	114·8	+4·1
III	107·7		100·8	93·6	115·9	+2·8
IV	108·5		101·9	93·9	117·8	+3·5
1959						
I	109·2		102·2	93·6	118·9	+2·9
II	110·0	+2·8	104·9	95·4	120·5	+4·9
III	110·7		106·3	95·8	122·0	+5·3
IV	111·4		109·1	97·9	124·7	+5·8
1960						
I	112·1		110·6	98·7	126·2	+6·1
II	112·8	+2·6	110·8	98·2	129·7	+7·7
III	113·5		111·4	98·1	132·7	+8·8
IV	114·3		112·1	98·1	133·9	+7·5
1961						
I	115·1		113·0	98·2	137·4	+8·9
II	115·9	+2·7	113·4	97·8	141·0	+8·6
III	116·8		113·7	97·3	142·6	+7·4
IV	117·8		112·8	95·8	143·9	+7·5

TABLE 8.5—*continued*

Year and quarter	Productive potential: 4th quarter 1955 = 100	Productive potential: Increase over previous year (%)	Output (4th quarter 1955 = 100)	Use of potential (%)	Income from employment: 4th quarter 1955 = 100	Income from employment: Increase over previous year (%)
1962						
I	118·7		113·3	95·4	146·2	+6·4
II	119·7	+3·3	114·6	95·7	148·2	+5·0
III	120·7		115·7	95·9	150·3	+5·4
IV	121·7		115·0	94·5	151·0	+5·0
1963						
I	122·7		(113·7)	(92·7)	(151·7)	(+3·7)
II	123·8	+3·4	117·8	95·2	154·9	+4·5
III	124·6		120·3	96·6	158·1	+5·2
IV	125·5	+3·1	122·2	97·4	161·1	+6·6
1964						
I	126·4		123·4	97·6	164·4	+8·4
II	127·3		125·0	98·2	167·5	+8·2
III	128·2		125·6	98·0	170·9	+8·1
IV	129·2	+2·9	126·8	98·1	174·4	+8·2
1965						
I	130·1		128·3	98·6	176·5	+7·4
II	131·0		127·4	97·3	180·8	+8·0
III	131·9		128·3	97·3	184·8	+8·1
IV	132·8	+2·8	129·5	97·5	188·5	+8·1
1966						
I	133·8		130·3	97·4	192·4	+9·0
II	134·8		130·1	96·5	196·1	+8·5
III	135·9		130·4	96·0	197·9	+7·1
IV	137·0	+3·2	129·6	94·6	195·8	+3·9
1967						
I	138·2		130·3	94·3	196·3	+2·1
II	139·5		131·6	94·3	200·0	+2·0
III	140·7		132·0	93·8	203·1	+2·6
IV	142·0	+3·7	133·7	94·2	207·1	+5·8
1968						
I	143·2		135·6	94·7	211·0	+7·4
II	144·4		135·0	93·5	214·0	+7·0
III	145·6		136·6	93·8	217·2	+7·0
IV	146·8	+3·4	138·1	94·1	220·0	+6·3

The extrapolation of the index beyond the end of 1967 will necessarily be tentative until sufficient evidence has accumulated to enable us to calculate changes between comparable periods. The underlying rate of growth of productivity, which was estimated to have increased from 2·7 per cent in 1962–3 to 3·7 per cent in 1966–7, may well continue to accelerate further. On the other hand, the causes of the acceleration in the past few years may prove to have been temporary, and the rate of growth of productivity may decline again. In either case, however, the rate of growth is unlikely to diverge so rapidly from the 1966–7 growth rate of 3·7 per cent as to make any significant difference in the level of the index of potential for the next year or two, and it seems safest to assume a continuation of a 3·7 per cent rate of growth of productivity until more evidence is available.

It is even more difficult to know how to treat the fall of about 0·3 per cent in the (seasonally adjusted) level of employment in the first three quarters of 1968. We can regard the fall either as cyclical, in which case it does not reduce the rate of growth of

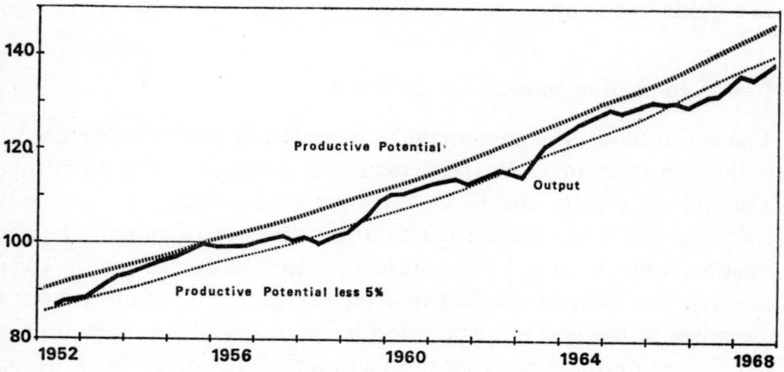

Fig. 8.2 Productive potential and output, 1952–68 (last quarter of 1955 = 100) (source: Table 8.5)

productive potential below the rate of growth of productivity, or as non-cyclical, in which case the rate of increase of potential is correspondingly reduced. In Table 8.5 and Fig. 8.2, the fall in employment has been treated as non-cyclical, and the estimated increase in productive potential between the last quarter of 1967 and the last quarter of 1968 has therefore been reduced to 3·4 per cent. This figure is rather above that suggested by the Department of Economic Affairs,[1] whose estimate of an average growth of productive potential of just under 3 per cent a year from 1966 to 1972 is obtained by extrapolating the average annual increase of output per head achieved in 1960–6, with an adjustment for changes in

[1] In *The Task Ahead* (H.M.S.O., 1969).

hours worked, but without any allowance for acceleration either within or after that period. It is, however, well within the margin of error the D.E.A. allow themselves.

In Table 8.5 and Fig. 8.2 the quarterly index of productive potential is compared with the quarterly index of gross domestic product, as measured from the output side. The output index is available quarterly in official statistics from the first quarter of 1955. For earlier years, it has been derived from the official annual figures with the help of the index of industrial production. In Fig. 8.2, a line indicating a 95 per cent use of potential has been added as a guide to the eye.

Use of productive potential as indicator

The variations in the percentage of potential in use provide a useful indication of changes in the pressure of demand in the economy. They show clearly the three business cycles between 1952 and 1967. In the first, from 1952 to 1958, the use of potential rises steadily from about 95½ per cent in 1952 to over 99 per cent in 1954 and 100 per cent in the last quarter of 1955. The disinflationary measures at the end of 1955 bring it down sharply in 1956, but it remains at above 97 per cent until a new disinflation in 1957 brings it down to under 94 per cent in 1958.

In the second cycle, from 1958 to 1962, the expansionist budget of 1959 brings a rapid rise in the use of potential, from under 94 in the first quarter of 1959 to over 98 per cent throughout 1960. The 1961 disinflation then brings it down to under 96 per cent in the first three quarters of 1962 and to under 95 per cent in the fourth. Except in the first quarter of 1963 (when an apparent percentage of 92·7 per cent is explained by the exceptional weather), it does not fall as low as in 1958–9.

The third cycle begins with the expansionist budget of 1963, which raises the percentage of potential in use again to over 98 per cent in 1964–5. The third cycle differs from the second in the longer duration of the period of high demand, and it is not until 1966 that the percentage of potential in use falls much below 97½. Since 1966, however, prolonged balance-of-payments difficulties have forced the Government to keep the use of potential continuously below 95 per cent for over two years – longer than in any previous cycle. It can probably be said that the cyclical process is now, at least temporarily, in abeyance.

Use of productive potential and rate of rise of incomes

If we express the index of output as a percentage of the index of productive potential, the resultant series of the percentage of potential in use provides us with the measure of the pressure of demand in the economy for which we are looking. We now need figures for the rate of rise of incomes with which to compare it. The most appropriate index for this purpose seems to be that of income from employment, easily calculated from the table of factor incomes included in the National Income estimates. This series has the advantage that, like those of productive potential and output, and unlike those of wage rates and earnings, it includes the effects of changes in the number employed. It is also more comprehensive than the index of weekly earnings, since it includes both the pay of the armed forces and employers' contributions to social security and private pension funds. The official figures are available quarterly from the beginning of 1955, while for earlier years it is possible to break the official annual figures down into half-yearly estimates with the help of the index of weekly earnings.

This index of income from employment, also based on 100 in the last quarter of 1955, is included in Table 8.5, together with a series showing its percentage increase over the corresponding quarter of the previous year. In Fig. 8.3(*a*) this last series is compared with that of the percentage of productive potential in use. The two curves are drawn so that a 2 per cent increase in income from employment is equated with a 92 per cent use of potential, and a 10 per cent increase in income with a 100 per cent use of potential. It will be seen that on these scales the two curves move closely together, both in the size and in the timing of the fluctuations. The two main discrepancies are in 1952–4, when the rise in incomes lags more than a year behind the rise in the use of potential, and in 1966–8, when the curve is distorted by the effects of the wage-freeze in the second half of 1966. In spite of these temporary discrepancies, the correlation between the curves is as high as 0·75.

The relationship between the percentage of productive potential

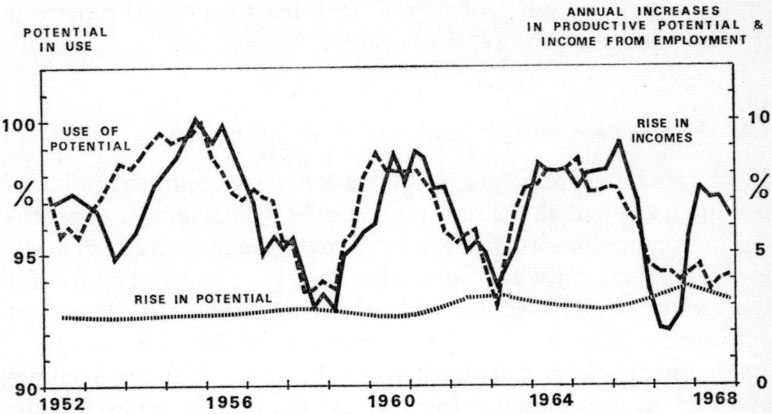

Fig. 8.3(a) *Productive potential and income from employment, 1952–68 (source: Table 8.5)*

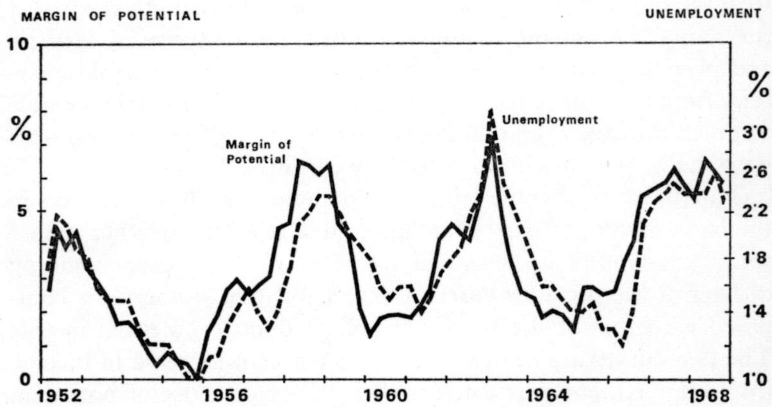

Fig. 8.3(b) *Margin of potential and unemployment, 1952–68 (source: Table 8.9)*

in use and the rate of increase of income from employment can also be shown in a different way. In Table 8.6 are shown the results of averaging the percentages of potential in use and the percentage increases in income in periods with given maximum or minimum uses of productive potential. The results range from an annual average income rise of 3·8 per cent for the 13 quarters in which the use of potential was 95 per cent or less to an average rise of 8·4 per cent in the 20 quarters in which the use of potential was over 98 per cent. The average use of potential in all the 66 quarters from the beginning of 1952 to the second quarter of 1968 was 96·7 per cent, and the average rise in employment income 6·6 per cent.

The results shown in Table 8.6 are plotted in Fig. 8.4. It will be seen that all the points lie very close to a straight-line curve, from a 2 per cent rise in income with a 92 per cent use of potential to a 10 per cent rise in income with a 100 per cent use of potential. As,

TABLE 8.6

USE OF PRODUCTIVE POTENTIAL AND RISE IN INCOME FROM EMPLOYMENT

Number of quarters	*Percentage of potential in use*		*Average annual percentage increase in income from employment*
	Range	*Average*	
13	95 and under	93·9	3·8
25	96 ,, ,,	94·7	4·9
30	97 ,, ,,	95·0	5·3
46	98 ,, ,,	95·9	5·9
66	All	96·7	6·6
53	Over 95	97·4	7·4
41	,, 96	98·0	7·7
36	,, 97	98·2	7·9
19	,, 98	98·7	8·4

however, we do not have data for an average use of potential much below 94 per cent or as high as 99 per cent, we should probably be wise to restrict our conclusions to uses of potential within this range, where we seem to have a reasonably reliable relationship between the percentage of productive potential in use and the rate of increase of income from employment. The reliability of the relationship naturally increases with the length of the period observed; for short periods, it can be considerably disturbed by random variations, especially of output.

It is sometimes asserted, although without much empirical evidence, that the reason for the slower rise of incomes when the margin of unused potential is high is not that the margin is high but that it has recently risen; and it is claimed that, if the margin were maintained at that level for a prolonged period, incomes would begin to rise faster without any fall in the margin. Unfortunately, apart from the period 1967–9, when comparison is invalidated by other factors (see pp. 215–23), a high margin of productive potential has never been maintained for long enough to test this contention. The longest period recorded before 1967 was from the second quarter of 1958 to the first quarter of 1959 (when the average margin of unused potential was 6·3 per cent and the annual rate of rise of income 2·9 per cent), which is too short to be conclusive.

It may, however, be possible to test this contention in another way. If it is true that, at any given average margin of unused productive potential, incomes rise more slowly when the margin has risen than when it has fallen, we should expect to find, at similar average margins of potential, that incomes would rise faster on the

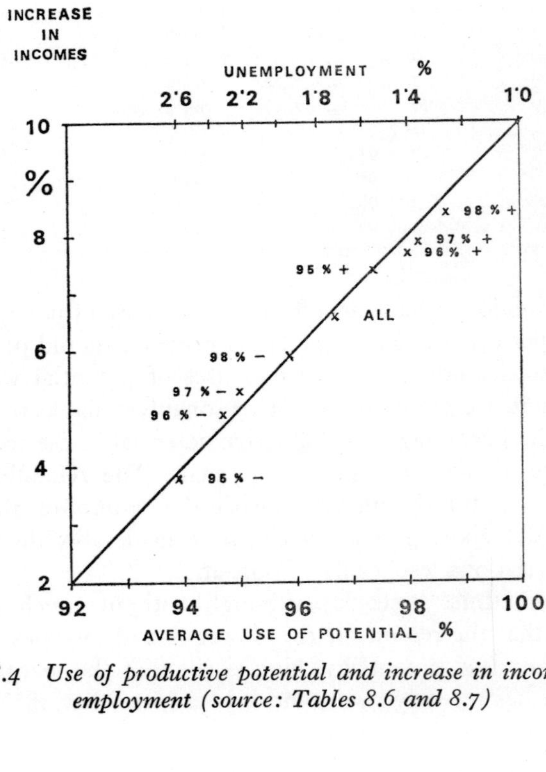

Fig. 8.4 Use of productive potential and increase in income from employment (source: Tables 8.6 and 8.7)

upswing of the cycle than on the downswing. This we can test from the data given in Table 8.5.

Since 1952 there have been three cyclical upswings, from the fourth quarter of 1952 to the fourth quarter of 1954, from the first quarter of 1959 to the first quarter of 1960 and (if we omit the snowy first quarter of 1963) from the last quarter of 1962 to the second quarter of 1964. There have also been three downswings, from the fourth quarter of 1955 to the second quarter of 1958, from the first quarter of 1961 to the fourth quarter of 1962 and from the first quarter of 1966 to the third quarter of 1967. We cannot, however, use this last downswing, for much of it was affected by the 'wage-freeze' of 1966.

In each cycle the top of the upswing was separated from the beginning of the downswing by a 'plateau', on which the use of potential was maintained at a consistently high level for an appreciable period. The average margins of potential and the average annual increases of income in each of these three stages of the cycle are shown in Table 8.7.

It will be seen that there is no significant difference between the upswing and the downswing of the cycle in the relationship between the average margin of unused potential and the average rate of income rise, though both periods are strongly differentiated from both the plateaus and the single (usable) example of a 'valley' in 1958–9.

Margin of unused productive potential and unemployment

The only step now needed to complete this section of the discussion is to relate the use of productive potential to the percentage of unemployment. This task is greatly facilitated by a recent paper by Mr J. R. Shepherd, of the Treasury, entitled 'Productive Potential and the Demand for Labour'[1] In this he concludes, *inter alia*, that

> at the margin, an increase of 1 per cent in output gives rise to a fall of about $\frac{1}{5}$ per cent in unemployment when unemployment is already low (300,000), but to a fall of about $\frac{1}{3}$ per cent when unemployment is somewhat higher (500,000).[1]

If we interpret an increase of 1 per cent in output as the equivalent of a fall of 1 per cent in the margin of unused potential, and assume

[1] *Economic Trends*, Aug 1968.

TABLE 8.7

MARGINS OF POTENTIAL AND INCREASES OF INCOMES

Period	*Average margin of unused potential*	*Average annual per cent increase in income from employment*
Upswings		
1952 (iv) to 1954 (iv)	2·1	6·3
1959 (i) to 1960 (i)	3·7	5·7
1962 (iv) to 1964 (ii)	4·0	6·4
Total upswings	3·1	6·2
Plateaus		
1954 (iv) to 1955 (iv)	0·5	9·7
1960 (i) to 1961 (i)	1·7	8·1
1964 (ii) to 1966 (i)	2·2	8·3
Total plateaus	1·6	8·6
Downswings		
1955 (iv) to 1958 (ii)	3·0	6·0
1961 (i) to 1962 (iv)	3·7	6·2
Total downswings	3·3	6·1

a ratio of 1 to $\frac{1}{4}$ at intermediate levels of unemployment, we can construct (Table 8.8) a rough scale between various percentage margins of unused potential and the equivalent percentages of unemployment.

TABLE 8.8

UNEMPLOYMENT AND THE MARGIN OF UNUSED PRODUCTIVE POTENTIAL

Unemployment		*Margin of unused potential*	*Unemployment*		*Margin of unused potential*
Number ('000)	%		*Number ('000)*	%	
233	1·0	0·0	443	1·9	4·0
256	1·1	0·5	466	2·0	4·3
280	1·2	1·0	489	2·1	4·6
303	1·3	1·5	513	2·2	4·9
326	1·4	2·0	536	2·3	5·2
349	1·5	2·4	559	2·4	5·5
373	1·6	2·8	582	2·5	5·8
396	1·7	3·2	606	2·6	6·1
419	1·8	3·6	629	2·7	6·4

TABLE 8.9

MARGIN OF UNUSED POTENTIAL AND UNEMPLOYMENT, 1952–68

Year and quarter	*Margin of unused potential* (%)	*Unemployed percentage (seasonally corrected)* Calculated *Current*	*Calculated Lagged 6 mths.*	*Actual*
1952				
I	2·7	1·6	1·3	1·7
II	4·4	2·0	1·4	2·2
III	3·9	1·9	1·6	2·1
IV	4·4	2·0	2·0	1·9
1953				
I	3·3	1·7	1·9	1·8
II	2·9	1·6	2·0	1·6
III	2·4	1·5	1·7	1·5
IV	1·6	1·3	1·6	1·5
1954				
I	1·7	1·3	1·5	1·5
II	1·4	1·3	1·3	1·3
III	0·8	1·2	1·3	1·2
IV	0·4	1·1	1·3	1·2
1955				
I	0·8	1·2	1·2	1·2
II	0·6	1·1	1·1	1·1
III	0·5	1·1	1·2	1·0
IV	0·0	1·0	1·1	1·0
1956				
I	1·4	1·3	1·1	1·1
II	1·9	1·4	1·0	1·1
III	2·7	1·6	1·3	1·3
IV	2·9	1·6	1·4	1·2
1957				
I	2·5	1·6	1·6	1·5
II	2·8	1·6	1·6	1·4
III	3·0	1·7	1·6	1·3
IV	4·5	2·1	1·6	1·4
1958				
I	4·6	2·1	1·7	1·7
II	6·5	2·7	2·1	2·1
III	6·4	2·7	2·1	2·2
IV	6·1	2·6	2·7	2·4
1959				
I	6·4	2·7	2·7	2·4
II	4·6	2·1	2·6	2·2
III	4·2	2·0	2·7	2·0
IV	2·1	1·4	2·1	1·9
1960				
I	1·3	1·3	2·0	1·8
II	1·8	1·4	1·4	1·6
III	1·9	1·4	1·3	1·5
IV	1·9	1·4	1·4	1·6

Year and quarter	*Margin of unused potential* (%)	*Unemployment percentage (seasonally corrected)* Calculated *Current*	*Calculated Lagged 6 mths.*	*Actual*
1961				
I	1·8	1·4	1·4	1·6
II	2·2	1·5	1·4	1·4
III	2·7	1·6	1·4	1·5
IV	4·2	2·0	1·5	1·7
1962				
I	4·6	2·1	1·6	1·8
II	4·3	2·0	2·0	1·9
III	4·1	1·9	2·1	2·2
IV	5·5	2·4	2·0	2·4
1963				
I[1]	(7·3)	(3·0)	1·9	(3·2)
II	4·8	2·2	2·4	2·5
III	3·4	1·8	(3·0)	2·3
IV	2·6	1·6	2·2	2·1
1964				
I	2·4	1·5	1·8	1·8
II	1·8	1·4	1·6	1·6
III	2·0	1·4	1·5	1·6
IV	1·9	1·4	1·4	1·5
1965				
I	1·4	1·3	1·4	1·4
II	2·7	1·6	1·4	1·4
III	2·7	1·6	1·3	1·5
IV	2·5	1·5	1·6	1·3
1966				
I	2·6	1·5	1·6	1·3
II	3·5	1·8	1·5	1·2
III	4·0	1·9	1·5	1·4
IV	5·4	2·4	1·8	2·1
1967				
I	5·7	2·5	1·9	2·3
II	5·7	2·5	2·4	2·4
III	6·2	2·6	2·5	2·5
IV	5·8	2·5	2·5	2·4
1968				
I	5·3	2·3	2·6	2·4
II	6·5	2·7	2·5	2·4
III	6·2	2·6	2·3	2·6
IV	5·9	2·5	2·7	2·3

[1] The figures for the first quarter of 1963 are effected by exceptional weather.

In Table 8.9 and Fig. 8.3(*b*) this scale is used to compare the margin of unused potential with the percentage of unemployment. It will be seen that, on this scale, the magnitude of the fluctuations in unemployment corresponds closely to that of fluctuations in the margin of unused potential. But the table and diagram also indicate that changes in unemployment frequently, though not invariably, lag behind changes in the margin. For the whole period the lag seems to average about six months, but its duration varies appreciably from period to period. In 1957, 1960 and 1964 the lag seems to have been considerably more than six months, while in 1952–3 and in 1961–2 it was almost nonexistent. In the early part of 1966 the lag seems to have been unusually long, but the gap was closed by the rapid rise of unemployment in the last quarter of that year and since then it seems to have been very small, although there were some signs of its reappearance in 1968.

If we insert in Fig. 8.4 the scale showing the relationship between margin of unused potential and the percentage of unemployment given in Table 8.8, we can read off the annual percentage by which (apart from time-lags) income from employment could be expected to increase at any given level of unemployment, ranging from 4 per cent a year with unemployment at about 2·6 per cent to 9 per cent with unemployment at 1·2 per cent.

A comparison of Figs. 8.3(*a*) and (*b*) shows that in the only years, 1958 and 1967, in which the rate of rise of income from employment slowed down to equality with the rate of growth of productive potential, the percentage of unemployment was about 2½ per cent. So long as the growth of productive potential is maintained at about its present rate, this seems to be the lowest level of unemployment which is, in the long run, compatible with an absence of inflation.

V. EQUILIBRIUM UNEMPLOYMENT IN COMPETITIVE LABOUR CONDITIONS

In the previous section it was estimated that, in the period from 1952 to 1966, the minimum percentage of unemployment compatible with a rise in income from employment of 4 per cent a year was about 2½ per cent. In this section an attempt is made to arrive at some idea of the percentage which would be compatible with this objective in a strictly competitive labour market.

We start with the assumption that, in a competitive market, a balance between the demand and supply of labour would result in stable efficiency earnings – that is to say, in a rise of real earnings equal to the rise of productivity, at present estimated at about 3·7 per cent a year. We can obtain some idea of the amounts of labour currently offered and demanded from the official monthly figure of registered unemployment and vacancies, although the unemployment figures cannot be used as they stand. It would seem that the published figures for unemployment considerably exaggerate the number available to fill the vacancies shown as available. There are two main reasons for this discrepancy. The first is that there is a large number of those registered as unemployed who suffer from various personal disabilities which make them 'likely to spend long periods on the registers even when the local demand for labour is high'. The number of such people is put by a survey conducted by the Ministry of Labour in 1964 at about 180,000, or 0·8 per cent of the total number of employees, both employed and unemployed (*Ministry of Labour Gazette*, April 1966).[1] Since many of the disabilities are connected with age, the rise since 1964 in the number of men in the age-group immediately below retirement age may have increased the number suffering from disabilities.

Regional unemployment variations

The other main reason for the difference between the number shown as unemployed and the number effectively able to occupy the situations vacant is the regional distribution of unemployment. Even if the number left after deducting those suffering from disabilities were exactly equal to the number of vacancies, a large surplus of vacancies over unemployment in some regions, accompanied by a large surplus of unemployment over vacancies in others, would be likely to lead to a faster rise in employment income per person employed than if unemployment and vacancies were in balance in each separate region. This is because an excess supply of labour is less effective in forcing earnings per head down than an excess demand in forcing them up. Instead of forcing earnings per head down until the excess supply of labour is absorbed, the excess supply has the effect merely of causing persistent local unemployment, with the unemployed neither able to obtain work locally at

[1] On this point, see also J. B. Wood, 'Labour Management and Economic Growth', *Il Politico* (University of Pavia) XXXII 1 (1967) 167.

TABLE 8.10

UNEMPLOYMENT AND VACANCIES, OCTOBER 1968

Regions	*Total unemployment*		*Non-effectives*		*Effective unemployment*		*Vacancies*		*Effective unemployment* less *vacancies*	
	('000)	(%)	('000)	(%)	('000)	(%)	('000)	(%)	('000)	(%)
A. High unemployment										
North of England	64	4·84	21	1·59	43	3·25	11	0·83	32	2·42
Scotland	79	3·59	35	1·59	44	2·00	17	0·77	27	1·23
Wales	39	3·90	12	1·20	27	2·70	8	0·80	19	1·90
Total A.	182	4·02	68	1·50	114	2·52	36	0·80	78	1·72
B. Moderate unemployment										
North-West	71	2·40	30	1·01	41	1·39	34	1·15	7	0·24
South-West	34	2·52	10	0·74	24	1·78	15	1·11	9	0·67
Midlands	74	1·99	17	0·46	57	1·53	41	1·10	16	0·43
Yorkshire and Humberside	53	2·60	14	0·69	39	1·91	21	1·03	18	0·88
Total B.	232	2·31	71	0·71	161	1·60	111	1·10	50	0·50
C. Low unemployment										
London and South-East	88	1·55	27	0·48	61	1·07	77	1·36	−16	−0·29
East and South	47	1·68	14	0·50	33	1·18	44	1·57	−11	−0·39
Total C.	135	1·60	41	0·49	94	1·11	121	1·43	−27	−0·32
Total Great Britain	549	2·36	180	0·78	369	1·58	268	1·15	101	0·43

the maintained wage rates nor sufficiently mobile to fill the excess of vacancies in other regions.

The 1964 survey found that the 180,000 unemployed whose disabilities prevented them competing effectively for the work available were distributed very unequally between regions, with the highest percentages in the regions of highest unemployment. In Table 8.10, the non-effectives are deducted from the unemployment totals for each region in October 1968, a month requiring very little seasonal adjustment. The resultant totals of effective unemployment are then compared with the number of vacancies in each region. We find that in the three regions with the highest unemployment percentages, the North of England, Scotland and Wales, there was a surplus of effective unemployment over vacancies of 78,000, or 1·7 per cent of the number of employees. In the regions with moderate unemployment, North-West and South-West England, the Midlands and Yorkshire and Humberside, there was an effective unemployment surplus of 50,000, or 0·5 per cent; and in the low unemployment regions, South-East England (including London) and South and East England, there was a deficiency of effective unemployment of 27,000, or 0·3 per cent. For Great Britain as a whole there was a surplus of effective unemployment of just over 100,000, or slightly more than 0·4 per cent.

We cannot just deduct this surplus from the October 1968 total of unemployment to obtain an estimate of what the total of equilibrium unemployment would be in conditions of competition and equal regional distribution. To do this we must estimate what the totals of unemployment and vacancies would be if they were exactly equated in each region separately. The results of this calculation are shown in Table 8.11. It will be seen that effective unemployment and vacancies are then equated at a total of 280,000, which, if we add back the non-effectives, gives a total of unemployment of 460,000, or just about 2 per cent.

The difference of 120,000, or 0·5 per cent, between this total and the total of 580,000, or 2·5 per cent, which we have estimated to be necessary in present conditions in order to prevent income from employment from rising by more than 4 per cent a year, is due to the combined effects of three factors: the unequal distribution of unemployment; the net monopoly power of labour; and government action to restrain the rise of incomes. In the following paragraph an attempt is made to estimate how much of this effect is due to each of these three causes.

To begin with, it can be said with some confidence that it is not wholly due to regional maldistribution. In October 1968, with unemployment at 549,000, or substantially below the required level of 580,000, the labour deficiency of 27,000 in the South-East, East and South was probably considerably more than offset by the

TABLE 8.11

EQUILIBRIUM UNEMPLOYMENT

Regions	*Effective unemployment*[1]		*Non-effective unemployment*		*Total unemployment*	
	('000)	(%)	('000)	(%)	('000)	(%)
A. North of England	12	0·91	21	1·59	33	2·50
Scotland	21	0·95	35	1·59	56	2·54
Wales	12	1·20	12	1·20	24	2·40
Total A.	45	1·00	68	1·50	113	2·50
B. North-West	36	1·21	30	1·01	66	2·22
South-West	17	1·26	10	0·74	27	2·00
Midlands	47	1·27	17	0·46	64	1·73
Yorkshire and Humberside	26	1·27	14	0·69	40	1·96
Total B.	126	1·25	71	0·71	197	1·96
C. London and South-East	69	1·22	27	0·48	96	1·70
East and South	40	1·43	14	0·50	54	1·93
Total C.	109	1·29	41	0·49	150	1·78
Total Great Britain	280	1·20	180	0·78	460	1·98

[1] Equals vacancies.

combined labour surplus of 128,000 in other regions. With total unemployment at 580,000, or 2·5 per cent, a deficiency of under 20,000 in the South-East, East and South would have been much more than outweighed by a surplus of over 140,000 in other regions. If we make a guess and say that a deficiency of labour in the South-East, East and South would just be balanced by a surplus of twice the size in other regions, we arrive at a figure for total unemployment of about 510,000, or 2·2 per cent, leaving 70,000, or 0·3 per cent, as the net effect of labour monopoly and government restraint.

Incomes restraint in 1966–8

We must now turn to the postponed discussion of the anomalous fluctuations in the rate of increase of incomes in 1966–8, revealed in Table 8.5 and Fig. 8.3(*a*). The period starts with the disinflationary measures of July 1966, which raised the margin of unused productive potential to a level which in previous cycles had been accompanied by a rise of employment incomes of not much more than 4 per cent a year. These measures have been accompanied by vigorous attempts to exercise direct government control over rises in both incomes and prices.

With a margin of unused potential sufficient to equate the supply of labour with the demand, the attempt to restrain rises in wage rates can be seen as an effort to offset the effects of labour monopolies, whether of trade unions or of unofficial groups of key workers. There is therefore no question of the desirability of the objectives of the policy, but merely of its methods and effectiveness. The case for an attempt to exercise direct control over prices is more arguable. Throughout the period, and especially since the devaluation of sterling in November 1967, government policy has been directed, not merely to slowing down the rise of incomes, but also to diverting large amounts of resources, mainly from personal consumption, to exports and to private-sector investment. The impact effect of a rise in prices of consumption goods and services is to reduce the volume of consumption. This check to consumption is not offset by a rise in profit margins and business profits, for much of it goes in taxation, some finances increased business investment, and only a small percentage goes to finance increased consumption by shareholders, and that after a long delay. The more successful the control of prices, the larger the increases in taxation needed to prevent consumption from rising.

On a longer view, however, there are two arguments on the other side. One is that the inability to take the easy way of offsetting higher costs by higher prices may force firms to try to offset them by increased efficiency. The other, which is probably more important, is that if employers know that they will, or even may, not be allowed to increase their prices, they may be induced to put up a stronger resistance to demands for wage increases. While these arguments may have some weight for home-based industries serving the home market, they seem to have little relevance to increases of rents, of prices charged for imports, or of prices charged by public authorities and nationalised industries.

Other measures which have accompanied the attempt to control wages and prices have been the heavier taxation of companies, tax discrimination against distributed profits and direct limitation of dividend increases. The purpose of these measures is mainly political; their effect on consumption is minimal.

Until April 1968, the office administering the prices and incomes policy was the Department of Economic Affairs. The responsibility was then transferred to the Ministry of Labour, re-named the Department of Employment and Productivity. Both before and after the transfer, these departments made considerable use of the National Board for Prices and Incomes, first established in April 1965. Up to July 1968, something like a hundred cases had been referred to the Board, almost equally divided between those concerned with prices and those concerned with incomes. The number of cases referred to the Board has increased over time, with almost half the total in the year ending July 1968. Reports have been issued on about three-quarters of the cases referred. Some of the recommendations of the Board have been implemented, especially those dealing with prices. Others have been ignored, or made the basis of a compromise. In a number of their reports, the Board have made recommendations for improving the productivity of the industries concerned. It is possible that these may have contributed to the rise in productivity discussed earlier in this paper, although the acceleration seems to have started some time before the Board was established.

Effectiveness of incomes policy

The extent to which the Board's recommendations have been implemented has depended largely on government policy. Since 1965 this has gone through four phases. Until July 1966, government action was limited to consultation and persuasion; this seems to have been no more effective than similar tactics by earlier Governments. In the second half of 1966, however, the Government successfully enforced an almost complete standstill on wages and prices, followed by an almost equally successful period of severe restraint in the first half of 1967. Since these measures of restraint were combined with a marked disinflation and a widening of the margin of unused potential, there seemed reason to hope that their effects would be permanent. Unfortunately, the return to voluntary methods in the second half of 1967 showed that the increases had been merely postponed, and in the second half of 1967 and the first quarter of 1968 incomes rose sharply. In March 1968, another strongly disinflationary budget was accompanied by a new period of severe restraint, to last until the end of 1969, with wage increases supposed to be limited to a maximum of $3\frac{1}{2}$ per cent a year, except where a larger increase could be justified by clear evidence of increased productivity.

As is shown in Table 8.12, the Government succeeded in limiting the rise in income from employment between the second quarter of 1966 and the second quarter of 1967 to no more than 2·0 per cent, as compared with rises of 4·1 per cent and 5·0 per cent respectively in the comparable periods of 1957–8 and 1961–2. In 1967–8, however, the postponed rises in wages brought the increase in employment income up to 7·0 per cent, as against 4·9 per cent in 1958–9 and 4·5 per cent in 1959–60. For the two years together, the 1966–8 rise of 9·2 per cent in employment incomes was exactly the same as in 1957–9, and slightly lower than the rise of 9·7 per cent in 1961–3.

After the second quarter of 1968 no valid comparison with previous cycles is possible, since the second halves of both 1959 and 1963 were periods of rapidly rising output and rapidly falling margins of unused productive potential, while in the second half of 1968 output is estimated to have risen only slightly faster than productive potential.

The rise in income from employment seems to have slowed down appreciably in the second half of 1968, from an increase of 7 per cent between the second quarter of 1967 and the second quarter of 1968 to an annual rate of $5\frac{1}{2}$ per cent (seasonally corrected) between the second and fourth quarters of 1968. Nevertheless, the rise remained a good deal faster than that of about 4 per cent a year which might have been expected, even without an 'incomes policy', on the basis of earlier experience with an average margin of unused productive potential of 6 per cent.

TABLE 8.12

PERSONAL INCOME AND CONSUMPTION, 1957–68
(Second quarters: £m. seasonally adjusted)

	Margin of unused potential	At current prices: Income from employment	At current prices: Total personal income	At current prices: Disposable income	At current prices: Consumption	Index of consumption prices (1958 = 100)	At 1958 prices: Income from employment	At 1958 prices: Total personal income	At 1958 prices: Disposable income	At 1958 prices: Consumption
1957–59										
1957	2·8	3,201	4,360	3,813	3,608	96·7	3,310	4,509	3,943	3,732
1958	6·5	3,331	4,612	3,975	3,804	100·2	3,324	4,603	3,967	3,797
Average 1957–8	4·2									
Increase 1957–8		130	252	162	196		14	94	24	65
do. %		4·1	5·8	4·2	5·4	3·6	0·4	2·1	0·6	1·7
1959	4·6	3,495	4,901	4,247	4,021	100·2	3,488	4,891	4,239	4,013
Average 1958–9	6·1									
Increase 1958–9		164	289	272	217		164	288	272	216
do. %		4·9	6·3	6·8	5·7	—	4·9	6·3	6·9	5·7
Average 1957–9	5·1									
Increase 1957–9		294	541	434	413		178	382	296	281
do. %		9·2	12·4	11·4	11·4	3·6	5·4	8·5	7·5	7·5
1961–3										
1961	2·2	4,096	5,722	4,899	4,436	103·8	3,946	5,513	4,720	4,275
1962	4·3	4,300	5,996	5,086	4,730	108·3	3,970	5,536	4,696	4,368
Average 1961–2	3·7									
Increase 1961–2		204	274	187	294		24	23	−24	93
do. %		5·0	4·8	3·8	6·6	4·3	0·6	0·4	−0·5	2·2
1963	4·8	4,495	6,334	5,360	5,021	109·7	4,098	5,774	4,886	4,579
Average 1962–3	5·1									
Increase 1962–3		195	338	274	291		128	238	190	211
do. %		4·5	5·6	5·4	6·2	1·3	3·2	4·3	4·0	4·8
Average 1961–3	4·5									
Increase 1961–3		399	612	461	585		152	261	166	304
do. %		9·7	10·7	9·4	13·2	5·7	3·9	4·7	3·5	7·1

	Margin of unused potential	Income from employment	At current prices: Total personal income	At current prices: Disposable income	Consumption	Index of consumption prices (1958 = 100)	At 1958 prices: Income from employment	At 1958 prices: Total personal income	At 1958 prices: Disposable income	At 1958 prices: Consumption
1966–8										
1966	3·5	5,695	7,919	6,576	6,089	121·7	4,675	6,505	5,400	5,003
1967	5·7	5,808	8,257	6,778	6,247	125·3	4,630	6,585	5,400	4,986
Average 1966–7	4·9									
Increase 1966–7		113	338	202	158		−45	+80	—	−17
do. %		2·0	4·3	3·1	2·6	3·0	−1·0	+1·2	—	−0·3
1968	6·5	6,217	8,909	7,227	6,543	130·7	4,750	6,810	5,540	5,006
Average 1967–8	5·9									
Increase 1967–8		409	652	449	296		+120	+225	+140	+20
do. %		7·0	7·9	6·6	4·7	4·3	+2·6	+3·4	+2·6	+0·4
Average 1966–8	5·4									
Increase 1966–8		522	990	651	454		+75	+305	+140	+3
do. %		9·2	12·5	9·9	7·5	7·4	+1·6	+4·7	+2·6	+0·1

Possible reasons for rapid rise of incomes

(i) *Restraints on consumption* On the face of it, these results suggest that the much more vigorous enforcement of an incomes policy in 1966–8 than in either 1957–9 or 1961–3 has on balance had no effect at all. Such an assessment would, however, probably be unjust. Conditions in 1966–8 differed from those of either 1957–9 or 1961–3 in at least two major respects. To begin with, in the earlier periods the Government was concerned only with checking inflation; it was able to obtain the resources needed for improving the balance of payments almost entirely by diverting them from a high rate of stock accumulation. In consequence, it was possible to allow personal consumption to rise quite rapidly in real terms, by an average of 3½ per cent a year or more. In 1966–8, however, the Government was faced with the necessity of diverting to exports very large amounts of resources, not from stock accumulation (which was already inadequate), but mainly from personal consumption. In this it has achieved very considerable success for, after a temporary rise in the last quarter of 1967 and the first quarter of 1968, personal consumption was checked back by the budget to almost exactly the same level in the second quarter as it had stood at in the second quarter of 1966. With the rise in the total (though not the working) population, this must have meant that the average standard of living was appreciably lower than it had been two years before.

This almost complete check to the rise in consumption was achieved partly by a rapid rise in prices of consumption goods and services and partly (contrary to the general impression) by an increase in personal saving, shown in Table 8.12 as a widening of the difference between disposable income and consumption. The rise in personal saving is in marked contrast with the experience of 1957–9, when there was no increase, and of 1961–3, when there was a fall. It is not surprising that the Government's successful efforts to prevent a rise in the standard of living should have provoked the more vigorous use of whatever monopoly power labour possesses, not only by trade unions but even more by unofficial groups of key workers. Mr Aubrey Jones, chairman of the Prices and Incomes Board, himself believes that the net effect of the

Government's incomes policy has been to reduce the rise of prices and incomes by 1 per cent a year below what it would otherwise have been. This claim may be on the optimistic side. But even if we assume that the effect of incomes policy has been to slow down the rise of incomes by only 0·5 per cent a year below what it would otherwise have been, the annual rate of increase of income from employment in the second half of 1968 would without it have been nearly 2 per cent faster than we should have expected on the basis of earlier experience. One possible explanation of this faster rise of incomes is that it is the effect of the increased use by labour of its monopoly power to resist the Government's efforts to hold down the standard of living. If this explanation is correct, the disinflationary measures of November 1968, necessitated by the rapid rise of personal consumption in the second half of the year, and the additional taxation imposed in the 1969 budget, are likely to be followed by maintained pressure for higher wages and a continuation of the over-rapid rise of money incomes.

(ii) *Redundancy payments* A second recent development which may have helped to induce a faster rise of incomes than was in the past consistent with present levels of unemployment may have been the result of the introduction of redundancy payments and more generous unemployment benefits. These may have reduced the urgency for some of the unemployed to obtain work and may therefore have reduced the pressure of supply on the labour market at any given level of unemployment. Some confirmation of this view is provided by the fact that in both 1967 and 1968 the number of employment vacancies was considerably larger than has in the past accompanied similar levels of unemployment. In Table 8.13 and Fig. 8.5 an attempt is made to measure the present divergence from earlier experience.

The number of unemployed tends normally to move inversely with the number of vacancies; the only development which tends to make them move in the same direction is a rise in the whole scale of the system as a result of an increase in the size of the working population. We can get rid of this distortion by expressing in Table 8.13 both unemployment and vacancies as percentages of the number of employees. It will be seen from Fig. 8.5 that, on the average of earlier experience, we should have expected the 1·1 per

TABLE 8.13

UNEMPLOYMENT AND VACANCIES IN GREAT BRITAIN, 1952–68

(Annual average percentages of number of employees)

Year	*Unemployment*	*Vacancies*	*Year*	*Unemployment*	*Vacancies*
1952	1·99	1·32	1961	1·51	1·42
1953	1·64	1·31	1962	2·03	0·93
1954	1·34	1·57	1963	2·49	0·85
1955	1·09	1·88	1964	1·65	1·38
1956	1·18	1·64	1965	1·40	1·66
1957	1·43	1·27	1966	1·53	1·60
1958	2·10	0·90	1967	2·40	1·07
1959	2·17	1·02	1968	2·42	1·16
1960	1·63	1·41			

cent of vacancies recorded in 1967 to be accompanied by an average level of unemployment of about 2·0 per cent, and the 1·2 per cent of vacancies in 1968 by about 1·9 per cent of unemployment, as against actual average unemployment of about 2·4 per cent in both years.

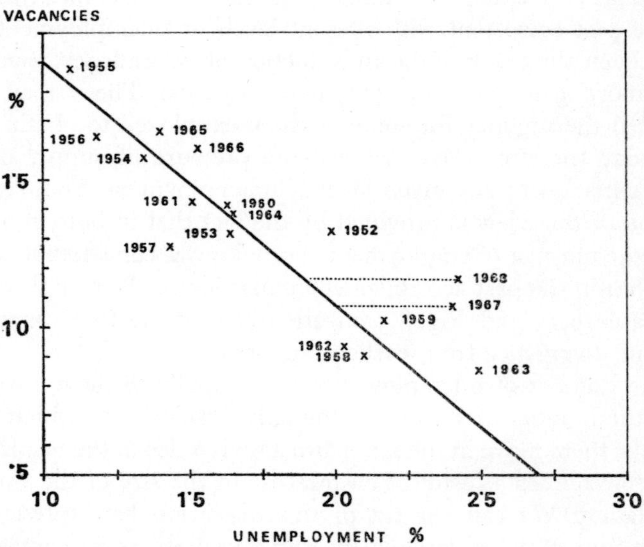

Fig. 8.5 Unemployment and vacancies: annual average percentages of numbers of employees (source: Table 8.13)

(iii) *Increase in structural unemployment* An alternative, or additional, explanation, put forward both by the D.E.A.[1] and by the National Institute[2] to account for the divergence in 1967–8 from previous experience in the relationship between unemployment and vacancies, is that an increased proportion of the unemployment recorded is structural rather than cyclical, and is due to the fact that an increased proportion of the unemployed is not of the type needed to fill the available vacancies – in particular, that the unsatisfied demand is for skills which few of the unemployed are able to supply.

It seems possible that both types of explanation may help to account for the over-rapid rise of incomes in 1967–8. The explanation that it has been due to labour's resistance to the Government's efforts to restrain consumption obtains some support from the fact that the slowing down of the rise of incomes in the second half of 1968 was accompanied by quite a substantial recovery in personal consumption. It also helps to account for the increase in the frequency of strikes, especially unofficial strikes, which has recently induced the Government to put forward measures designed to discourage them. If it is correct, the effectiveness of the Government's measures to discourage strikes may be small so long as it is obliged to continue to hold down personal consumption.

While the checking of the rise of personal consumption may account for the increased pressure for higher money incomes and for the increased frequency of strikes, it does not explain the change which seems to have taken place in the relationship between unemployment and vacancies, as do the second and third explanations. One test of the relative importance of the different explanations will be to see what happens when, at last, consumption can again be allowed to rise proportionately with national income. In so far as the first explanation is valid, the relationship between the level of unemployment and the rate of rise of incomes can then be expected to return towards that shown in Fig. 8.4. If, on the other hand, either the second or the third explanation is correct, the level of unemployment corresponding to any given rise of incomes will be found to have permanently increased to above that found in the period 1952–66.

[1] *The Task Ahead*, p. 42.

[2] *National Institute Economic Review*, Feb 1969, p. 28.

VI. EXCESS DEMAND AND THE BALANCE OF PAYMENTS

The effects on the balance of payments of an over-rapid rise of output and a consequent shrinking of the margin of unused productive potential seem to take three forms. The first appears as a direct result of the faster rise of output, which increases the demand for important materials. This effect is accentuated by a rise in the rate of stock accumulation. The rises, both in imports and in stocks, usually appear only after a time-lag of about nine months, and therefore affect the annual totals only in the second year of the upturn. Since this worsening of the balance of payments usually brings with it the first tentative steps to restrain demand, and since these are shortly followed by a slowing down of the rise of output, the check to output is usually attributed to the effects of the worsening balance of payments. However, by the second year of each upturn (1954, 1960, 1964) the margin of unused potential had already fallen so low that the rate of growth of output had in any case to fall towards that of potential. The most, therefore, that a restriction of demand could do at this stage was to anticipate by a very few months the inevitable slowing down of the rise of output.

In the 1958–61 and the 1962–6 cycles, as will be seen from Table 8.14, the main rise in the rate of stock accumulation and the main worsening of the balance of payments appeared in the second years of the upturn, 1960 and 1964. In the 1952–7 cycle, exceptionally, these developments did not appear until 1955, the third year of upturn. There was a special reason for this postponement. In 1954 the Government sold off large quantities of reserve stocks accumulated during the Korean War, so that the sharp rise in private-sector stocks was more than offset by the fall in government stocks, and total stock accumulation fell. The smaller further fall in government stocks in 1955 again kept total stock accumulation below that of the private sector, and probably prevented the adverse balance of payments from being larger than it was.

The inverse cyclical relationship between the balance of payments and the rate of stock accumulation, which is clearly shown in Table 8.14, implies that a favourable balance of payments which

TABLE 8.14

BALANCE OF PAYMENTS AND STOCK ACCUMULATION, 1952–68

Years	Increase in output over previous year (%)	Average margin of unused productive potential (%)	Balance of payments on current a/c		Stock accumulation				Balance of payments plus stocks	
			£m.	% of G.N.P.	Public Sector £m.	Private sector £m.	Total £m.	Total % of G.N.P.	£m.	% of G.N.P.
1952	−0·7	3·8	+163	+1·2	+128	−78	+50	+0·4	+213	+1·5
1953	+4·0	2·5	+145	+1·0	+27	+98	+125	+0·8	+270	+1·8
1954	+4·2	1·1	+117	+0·7	−188	+244	+56	+0·4	+173	+1·1
1955	+3·4	0·5	−155	−0·9	−93	+393	+300	+1·8	+145	+0·9
1956	+0·9	2·2	+208	+1·1	−8	+267	+259	+1·4	+467	+2·5
1957	+1·7	3·2	+233	+1·2	+18	+220	+238	+1·2	+471	+2·4
Average 1952–7	**+2·3**	**2·2**	**+118**	**+0·7**	**−19**	**+191**	**+172**	**+1·0**	**+290**	**+1·7**
1958	−0·1	5·9	+344	+1·7	+28	+83	+111	+0·5	+455	+2·2
1959	+4·5	4·3	+143	+0·7	+1	+173	+174	+0·8	+317	+1·5
1960	+5·4	1·7	−265	−1·2	−42	+637	+595	+2·6	+330	+1·4
1961	+1·8	2·7	−4	—	+4	+319	+323	+1·3	+319	+1·3
Average 1958–61	**+2·9**	**3·6**	**+55**	**+0·3**	**−2**	**+303**	**+301**	**+1·3**	**+356**	**+1·6**
1962	+1·3	4,6	+112	+0·4	+11	+58	+69	+0·3	+181	+0·7
1963	+3·3	4·5	+111	+0·4			+228	+0·8	+339	+1·2
1964	+6·0	2·0	−399	−1·4			+677	+2·3	+278	+0·9
1965	+2·4	2·3	−91	−0·3			+436	+1·4	+345	+1·1
1966	+1·3	3·9	+5	—			+259	+0·8	+264	+0·8
Average 1962–6	**+2·9**	**3·5**	**−52**	**−0·2**			**+334**	**+1·1**	**+282**	**+0·9**
1967	+1·4	5·9	−399	−1·2			+184	+0·5	−215	−06·
1968	+3·4	5·9	−419	−1·2			+236	+0·7	−183	−0·5

is accompanied by an abnormally small rise in stocks is likely to be a precarious one; while, given adequate foreign exchange reserves, an adverse balance which is accompanied by an exceptionally large rise in stocks should not, by itself, give rise to undue anxiety. Even apart from the need to repay the foreign short-term debts incurred in recent years, the U.K. needs a current account surplus of something like £300 million a year, or rather over 0·8 per cent of the present gross national product, to permit the removal of restrictions on long-term foreign investment. With an average rate of stock accumulation equal to about 1·2 per cent of G.N.P., the aggregate of balance of payments plus stock accumulation needed for long-term viability is thus rather over 2 per cent of G.N.P. With the additional need to repay short-term foreign debts, the Government has set its sights higher than this, at a balance-of-payments surplus of £500 million or about 1·4 per cent of G.N.P. This implies a total of balance of payments plus stock accumulation equal to about 2·6 per cent of G.N.P. – a level which has been approached since the war only in the period 1956–8. Provided that the combined total can be raised to, and maintained at, this level, temporary changes in the relative proportions of the two items can be disregarded.

If this first effect on the balance of payments were the only result of an over-rapid rise of output, it would be possible for a country with adequate reserves of foreign exchange to disregard it. Unfortunately there are two others. Even after the rate of rise of output has fallen to equality with that of productive potential, the maintenance of an inadequate margin of unused potential is likely to be accompanied by long order-books, delays in delivery, and the development of bottlenecks. It therefore tends both to lose exports and to cause local users to obtain urgently needed goods from abroad. Statistical evidence of this effect is difficult to obtain, since, in the short run, developments abroad may be as important as those at home. Some evidence is perhaps provided by Table 8.14, with the progressive fall of balance of payments plus stocks, as a percentage of G.N.P., from 1953 to 1955 and from 1959 to 1961. A similar fall in 1964–6 seems to have been temporarily interrupted by 1965 by the imposition of the import surcharge.

Inflation, export costs and the balance of payments

Most serious of all the effects of a period of excess demand is a permanent rise in the level of costs and prices. If the rise in costs is faster than that in other industrial countries, the competitive power of domestic producers will be permanently impaired, both in home and export markets. As Table 8.15 shows, the rapid rise in British labour costs per unit of output has caused both British costs to rise faster than export prices, thus making exports less profitable, and prices of British manufactured exports to rise faster than those of most other countries, thus making British exports less competitive.

It is this rise in British costs which has probably been the main reason for the deterioration of the balance of payments, especially

TABLE 8.15

U.K. LABOUR COSTS AND DOLLAR EXPORT PRICES OF MANUFACTURES 1952–68

(1958 = 100)

	U.K. labour costs			*Dollar export prices of manufactured goods*					
	Output	*Income from employment*	*Labour cost per unit of output*	*U.K.*	*U.S.A.*	*Germany*	*France*	*Italy*	*Japan*
1952	87·0	67·6	77·7	94	89	106	104	119	115
1953	90·5	71·5	79·0	91	89	100	98	115	108
1954	94·3	76·3	80·9	90	88	96	97	111	103
1955	97·5	83·4	85·5	92	90	96	97	106	98
1956	98·4	91·0	92·5	94	94	99	102	100	101
1957	100·1	96·1	96·0	99	99	100	102	104	105
1958	100·0	100·0	100·0	100	100	100	100	100	100
1959	104·5	104·7	100·2	100	103	100	94	93	100
1960	110·1	112·6	102·3	102	105	102	97	96	102
1961	112·1	121·6	108·5	103	106	107	97	93	98
1962	113·6	128·4	113·0	105	106	108	97	88	95
1963	117·4	134·7	114·7	107	106	107	98	94	93
1964	124·4	146·0	117·5	109	106	108	101	96	92
1965	127·7	157·4	123·2	112	110	110	103	94	92
1966	129·4	168·4	130·1	117	113	112	106	93	90
1967	131·2	173·7	132·1	116	116	111	106	93	92
1968	135·7	185·8	136·9	108[1]	118	111	105	89	92

[1] Sterling price index = 126.

since 1962. It is true that, as Table 8.16 shows, the progressive rise of government expenditure abroad has been an important contributory factor; but of the deterioration of £108 million in the average balance on current account between the 1958–61 and 1962–6 cycles, £65 million was due to the worsening of the visible balance, and only £43 million to the faster rise in government expenditure abroad than in the net invisible earnings of the private sector. It is likely that the visible balance would also have fallen sharply between the 1952–7 and the 1958–61 cycles if it had not been for the substantial improvement in the terms of visible trade, due mainly to the sharp fall in 1957–8 in prices of imported foodstuffs and raw materials, which much more than offset the deterioration in the terms of trade for services. Between the 1958–61 and the 1962–6 cycles, on the other hand, a moderate further

TABLE 8.16

TERMS OF TRADE AND BALANCE OF PAYMENTS, 1952–68

TERMS OF TRADE (1958 = 100)

	Average 1952–7	*Average 1958–61*	*Average 1962–6*	*1967*	*1968*	
					Jan–June	*July–Dec*
Goods						
Export prices	95	100	107	115	123	126
Import prices	106	99	102	106	118	120
Terms of trade	90	101	105	108	104	105
Services						
Export prices	98	102	104	108	114	115
Import prices	93	107	117	130	145	145
Terms of trade	105	95	89	83	79	79
Goods and Services						
Export prices	96	101	106	113	121	123
Import prices	103	101	106	112	123	126
Terms of trade	93	100	100	101	98	98
BALANCE OF PAYMENTS ON CURRENT ACCOUNT (£ million)						
Commodity Trade						
Exports and re-exports	3033	3638	4525	5026	2927	3176
Imports	3202	3799	4751	5661	3387	3512
Visible balance	−169	−161	−226	−635	−460	−336
Net Invisibles						
Government	−119	−265	−418	−466	−237	−225
Other	+407	+481	+591	+702	+428	+411
Invisible balance	+288	+216	+173	+236	+191	+186
Balance of payments	+119	+55	−53	−399	−269	−150

improvement in the terms of visible trade was entirely offset by the further deterioration in the terms of trade for services.

As Table 8.15 shows, the devaluation of sterling in November 1967 seems to have about restored the competitive position of British exports, and, which is perhaps at least as important, to have appreciably improved the profitability of exporting. It is essential that these improvements should be maintained, especially until the enormous foreign short-term debts contracted in recent years have been repaid. This repayment seems likely to take many years to achieve. The Treasury's economic forecasts, which accompanied the 1969 budget, indicated that the balance of trade in goods and services, at 1958 prices, seasonally corrected, was expected to improve from an import surplus of £140 million in the second half of 1968 to an export surplus of only £30 million in the first half of 1970, in spite of the fact that consumption expenditure was expected to rise by little more than one half of one per cent over this period.

Britain's trading prospects

In the absence of an improvement, of which there has hitherto been little sign, in the terms of trade for goods and services combined, of a substantial further increase in net investment income from abroad or a substantial decrease in transfer payments (mainly on government account) to abroad, an estimated balance-of-trade surplus in goods and services at 1958 prices of £30 million implies a current account surplus at current prices of barely £50 million in the first half of 1970. This would be an improvement of barely £200 million in eighteen months over the current account deficit of £150 million in the second half of 1968. A current account surplus at the rate of barely £100 million a year would be only just enough to cover normal net exports of long-term capital even under present restrictions, and would leave nothing for the net repayment of foreign short-term debt. A continuation of the improvement in the half-yearly current account balance at the rate of £200 million every eighteen months would mean that the target of a £500 million surplus would be reached about the second half of 1971. On these assumptions which, on the trading results for the first four months of 1969, look over-optimistic, net repayments of short-term debt could probably begin on a small scale in the second half of 1970, but the repayment of the whole debt of something like £3,000 million would not be completed until towards the end of the 1970s.

It is true that, appreciably before then, increasing confidence in sterling might have removed our foreign creditors' desire for repayment. But, even so, it would be necessary, in order to permit the removal of restrictions on exports of long-term capital and to maintain confidence in sterling, to maintain a current account surplus of £300 million a year or more. This means that the country must never again allow incomes to rise as much faster than output as they have done in recent years. And this again implies, as does the Treasury projection for the period up to 1970, that the country must from now on be prepared to maintain a larger average margin of unused productive potential, and a higher average level of unemployment, than those to which the post-war generation has become accustomed.

FURTHER READING

Dow, J. C. R., and Dicks-Mireaux, L. A., 'The Determinants of Wage Inflation in the United Kingdom, 1946–56', *Journal of the Royal Statistical Society*, series A, Pt 2 (1959). (Republished by National Institute of Economic and Social Research, Reprint Series no. 23.)

Dow, J. C. R., *The Management of the British Economy, 1945–60* (National Institute of Economic and Social Research and Cambridge University Press, 1964).

Godley, W. A. H., and Shepherd, J. R., 'Long-term Growth and Short-term Policy', *National Institute Economic Review*, Aug 1964.

Lipsey, R. G., 'The Relation between Unemployment and the Rate of Change of Money Wage-rates in the United Kingdom, 1952–1957: A Further Analysis', *Economica*, Feb 1960.

Matthews, R. C. O., 'Why Has Britain Had Full Employment Since the War?', *Economic Journal*, Sep 1968.

Paish, F. W., *Studies in an Inflationary Economy* (Macmillan, 1962) chap. 17.

Pearce, D. W. and Taylor, J., Spare Capacity: What Margin is Needed?', *Lloyds Bank Review*, July 1968.

Phelps, E. S., 'Phillips Curves, Expectations of Inflation, and Optimal Unemployment Over Time', *Economica*, Aug 1967.

Phillips, A. W., 'The Relation between Unemployment and the Rate of Money Wage-rates in the United Kingdom, 1861–1957', *Economica*, Nov 1958.

Romains, A., 'Cost Inflation and Incomes Policies in Industrial Countries', *I.M.F. Staff Papers*, Mar 1967.

Shepherd, J. R., 'Productive Potential and the Demand for Labour', *Economic Trends*, Aug 1968.

Shultz, G. P., and Aliber, R. Z., *Guidelines, Informal Controls, and the Marketplace* (University of Chicago Press, 1967).

Index